红山文化古玉收藏研究俱乐部

Research and Collection Clud of HongShan-Culture Jade Articler

HONGSHAN-CULTURAL ANCIENT JADE APPRAISAL

红山文化古玉鉴赏

徐强 书

华夏出版社

HUA YI PUBLISHING HOUSE

图书在版编目（CIP）数据

红山文化古玉鉴定／徐强 著. —北京：华艺出版社，2007.8

ISBN 978-7-80142-865-3

Ⅰ.红… Ⅱ.徐… Ⅲ.红山文化 - 古玉器 - 鉴定 Ⅳ.K876.84

中国版本图书馆CIP数据核字(2007)第116601号

红山文化古玉鉴定

作　　者：	徐　强
责任编辑：	郑治清
装帧设计：	三和元点文化
本书策划：	骆彦卿
印　　刷：	北京威灵彩色印刷有限公司
出版发行：	华艺出版社
地　　址：	北京北四环中路229号海泰大厦10层
邮　　编：	10083　　电话：82885151
开　　本：	889 × 1192
字　　数：	120千字
印　　张：	19.5
版　　次：	2007年10月第1版　2007年10月第1次印刷
书　　号：	ISBN 978-7-80142-865-3/Z·436
定　　价：	380.00元

作者简介

徐强（听雨堂主人），1946年生人，籍贯山东掖县。1965年进军工企业当工人。1969年调沈阳军区赴中苏边界从事战地摄影记者工作。1977年为辽宁电影制片厂导演，摄影师，直到2004年退休。

由于自小受祖父影响，酷好对中国古玉器的收藏与研究。从七十年代开始收藏中国古玉器，每得一玉必置案头数月，反复潜心分析研究。为证其根本，验证他人对古玉鉴论，亲自做过数十种实验，写下近50万字古玉鉴赏笔记。

1983年，辽宁电影制片厂受辽宁考古研究所委托拍摄"牛河梁红山文化考古发掘"纪录片，因此便接触与开始了对红山文化古玉的收藏与研究。二十多年，他先后数次赴辽西和内蒙古三县七旗进行实地考察，从中掌握了大量有关红山文化方面第一手资料。

徐强先生共收藏中国古玉器1600余件。2002年由沈阳市文化局、文物局组织本人藏品在沈阳故宫博物院展出一年。2003年他所著《红山文化古玉精华》，2004年所著《中国古玉珍藏》分别由蓝天出版社出版。并先后为"收藏界"、"艺术与收藏"杂志社撰写《红山文化古玉鉴识》文章。应广大古玉收藏者要求，2007年将出版《红山文化古玉鉴定》。2005年，中国图书总公司赴法国进行图书展期间，将徐强先生所著《红山文化古玉精华》一书亲自赠与法国总统希拉克，希拉克看后十分兴奋，并对中国古文化大加赞赏。

做为古玉收藏家与鉴赏家，徐强先生为弘扬和传播中华民族优秀文化，数十年来进行着不懈而艰辛的努力。2005年徐强先生成立《北京听雨堂文化发展中心》。他提出《关于成立红山文化古玉收藏研究俱乐部》的申请，经中国文化管理学会会长办公会议研究决定，于2006年4月报文化部社会团体管理办公室备案正式批准成立，并聘其为俱乐部主任。俱乐部建立《红山文化古玉珍品馆》，长年供会员与红山文化爱好者免费参观。在不到一年时间里，先后受邀在江苏昆山和北京中华世纪坛展出红山文化古玉精品，亲自讲授红山文化古玉鉴定知识。

数年来，陆续接待来自美国、德国、法国、日本、赤道几内亚、刚果等国家及港台地区古文明研究学者、红山文化爱好者的造访和进行文化交流。前不久，又接受墨西哥国家电视台录像采访。

徐强先生为世界收藏家联合会国际会员。

Author Brief Introduction

Xuqiang(the host of rain-hear hall), who was born in 1946, and his hometown is at ye county in Shandong province. In 1965, he entered into a Military enterprise to be a worker. In 1969 he was transferred to Shenyang military region to be a battlefield photograph Reporter in the boundary between China and the Soviet Union. He was the director and photographer for Liaoning Film Studio in 1977, until retiring in 2004.

Because of the influence of his grandfather while a child, he would love collecting and studying of Chinese ancient jade article. Since 1970s, he has begun to collect Chinese ancient jade article. Every time he got a jade, he must would put it on his desk a few months to analyse and research again and again with great concentration. To prove its source and verify other person for the conclusion of ancient jade appraisal, he personally carried on tens of experiments and wrote down near five-hundred-thousand-words note about ancient jade appreciation.

In 1983, Liaoning Film Studio was entrusted by Liaoning Archaeological Institute with taking Documentary film "Niuheliang Hongshan cultural archaeological unearthing". Therefore he began to contact with collecting and studying the Hongshan cultural ancient jade. During more than 20 years, he went to East of Liaoning and san county qi flag in Mongolia for many times to carry out field explorations, From it, he have grasped plenty of relevant Hongshan culture firsthand information.

Mr. Xuqing collects totally more than 1600 Chinese ancient jade articles. In 2002, orginzed by Shenyang Cultural Bureau and Cultural Relics Bureau, his most-prized holdings would be on display in Shenyang Palace Museum for one year. The "Hongshan Cultural Ancient Jade Cream" composed in 2003 and " China Ancient Jade Treasure" composed in 2004 separately published by the Press of Blue Sky. And he also composed article "Hongshan cultural ancient jade appreciation and identification" for the magazine "Collection World" and "Artist and Collection". For the requirement of large-scale ancient jade collector£¬he will publish the book "Hongshan Cultural Ancient Jade Appraisal " in 2007. During 2005, Chinese Book Main corporation exhibited books in France, they presented the book "Hongshan Ancient Jade Treasure" composed by Mr.Xuqiang to French president Jacquea Chirac. Jacquea Chirac is very glad after reading, and he appreciated substantially for Chinese ancient culture.

As ancient jade collector and connoisseur, Mr. Xu Qiang has been making unremitting efforts and hard work for the past few decades in order to develop and disseminate Chinese excellent culture. In 2005, Mr. Xuqiang setted up "Beijing rain-hear hall culture developing center". He put forward the application "about founding Research and Collection Club of Hongshan-Culture Jade". Through research of official business and decided by the China cultural Administration Association president meeting, On April in 2006 they notified the Culture Ministry social group Management office to keep on record and formally approved, and they appointed him as club director. The club establishes "Hongshan cultural ancient jade treasure house", let members and Hongshan cultural fan would be free to visit it. In less than one-year period, he was invited to be on display Hongshan cultural ancient jade high-quality holdings in Kunshan Jiangsu province and century platform of China in Beijing, and personally taught Hongshan cultural ancient jade appraisal knowledge.

For many years, we have received successively that coming from America、 Germany、 France、 Japan、 Equatorial Guinea, Congolese, other countries etc. and Hong Kong or Taiwan areas, the ancient civilized studies scholar、 Hongshan cultural fan paid a visit for and carried out cultural exchange. Recently, we also accepted the Video interview of Mexico National Television Broadcast Station.

Mr. Xuqiang is an international member of the world collector federation.

目 录 Contents

前　言

当一件件玉器摆放在你面前的时候，我们的专家需要逐一对其进行分析研究，最终做出正确判断，以认定其中真伪，这就是古玉鉴定。

鉴定专家的责任重大，他像医生，同时又像法官。任何不负责任的诊断和误判，都将产生严重的后果甚至导致生命的终结。

红山文化距今 5000 — 6000 年，在文字尚未出现和没有任何文字记载情况下，仅凭主观想象即能对红山文化玉器做出正确鉴定显然是不现实的。一个真正的古玉鉴定专家，任何时候都不能脱离实际和主观臆断从事，而必须以历史的、唯物的、科学的态度来客观地分析问题和认识问题。

研究红山文化古玉器，要涉猎多学科知识。要真正做到对红山文化玉器做出正确鉴定，必须首先学习与研究人类学、考古学、气象学、地质学、矿物学、物理学、工艺学、美术学、宗教学等，甚至还需要基本了解和掌握远超过以上学科所包含的更多知识，因为这些知识与我们的古玉鉴定工作密切相关。只有充分了解了远古时期我国北方地区当时的气候条件、生态环境变化、人类的生存与生产方式、原始宗教意识与图腾观，以及玉石形成年代与结构、玉石矿物成分与硬度、玉石在外因条件下收缩与膨胀原理、玉器的工艺造型与意境、土壤中多种元素对玉器的侵蚀与危害、玉石所含的矿物成分与其它物质相溶合所发生的化学变化等与红山文化玉器鉴定相关大量信息，才能称为真正意义上的科学鉴定。

民间所收藏红山文化玉器，大都出土时间、地点、环境不明确。因此我们在鉴定工作中必须以科学考古发掘报告、出土玉器实物及相关图片资料做为鉴定基础与重要依据。任何严重脱离科学考古实际、违背时代特征、玉质特征、造型特征、工艺特征、沁象特征之器物，皆不能被认定为红山文化真古玉器。

鉴定专家，是特定领域与工作范围内被授予了特殊权利的执法者，他代表着行业中的技术最权威。专家鉴定，是对所鉴器物经过认知、印证后的意见总结，把握和决定着被鉴物品生、杀命运的有效判决权。鉴定专家在倍受人们尊重的同时，眼下更多的是让人深感惶恐。因为在社会经济大潮中，有些鉴定专家过当利用了自己的权利，私欲与贪婪往往使一些人严重丧失了理智与职业道德。

鉴定专家应该对自己的职责与行为负责。因为任何错误鉴定，都将给我们的国家和民众利益造成永远无法弥补的损失。为此我们的鉴定专家在提供有偿服务的同时，必须承担相应的法律责任与经济赔偿责任，以推动社会进步和避免人类犯更大的错误。

古玉鉴定，是严谨的学术研究和科学认证，是一项严肃认真和需要付出艰辛的工作，对此来不得半点虚伪与含糊。在红山文化古玉鉴定工作中，以法律责任与经济赔偿约束自己的行为势在必行，首先从本书和从我做起。

徐强 于北京《听雨堂》

2007.3.3

Preface

When jade wares are put in front of you, they needed to be analyzed and studied one by one for correct judgement whether they are real and fake. This is ancient jade identification.

Experts are significant in the identification of jade wares, and they are like the doctor, as well as the judge at the same time. Any irresponsible diagnosis and judgemen will lead to serious consequence, even the end of life.

It has been 5000-6000 years since the occurrence of Hongshan culture, and it was not realistic to make correct identification for jade wares at that time just through subjective imagination without characters and letters. A genuine ancient jade appraisal expert should not lose contact with reality and rely on subjective imagination, and he/she must objectively analyze and recognize problems with the historical, scientific and materialistic attitudes.

Various subjects of knowledges are needed to study Hongshan culture. To be competent for the identification of Hongshan-cultural jade wares, anthropology, archaeology, meteorology, geology, mineralogy, physics and technology, fine arts, religion and so on should be firstly studied, even more. For the above knowledge closely relates to the appraisal of ancient jade wares. Only when we have known fully about the climate condition, ecological environment, and the survival production ways of mankind, and original religious consciousness and totem sight of the ancient period in the north area of our country, as well as the related information including the jade formation time and structures, jade mineral composition with hardness, the contraction and expansion principle of jade wares under the external and internal condition, sculpture and artistic conception of jade wares, various elements in earth that corrodes and endangers jade wares, mineral compositions contained in jade wares and their reaction with other materials, complete identification can be achieved.

The excavated time, sites and environment of most folk Hongshan cultural jade wares are not clear, so we must consider the excavated report, jade wares and related picture documents as the identification basis. Any jade ware, which seriously disengage scientific archeology practice, violate time characteristics, jade property, sculpture features, technology characteristics, etc. can not be considered as the real Hongshan jade ware.

Appraisal expert, who is the law-executor in specific field and has been conferred special right, represents the highest technology authority in his field. Expert appraisal, which is the conclusion of opinions for the identified articles after recognition and verification, determines the destination of the identified wares. The experts should be respected very much, while some of them make people worried. In social and economic tides, some experts are abusing their rights, and selfish desire and greediness lead to loss of senses and professional ethics.

Appraisal expert should take the responsibility for his own duty and behavior, because any incorrect appraisal will cause huge benefit loss of our country. Therefore, while offering paid service, our appraisal expert must undertake the corresponding legal responsibility and economic liability to pay compensation in order to promote social advance and avoid human mistakes.

Ancient jade appraisal, which is strict academic research and scientific certification, is a serious and hard job, so it must not be even a little bit hypocritical and ambiguous. In the identification of Hongshan-cultural jade wares, it is imperative under the situation to restrict our behaviors using legal responsibility and economic compensation. Firstly, we should start from this book and ourselves.

Qiang Xu Hear Rain Hall
Beijing 2007-3-3

红山文化简介

红山文化，因首次发现于中国内蒙古赤峰红山而得名。其覆盖范围，西起西拉木伦河、老哈河，南到大凌河流域，地处辽宁省西部、内蒙古东部四盟及河北省北部地区。

红山文化遗址经树轮校正，其年代距今为5485±110年，碳14测定年代数据为距今4895±70年，应处在新石器时代中期，由母系氏族公社向父系氏族公社过渡阶段，时间大约跨自公元前4000—公元前3000年的一千余年。

红山文化的发现可以追溯到20世纪初。1908年日本人类学家鸟居龙藏在内蒙古林西县和赤峰县英金河畔调查，曾发现红山文化遗存。1919年法国学者桑志华、德日进也在内蒙古东南部发现多处新石器时代遗址，并曾到赤峰东北郊的红山前作过调查，对沙锅屯洞穴遗址和红山后遗址进行了发掘。1921年，应聘来华进行矿产资源调查的瑞典地质学家安特生在进行煤矿调查的同时，在南票煤田附近发现石灰岩洞穴数个，并对洞内堆积进行了发掘。1935年日本东亚考古学会滨田耕作、水野清一在赤峰红山后遗址发掘，1939年发表考古报告书。

中国学者在早期对红山文化的发现，特别在研究方面有着不可磨灭的贡献。1930年中国考古学家梁思永在内蒙古林西县和英金河流域调查新石器时代遗存，他和考古学家裴文中、尹达对这类遗存给予了了极大的关注，并于40年代提出，沙锅屯、红山后的遗存是中原彩陶文化与北方细石器文化在长城地带相遇产生的一种"混合文化"，是一种新型的考古学文化，并正式定名为"红山文化"。1951年北京大学历史系考古专业在吕遵谔带领下调查并发掘了红山后遗址，于1958年在《考古学报》上发表报告时，使用了"红山文化"的名字。

红山文化，自从20世纪30年代被发现以来，作为我国北方地区新石器时代一个主要考古学文化，已经为世人所公认，由此更引起国内外考古、史学、美术、收藏界等诸多方面的关注和重视。辽宁省考古工作者更为此进行着不懈的努力，到70年代中期终于发现了红山文化时期的建筑址和墓葬群，在经过数十年的努力之后,红山文化才逐渐揭开那神秘的历史面纱。

牛河梁冢、庙、坛的重大发现，推动了对红山文化研究的进程，并提供了更准确的科学依据。可以认为，以牛河梁陵庙为主要地点，其附近地区为红山文化时期的政治、宗教、祭祀、陵墓的所在地和中心，其文化辐射范围波及东三省和内蒙古东四盟及河北省北部地区.

红山文化玉器种类繁多，功能广泛，工艺精良，风格鲜明，是我国古代文明的奠基石，已显露出人类走向文明的曙光，同时也是古代玉器艺术赖以发展的源泉和基础。

近三十年来，通过考古发掘和从民间征集到的红山文化典型玉器主要有：C型玉龙、兽形玦、勾云形玉佩、马蹄形玉箍、玉鸟、玉鸮、玉龟、玉璧、丫形器、玉蚕、玉蝉、玉熊、虫形玉、玉神面、玉神祖等。尤其动物形玉，是构成红山文化玉器群的核心。一些动物大都被抽象化，或做了夸张处理，并且极具神秘感。但它们显然都不是随意之作。经研究，它们都是先民们特意以玉制成的具有某种超自然力的图腾象征物。而且这些玉器大多与神灵崇拜、

都是先民们特意以玉制成的具有某种超自然力的图腾象征物。而且这些玉器大多与神灵崇拜、自然崇拜、祖先崇拜、生殖崇拜有着密切的联系。

红山文化的考古发现，填补了我国北方地区历史、文化延续的空白，确定了以大辽河流域及其支流大凌河、老哈河为主要地带的我国新石器时期的文明起源，为我国五千年的文明史找到了最可靠的依据。

红山文化时期，先民们不但创造了农牧业生产工具，创造了民族文化，更重要的是创造了人类文明。红山文化玉器是特定历史时期的产物，我们通过分析和研究红山文化玉器，其目的在于了解社会发展史、文化发展史、宗教发展史和中华文明发展史。这是历史所赋予我们的重任。

徐强　于北京《听雨堂》

2007.3.6

Hongshan-Culture Brief Introduction

"Hongshan-culture" has its name through the discovery in Hongshan which is in Chifeng city of Inner Mongolia. It covers from Xar Moron River in the west to Dalinghe River in the south, including the west of Liaoning province, eastern four leagues of Inner Mongolia as well as the north of Heibei province.

After the proof of growth ring of Hongshan sites, we found that it has been dated from 5595-5375 years ago. According to the result of C_{14} detection, it has the history back to 5965-4825 years which are in the middle of New Stone Age, and during the age of matrilineal ethical community to patrilineal ethical community, which dated from 4000-3000 BC.

The discovery of Hongshan-culture can trace back to the beginning of the 20th century. In 1908, Japanese anthropologist Torii Ryuzo discovered the existence Hongshan culture when he was doing his investigation at the waterside of YingJinhe River in Linxi and Chifeng county of Mongolia. In 1919, French scholar Emile Licent and Pierre Teilhard de Chardin also discovered many sites in the southeast of Mongolia and they made investigation and discovery of Hongshan sites in the northeast of Chifeng. In 1921, Andersson, Swedish geologist, employed by Chinese government, came to China for investigation of mineral resource, and many Limestone holes had been found and excavated. In 1935, Hamada sosaku and Mizuno Seiichi from Japanese eastern Asia Archaeology Institute discovered the sites behind Hongshan mountain in Chifeng county and in 1939, archaeology statement was published.

Chinese scholar contributed a lot in the early discovery of Hongshan culture, especially in the aspect of research. During 1930 Chinese archaeologist Si-Yong Liang was investigating the sites of New Stone Age in Linxi county and Yingjin river region of Mongolia, and he together with archaeologist Wen-Zhong Pei and Da Yin paid great attention to this kind of existence. In 1940s, they indicated that Shaguo village and Hongshan cave ruins had suggested "a kind of mixed culture" that generated from Central Plains pottery culture and north microlithic culture in the region of the Great Wall. That was a new kind of archaeology culture, formally named as " Hongshan culture ". In 1951, historical department archaeology division of Beijing University, led by E-Zun Lv, investigated the Hongshan sites, and then they used the name "Hongshan culture" in the report published in1958.

Since 1930s, Hongshan culture as a main archaeology culture of the New Stone Age in the north area of our country has been recognized, and from then it attracted more and more attention from domestic and international archaeology, science of history, fine arts and collection fields. Archaeology workers from Liaoning province carried out unremitting effort, and finally in 1970s, the discovered the building and grave sites of Hongshan-cultural period. After tens of years of efforts, the mysterious Hongshan culture was revealed gradually.

The significant discovery of Niuheliang Tomb, Temple and Platform has promoted the research process for Hongshan-cultue, and offered more accurate science basis at the same time. We may think that Niuheliang temple and its nearby area were locations and centers of politics, religion, sacrificing and grave during Hongshan-cultural period, and its cultural scope including the northeast of China, tour eastern alliances of Mongolia and the north area of Hebei province.

The jade wares of Hongshan-culture are of various kinds with has wide functions. Moreover, the technique is exquisite and style is bright. So the jade wares of Hongshan-culture are the very important proof of the archaic civilization and the dawn of the process to civilization. At the same time, they are also the source and foundation of the ancient art of jade wares.

In the past thirty years, there were some typical jade wares which were collected from the folk, such as: jade dragon, jade bird, jade animals, jade clevis hoop, jade tortoise, jade cicada, jade numen and compound jade baldric and so on. The animal jade wares are the main elements of Hongshan-culture jade wares. These animal jades are nonobjective, exaggerative and have great sense of mystery. After research, people have found that they are symbols for totem and supernatural power. Furthermore, these jade wares have some close relations with divine worship, nature worship, ancestor worship and sex worship.

The archaeological discovery of Hongshan-culture has filled the blank of the historical and cultural continuity in the north area our country, determined the civilized origin of New Stone Age along as the Daliao river and its tributary Daling, Laoha river in our country, which provides the most reliable basis for the 5000-year civilized history of our country.

During Hongshan-cultural period, people had not only invented the farming tools, created national culture, but also created human civilization, which was more important. Hongshan-cultural jade ware is the outcome of specific historical period. By analyzing and studying Hongshan-cultural jade ware, we aimed to understand the history of social development, cultural development, religious development and Chinese civilization development. This is our historical task.

Xuqiang

〈Hear rain hall〉

2007.3.6

图1 辽西山区鸟瞰
Picture 1 looking down from above of the mountains in western Liaoning

图2 红山文化积石冢
Picture 2 the stone grave mounds of Hongshan culture

　　辽宁西部连绵起伏的丘陵，在大凌河与老哈河之间，分布着古老而神秘的红山文化。独特的地理环境，让这里汇聚了不同经济类型、不同文化传统的古文化。在中华古代文明发展史中，红山文化已成为印证我国北方地区人类走向文明的重要佐证。

　　积石为冢，是红山文化时期原始先民葬墓的主要特征。这一特殊形式为它的存在做下了明显标记，又由于葬墓距地表较浅容易暴露和许多客观因素，致使大量红山文化玉器散失民间。

There are continuous hills rising and falling between Daling river and Laoha river in the west area of Liaoning, in which distributed ancient and mysterious Hongshan culture. Its unique geography environment let here have gathered ancient culture of different economic type and cultural tradition. In Chinese ancient civilization developing history, Hongshan culture has become the important evidence that confirm the human in the north area of our country being civilization.

Amassing stone is being to grave mounds, which is the major feature of original late the people to bury in tomb during Hongshan-culture period. This special form have marked obvious mark for its existence, and also as the tomb is near from the earth face easy to be exposed and a lot of objective factors, which caused plenty of Hongshan-culture jade wares lost in non-governmental circles.

图3 牛河梁第二地点二号冢中心大墓
Picture 3 The central tomb of the No.2 stone grave mound at the No.2 location in Niuheliang

图4 中心大墓近景观察
Picture 4 The close-range view of the central tomb

二号冢 中心大墓上部有用石块砌筑的规模庞大的方台式石椁，墓穴深入地下1.4米，棺长2.21米，宽0.85米，系用石块和平铺的石板砌成。此墓规模庞大，可见规格甚高。

引起我们格外注意的是：墓中未出任何随葬品，因为此墓已在早年被盗。按照此墓规格来看，墓中至少要随葬数十件红山文化玉器，这些玉器无疑早已散失民间。经过若干年，散失在民间的红山文化古玉究竟有多少？这需要经过细致而严谨的调查与统计，而不是仅靠几位考古学家不切实际的推论所能决定的。因此，"红山文化玉器只存世300件"的说法不能成为正确的科学定论广为应用。

正因为民间散失着大量红山文化玉器，在真品、赝品混杂的茫然中，需要我们的古玉鉴定专家去伪存真，以挽救中国古代历史中的瑰宝。

There is large scale outer coffin of square flat type building by laying stones on the top of the central tomb, and its tomb is underground 1.4m deep, 2.21m long, and 0.58m wide, building by laying stones and spreading slabstone. The scale of this grave is huge, which evidently can be seen very high standards.

It arousing us especial notice: There wasn't any unearthed wares in tomb, for this grave has been stolen in early years. According to this tomb standards, there was at least tens of Hongshan-culture jade wares following to bury, and those jade wares undoubtedly were lost in non-governmental circles long ago. After certain years, how many Hongshan-culture ancient jade wares were lost in non-governmental circles actually? This need to be careful and strict investigation and statistics, instead of relying on some of archaeologists" impractical inference can decide. Therefore the saying of " Hongshan-culture jade wares exist only 300 articles in the world" can not become correct scientific final conclusion to apply broadly. Just because there are plenty of Hongshan-culture jade wares in non-governmental circles. Between the real and false confusion, it need our ancient jade appraisal expert to winnow truth from falsehood, in order to save the rarity in Chinese ancient history.

这件现陈列于北京国家博物馆的玉龙，被称为目前所见红山文化玉器中最大的器物，曾引起国内、外极大的轰动与关注，被奉为国宝级文物。究其身世，并非科学考古发掘之器。而是 70 年代在民间征集所得。

玉龙造型生动，线条流畅，沁象真实自然，加工工艺符合新石器时代特征。诸多因素确定此器为红山文化真古玉器无疑。

散失在民间的红山文化玉器有很多。由于出土环境、地点、时间不明确等原因，尽管被收藏，但并不被专家所认可，甚至对民间藏品给予彻底否定。同样来自于民间，文管部门征集为真，民间收藏为假，这不是唯物主义者应有的态度。领导者们需要转变观念，鉴定专家们的业务素质需要得到进一步提升。

This jade dragon now displays in Beijing National Museum, which is called the biggest implements of all the present Hongshan cultural jade ware. It arouse domestic and international maximum sensation and solicitude, and had been received for the national cultural relic. Studying its life story, is not scientific archaeology unearthed ware. But it is non-governmental collection in 1970s.

Jade dragon modelling is lively, has smooth line, its infiltration phenomenon is true and natural, and processing technology accords with the feature of the New Stone Age. Many factors definite that undoubtedly this ware is Hongshan cultural real ancient jade ware.

There are many Hongshan cultural jade wares lost in non-governmental circles. Since unearthed environment, place and time not clear, even though the ware is collected, but could not be accepted by the expert even giving negation for nongovernmental collection thoroughly. Also coming from non-governmental circles, the culture administration department collection is true, but the non-governmental collection is false, which does not be the deserved attitude of the materialism people. Leaders need change ideas, and the business quality of appraisal experts need to get further promote.

红山文化玉器鉴定要点
Hongshan-Culture Jade Ware Appraise Main Points
（要以考古出土玉器做为参照标准）
(With archaeology excavate jade ware as reference standard)

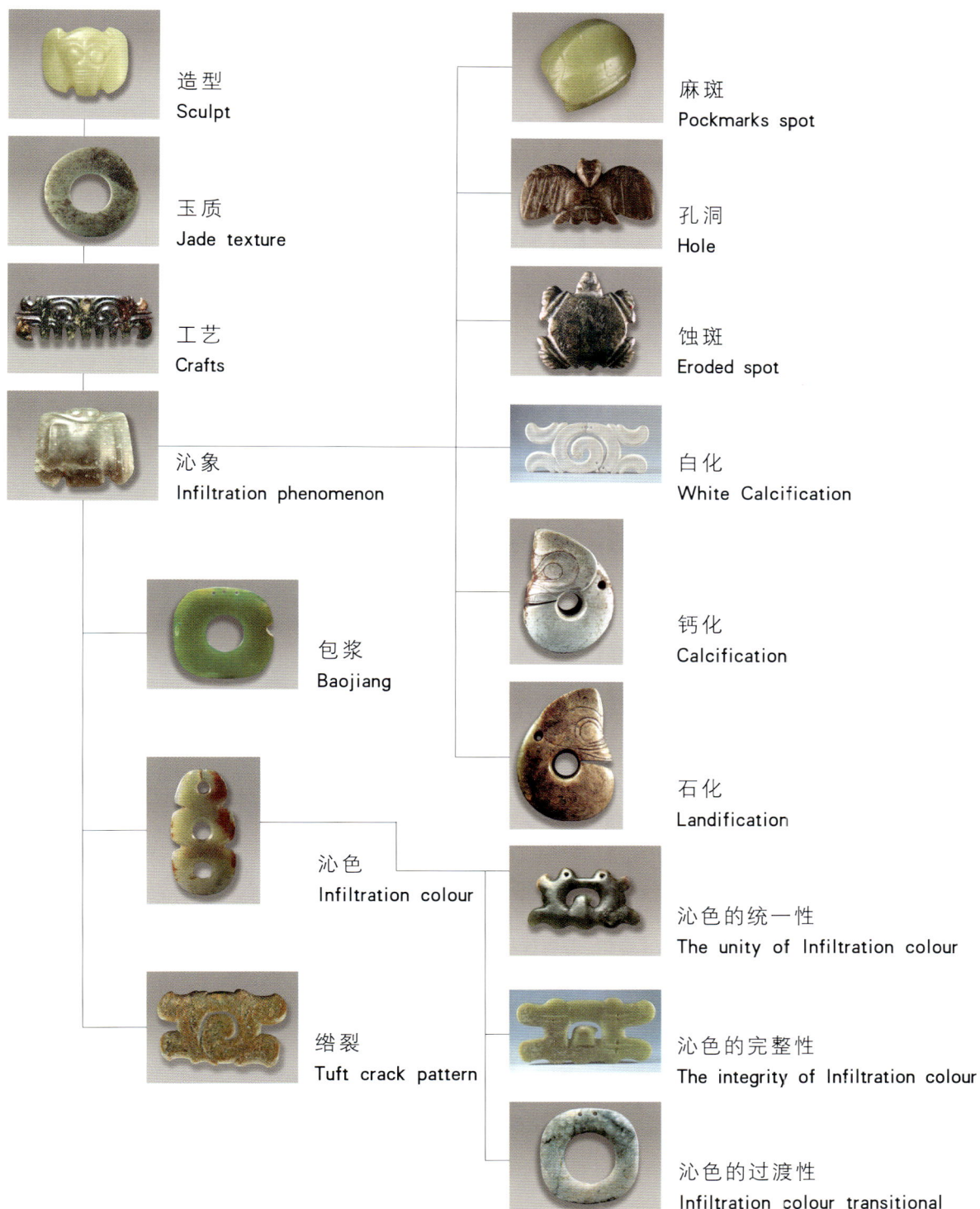

造型
Sculpt

玉质
Jade texture

工艺
Crafts

沁象
Infiltration phenomenon

包浆
Baojiang

沁色
Infiltration colour

绺裂
Tuft crack pattern

麻斑
Pockmarks spot

孔洞
Hole

蚀斑
Eroded spot

白化
White Calcification

钙化
Calcification

石化
Landification

沁色的统一性
The unity of Infiltration colour

沁色的完整性
The integrity of Infiltration colour

沁色的过渡性
Infiltration colour transitional

《红山文化古玉鉴定》常用术语解释

《Identification of Hongshan cultural ancient jade》Explain frequently with terminology

造型：经过设计、雕琢后所显示的玉器形象。
Sculpt: Through designing and carving the rear jade ware demonstrated image.

玉质：玉石的质地。（包括颜色、硬度、矿物结构与成分等）
Jade quality: The texture of jade. (Include color, hardness and mineral structure and composition etc)

工艺：玉器的加工方法与表现形式。
Technology: Expression form and the processing method of jade article.

沁象：玉器受到浸蚀后所呈现出的多种形态变化。
Infiltration phenomenon: the various changes formed After jade ware gets etch.

包浆：玉器在温度变化下，由于"出汗"所产生矿物质内分泌，久之在玉器表面结成的亮膜。
Baojiang: Jade ware is under temperature change, because of " perspire " the endocrine phenomenon of mineral matter produced, for a long time in the surface of jade article the bright membrane formed.

沁色：由于各种因素，土壤中的微量金属元素与非金属元素对玉器浸染所形成之颜色。
Infiltration colour: Because of various factors, nonmetal elements and the trace metal elements in soil for jade ware is contaminated the color formed.

绺裂：在相对湿度下，玉器由于内、外温度不能平衡，热胀冷缩原理使玉器表面产生的呈起层状纹裂。

Tuft crack pattern: Under relative humidity, Jade ware can not be balanced because of internal and external temperature, Heat expands, which is cold to draw back principle and to make the surface of jade article to produce a level of first floor shape split veins.

麻斑：无论玉质何等坚密，土壤中的多种元素皆能对其表面造成浸蚀。当逆光观察器表时，会看到许多微小麻坑，形似桔皮。

Numb spot: No matter how hard and dense the jade quality is, the various elements in soil can be etched as it surface causes. When observe ware surface conversly, you can see a lot of small numb hollows and shape which seems orange skin.

孔洞：玉器由于受到酸、碱、生石灰等化学物质浸蚀，由表及里形成深浅不一、孔周参差不齐形似虫蛀之孔。

Hole: Because of geting the chemical materials such as acid, soda and raw lime, Jade ware etches from surface to depth differently, different size shape different holes

蚀斑：玉器表面绺裂处玉皮剥落，由于玉石分泌物长期集存所形成的褐色斑痕。

Eroded spot: Surface tuft crack pattern of jade ware, jade skin is peeled off,Because jade secretes material for long-term concentration which has the brown a little trace of color spot formed.

白化：当某种元素作用于玉器时，这种元素恰与玉石所含有元素快速溶合并发生化学反应，改变玉石质地成为白色。

White Calcification: When certain kind element takes affect in jade ware, this kind of element exactly with the element contained by jade dissolve fast to merge occur chemical reaction, Change jade quality to become white colour.

钙化：碳酸钙等类物质对玉石所造成的侵害，其颜色界于白化与石化之间。

Calcification：The kind of materials such as calcium carbonate for jade cause hurt, Its color between circle in white calcification and stone calcification.

石化：玉器在白化或钙化后，泥浆随之浸入并凝结，玉石微透明特性发生质变。呈石质的玉器，其色如土。

Stone Calcification: After jade ware in white calcification or calcification, mud along with soak to enter and condense, jade tiny transparent property occured. The jade ware like stone, and the colour like earth.

沁色的统一性：特定环境下，各种微量元素在土壤中通常是均等分布的。当玉器整体被土覆盖，受沁后的玉器应该保持沁色的相对统一。

Infiltration the unity of colour: Under specific environment, various trace elements are usually equal distribution in soil. When the whole of jade ware cover by earth, receive the jade ware after infiltration the relative unification that should maintain infiltration colour.

沁色的完整性：在相同环境与条件下，一件玉器的受沁变化应该是全面而完整的。无论器面的突起或凹下，甚至系佩孔处都不会出现"断沁"现象。

Infiltration the integrity of colour: Under the same of environmental and Condition, A jade ware get infiltration change should be complete all-sidedly. Regardless of ware surface convexity or concave go down, even to wear hole place will not arise the phenomenon " infiltration breaks ".

沁色的过渡性：当沁色通过玉器表面瑕疵处进入玉理后，要经过漫长时间方能深入和扩展开来，因此形成了沁色的逐渐过渡。其特征类似喷绘。

Infiltration colour transitional: After Infiltration colour enters jade through the surface flaw place of jade ware, for a long time, which is going to deeply and expanded, Therefore have formed infiltration colour transform gradually. Feature is similar to spray to paint.

活沁与死沁：凡活沁，沁色皆有进入点，由一点而逐渐扩展成面。活沁为露头沁，浸入点颜色较重。如水银浸入，可见进入处泛锡光。死沁，沁色内含玉理，无进入点。所见黑斑、杂质、颜色皆为玉石生成时原生包裹体。活沁，生动活泼。死沁，僵滞呆板。

Live infiltration and dead infiltration: All live infiltration, Infiltration colour enter point and expand surface gradually. Live infiltration shows infiltration of head, Soak into a dark color. For instance, mercury soaks enter, you can see the tin light.

dead infiltration, contains jade skin texture , have no enter point. You can see black spot、impurity、and raw parcel body with jade color. Live infiltration, it is lively. Dead infiltration, it is stiff and rigid.

开门：古玩行语。形容开门见山，一目了然。

Open the door: Antiques profession terminology. described to come straight to the point, is clear at one sight.

通过原始遗存物质对玉器科学鉴定

现今高科技的仪器和先进设备，完全能够为玉器鉴定提供切实可靠的参考数据。但这种行之有效的方法，必须在玉器本身所具备一定条件下方能完成。例如，在玉器系佩孔与表面所发现的原始遗存土样与粘附腐殖物，通过这些，可以科学分析土质与玉器受沁变化是否存在必然关系；沉积土在玉器表面的压实程度是否具备客观形成年代；腐殖物纤维成分是否符合特定年代特征。以此分析与最终确定玉器的制作完成时间。

玉器原始遗存物质，是科学鉴定的重要物证和今后鉴定工作的方向，并具有全球统一性的重要意义，切不可忽视。

Scientific Appraisal of Jade Articles by Original Remains

Nowaday,the high-tech instnment and advanced equipment can offerpractical reliable reference data tor the appralsal of jade artlcles completely.But this kind of effectire method that can be completed mustbe in a certain condition possessed by jade articles themselves.

For instance,original remains of soil sample and sticking rottenmaterials that wrere discovered in the wearing hole and the surface ot jadearticles.through these,can scientlflcally analyze soil quality and Jadearticles received ooze changes whether there is inevitable relation;Whether the squeezing compact degree of depositing soil on the surface ofjade articles has objective forming ages; Whether the rotten fiber compositionaccorbs with specific ages feature. For this we can analyze and finally determine the time of finishing jade articles.

The original remains of Jade articles are the working birection of the appraisal in the future and the important material evidence of scientific appraisal,and have impoortant meaning of global unity,so not to be ignored.

图6 玉镯
(牛河梁第二地点一号冢14号墓出土)
尺寸：直径6.8cm（右） 7.3cm（左）
Picture 6 Jade Bracelet
(unearthed in the No.14 tomb from the No.1 stone mound at the No.2 location of Niuheliang)
Size: diameter6.8cm (right)7.3cm(left)

图7 玉镯局部放大
Picture 7 Jade Bracelet partly enlarged

原始出土玉器上的残留物，可成为我们鉴定玉器的重要科学依据。

如泥沙、腐烂物、附着物，我们可以通过它所含有的元素和成分化验,检测出玉器受沁变化的合理性。并通过碳14测定出玉器的制作年代。

我们所见玉镯器表的附着泥土十分坚固，须用竹刀方能除去，成片剥落、不松散、呈粘结状。

The residuum of original unearthed jade wares can become the important scientific basis on which we appraise them.

As silt, rotten things and attachment, we can examine to conclude the rationality that jade ware received infiltration through the test of its composition and element and determine the producing age time of jade wares through carbon 14.

The soil attached on the surface of jade bracelet ware is very firm, which must use bamboo knife to exclude, and it flakes off not loosely to submit binding form.

图 8 玉蝗
尺寸：高 8.8cm
玉质：青玉
〔听雨堂珍藏〕

Picture 8 Jade locust
Size: 8.8cm high
Jade texture: blue-green jade
(Collection of "rain-hear hall")

图 9 玉蝗背面
Picture 9 The back of jade locust

图 10 玉蝗系佩孔处局部放大
Picture 10 the hole of hanging and wearing of Jade locust
partly enlarged

许多红山文化玉器的系佩孔、镂空处存有遗留物。它为我们今后的 科学仪器鉴定提供了很好的原始资料。

这件玉蝗系佩孔处，可明显看到麻丝状腐烂物。以此可测定出玉器的制作年代。

A lot of hanging and wearing holes and hollow place of Hongshan-culture jade wares remains other matters. It has offered very good source data for our scientific instrument appraisal in the future.

This hanging and wearing hole place of jade locust can be seen rotten hemp silk material obviously. With this we can determine the producing age of jade ware.

图 11 玉鸟
尺寸：高 4.2cm
玉质：青玉
（听雨堂珍藏）
Picture 11 Jade bird
Size: 4.2cm high
Jade texture: blue-green jade
(Collection of "rain-hear hall")

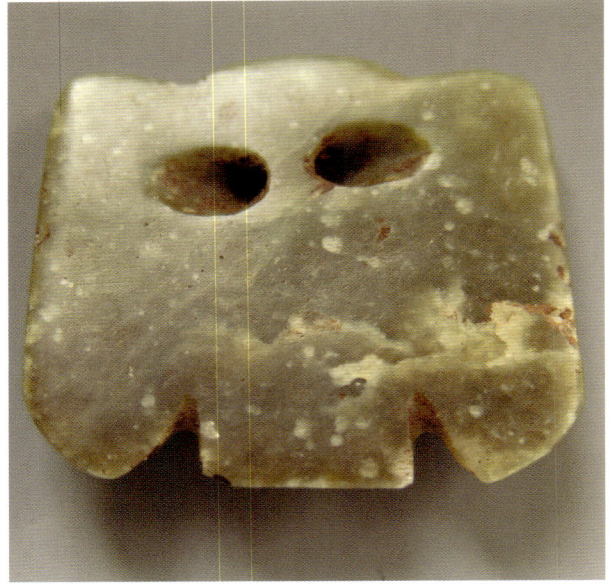

图 12 玉鸟器背
Picture 12 The back of jade bird

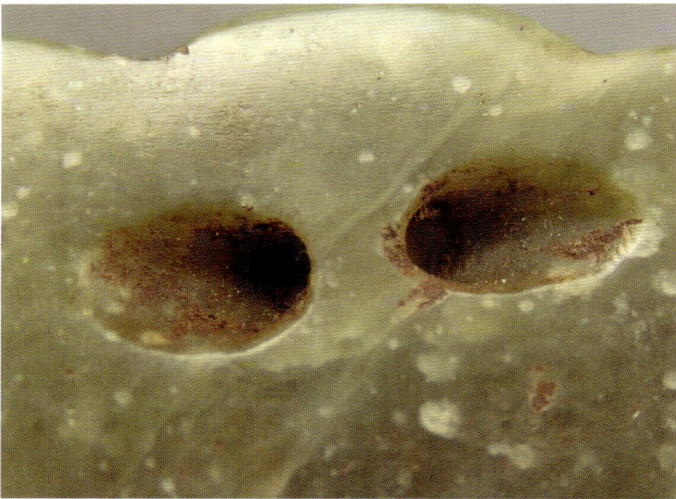

图 13 玉鸟系佩孔处局部放大
Picture 13 the hanging and wearing hole of Jade bird partly enlarged

玉鸟受沁后可见绺裂痕、钙化斑，并且包浆明显。

这是一件未经盘化保持原始出土状态的红山文化玉器，尽管土锈未除，但仍能够看出温润亮泽的包浆。

After jade bird receives infiltration, we can see the trace of tuft and crack、Calcification spot, and like thick liquid around the jade ware is obvious.

This is a non-made Hongshan-culture jade ware maintains original unearthed state, though the soil rust does not be excluded , but can still find out mild baojiang.

图 14 玉鳄
尺寸：高 5.3cm
玉质：青玉
（听雨堂珍藏）

Picture 14 Jade crocodile
Size: 5.3cm high
Jade texture: blue-green jade
(Collection of "rain-hear hall")

图 15 玉鳄背面
Picture 15 The back of Jade crocodile

图 16 玉鳄系佩孔处局部放大
Picture 16 the hanging and wearing hole of Jade crocodile partly enlarged

玉鳄玉质坚密，但受沁后仍可见器表微小麻斑。

系佩孔内沉集泥土粘结牢固，由此可以分析土质和大致形成时间，并可为科学仪器鉴定提供考证土样。

The texture of Jade crocodile is firm and dense, but after infiltration there is still small numb spot on the ware surface.

There is soil depositing in the hanging and wearing hole and binding firmly, so it can be analysed soil texture and approximate form time, and can offer archaeology verification soil sample for scientific instrument appraisal.

图17 玉鸟
尺寸：高 4.5cm
玉质：青玉
（听雨堂珍藏）
Picture 17 Jade bird
Size: 4.5cm high
Jade texture: blue-green jade
（Collection of "rain-hear hall"）

图18 玉鸟背面
Picture 18 The back of jade bird

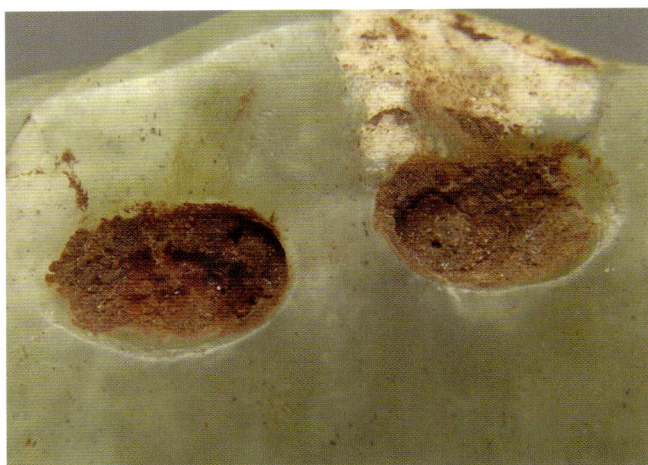

图19 玉鸟系佩孔处局部放大
Picture 19 the hanging and wearing hole of Jade bird partly enlarged

玉鸟受沁后可见器表遍布钙化斑与局部绺裂痕。

系佩孔内积存较多腐土，可供仪器分析、测定玉器制作年代。

很多人认为，包浆是由盘化而出。其实并不然，这件玉器未经盘化，包浆依然温润亮泽。

After jade bird receives infiltration, we can see the trace of tuft and crack、Calcification spot, and like thick liquid around the jade ware is obvious.

There is much rotten soil in the hanging and wearing hole for instrument analysis and mensuration of producing time of jade ware.

Many people think that baojiang is to made. Actually not, this jade ware do not be made, and baojiang still moist and bright.

红山文化玉器造型

Ornamental Mould of Hongshan-Culture Jade

红山文化玉器造型

在我们谈红山文化玉器的造型之前，首先要了解这一时期的历史背景。当母系氏族社会的权力逐渐转移到父系氏族以后，人们的原始宗教意识又进一步得到向前发展，这种发展仍然延续着原始先民对抵御自然灾害的束手无策和执政者权力的不可侵犯。这一时期的宗教活动不但频繁，而且犹为神圣。人们不但崇拜神灵，而且相信神灵主宰着生命及不同领域的一切。

对神灵的崇拜主要分为三个方面：自然图腾崇拜、祖先图腾崇拜和生殖图腾崇拜。

自然图腾崇拜：就是源自于大自然中的各种动、植物或其他物体。他们相信这些东西能够给人们带来好运或者安全感。例如，当他们看到鸟类在天空中自由飞翔时，希望自己也能够那样随心所欲。进而又想到，人死后鸟儿能够将自己的灵魂带入天上，进入那个神秘莫测的美好世界。并因此崇拜鸟类动物为天神。兽类动物是原始先民赖以生存的主要食粮。对于游牧民族来说，离开动物他们就不能存活，因此他们又将兽类动物崇拜为地神。天、地之神的产生，说明当时人们所追求的精神寄托和物质保障。

祖先图腾崇拜：按照弗洛伊德学说应该来自于梦境。当某一天人们在梦境中幻觉到自己已逝去的祖先时，首先感到的是惊奇和恐惧，进而相信人虽已去，但灵魂永存。另一方面又使人们增加对祖先的崇敬与思念，长时期以来这种传统意识一直在延续着。从对祖先神的敬畏到对祖先神所寄于的希望，人们在尽量表达自己的意愿。以玉制成神器或佩带，或供奉，或祭奠。这些想象中具原始形象的人物、动物或与人复合而成的图腾器，人们寄希望祖先的灵魂永存和得到祖先神的保护，或者期望自己死后灵魂能够追随祖先，从而得到再生。

生殖图腾崇拜：生殖被原始先民视为最神秘而神圣的领地。在新石器时代，不同地域的部族不但有着严格的婚姻制度，同时又希望自己的部落与部族得到更快的发展与壮大。因为疾病和自然灾害严重威胁着人们的生命，此时生殖与繁衍尤显得格外重要。这一时期的人们不仅只关注人类的繁衍，同时与自己生命息息相关，象征部族财富的动物生殖与繁衍同样成为人们的热切企盼。人们之所以对生殖产生崇拜，因为生殖延续着生命，能够创造财富，而且更大的群体对战胜自然灾害非常有利。

在红山文化玉器群中，属自然图腾崇拜的玉器很多。我们见到最多的则是鸟形玉和兽形玉，因为它们象征着天神和地神。比较常见的有：玉鸟、玉鹰、玉鸮、玉凤及各种不同动物形态的玉兽。玉鸟多呈飞翔状，玉兽多为卷体。鸟类玉器所钻系挂孔多在鸟的颈后，悬挂起来时，鸟头朝向上方，多呈俯瞰状。而兽类玉器系挂孔多在兽背偏上方，悬挂起来时，兽头多朝下。鸟与兽头部的朝向不同，显然其中有着一定寓意。

红山文化玉器中常见到人面或兽面人物造型玉器。这些人物形玉器很多头部生角，双臂交于胸前，双腿弯曲呈倚蹲状。有人称此类玉器为太阳神，这些神祖类玉器极具神秘感。从玉器造型基本特征分析认为，原始先民相信他们的祖先是由某种动物演化而来。尤其头生双角的牛，它的特征极与神祖相似。角立于头顶，从某种意义上解释，象征着至高无上。角，直对苍天，同时又寓意着可与天对话，与神灵相沟通。角，还是保护自己抵御外侵的武器，是否与权力有关，还需进一步分析与研究。

总之，这些不同造型和神态各异的祖先神像的出现，说明当时人们对祖先的敬仰与崇拜，并进一步幻化为神灵，以求得到祖先神的充分保护。

生殖图腾崇拜在红山文化玉器中范围比较广泛，除一些较直观表现男性与女性的生殖器外，其它大多以动、植物或几何形状出现在红山文化玉器群中。这些造型奇特，寓意深刻，具象或抽象的玉器，皆以不同方式直观或隐喻的手法展示着男性与女性的生理特征，揭示着人类及一切生物生殖繁衍的神秘性及重大社会意义。例如我们在红山文化中常见到的，也是造型最简单的璧、环类玉器则是表现女性生殖器的。一些管、玉瑑类玉器则是表现男性生殖器的。笔者在所著《中国古玉珍藏》一书前言中对此进行了详尽分析。另外，红山文化古玉中的蝉、蚕、螳螂、蛙等因其繁殖能力极强，也被做为生殖繁衍的典范而得到崇拜。

在红山文化玉器群中还多见一些复合形器，这些复合形器多呈片状。也时常见到一些圆雕作品，这些玉器大都为抽象的鸟与兽复合而成，象征着天地合一之神。

红山文化玉器主要以动物为主。这些形态各异、风格朴拙、工艺精湛、抛光亮丽的动物形玉器、不但充满了神秘感，而且充分展现了时代气息。简练而高度概括的艺术造型，将雕塑艺术推向了一个永远不败的颠峰，让我们的后人望而兴叹，甚至怀疑为外星人所为。

红山文化玉器种类繁多，由于地区的不同、部族的不同、年代的不同、在玉器的造型及制作工艺方面或多或少存在一些较小的差异。尤其对一些尚未见到的其他造型的玉器，不要给予一概否定。因为我们相信没有正式发掘出来的东西还很多。比如前些年，我们的专家还不承认红山文化玉器中有人物形玉器，但没过两年正式发掘时就出现了，这应当不足为奇。还有，我们一些专家常常以正式发掘出土器为样品，在鉴定工作中按图索骥，与出土器稍有不同，则给予全面否定。做为历史唯物主义者，我们必须学会客观的分析问题和处理问题。武断霸道不能单纯理解为对事物的客观认知问题，水平问题。实际上反映出来的是思想意识问题，工作作风问题。任何主观武断、吹毛求疵、故弄玄虚、装腔作势，势必将古玉鉴定工作引入只有少数专家说了算的死胡同。长期以来，人们认为只有"专家"最权威。其实并不然，真才实学完全是在实践中不断摸索出来的。哲人说过："实践出真知"，就是这个道理。当然，理论也万不可忽视，尤其对红山文化古玉研究来说，要在实践中不断的学会分析和总结，从而升华理论。完全靠书本理论指导实践难免不走弯路，因为有些理论并没有经过充分验证，没有经过实践所产生的。这些空头理论或者错误的理论就不能够指导我们的实践，尤其古玉鉴定，实践更为重要。

红山文化玉器的造型千变万化，然而其神韵却是永远不变的。神韵是时代所留下的特殊印记，它包含玉器的用材、造型、神态、工艺、沁象等。同时神韵又是形态与神态、意念与理念综合的表露和内涵。正是这些潜移默化的有形和无形 "美"，成为构成神韵的主要条件和因素。

神韵是意境，是古玉的灵魂和生命。灵魂，是无形的，它没有特定的标准和衡量尺度。我们强调红山文化玉器的神韵，重在分析和观察构成神韵的诸要素是否达到一定要求。神韵固然很重要，但不能做为衡量玉器真伪的惟一理由。

我们说红山文化玉器的神韵是生命，是因为每一件玉器都并非随意之作，而与神灵崇拜有着密切的联系。作为神器，其中蕴含着极为深刻的寓意。正是通过这些神秘莫测的玉器，原始先民溶入了自己的愿望与意识，充分表达着自己的的憧憬与意愿。因此我们说，每一件红山文化玉器都是具有生命力的器物。

红山文化玉器不但充分展现了中国最原始的造型与雕塑艺术，而且充分体现了原始先民们高超的雕琢技艺与先进的生产能力。

通过对红山文化玉器造型的分析研究，能够让我们从中了解和掌握距今五、六千年前的历史史实及原始文化。比如，在动物形玉器中我们时常发现一些今天已不复存在的动物形象，这些动物在五、六千年前是否客观存在，而后来逐渐灭绝？红山文化玉器有大象，这种生活在亚热带地区的动物，是否远在新石器时代北方地区也有生存？如此等等，这于我们对原始社会气象学研究及生物科学研究都提供了十分难得的资料。还有，红山文化神祖类玉器为什么这些人物多双手交于腹处，双腿弯曲呈倚蹲状？为什么他们头顶多生有角？这些对于研究我国宗教历史发展应该有着特殊的意义。

通过对红山文化玉器造型分析与研究，不但能够让我们从中了解新石器时代的政治、经济、文化、宗教等诸多方面的历史史实，更让我们从中了解中华民族的发展历史和文明历史。

Modeling of Hongshan-Culture Jade

Before talking about shape of Hongshan-Culture jade, we should know the back ground of Hongshan culture first. When the evolutions of society from Matriarchal clan to Patriarchal clan, people□ religion consciousness got a big progress, but which still let our ancestors felt helpless against Natural disasters and inviolability of ruler. Religionary activities at this time were not only frequent but divine. Ancestors worshiped and believed god, which can control lives and everything of the trips.

God worship can be divided into three aspects: totem of nature worship, totem of primogenitor worship and totem of procreation worship.

Totem of nature worship came from natural animals and plants or other kind of things, which ancient people believe that would bring good luck or safety. For example, they wished they were as free as bird flying in the air. And they imagined that bird could bring their soul into the wonderful and mythic heaven after death, so they worshipped bird as god of heaven. Ancestors' main food was beast, and they couldn't live without their main food. Therefore, they adored beasts as gods of earth. Those totems indicated their desire of spiritual reposing and materials safety.

According to Floyd theory, totem of primogenitor worship comes from dream. Someday when pepole dreamed of their forefathers, the first reaction was fear and surprise, then they believed that the soul of the person still exist though his body has gone. On the other hand, such dreams make their worship and nostalgia of their primogenitors more deep. So they, through the human shaped jade, expressed that their wishes that the soul of primogenitor would last forever and get blesses from primogenitor and their own souls would follow their primogenitor and relive.

Totem of procreation worship: Procreation is the most mystic and divine field for the ancestors. In New Stone Age, different tribes not only had strict marriage system, but they also wished their trips thrived. Since their lives were threatened by all kinds of diseases and natural disasters, procreation were very important at that time. They also concerned procreation of animals, which linked their lives closely and symbolized their treasure would boom up. People worshiped procreation because it created life and treasure.

Most of Hongshan-Culture jade objects are nature worship totem, in which jade bird symbolized god of heaven, and jade animals symbolized god of earth. Among them most are jade bird, jade hawk, jade howlet, jade phoenix and various kinds of animals. Feature of those birds are flying, while animals are crouching. Holes in bird jade are in its back neck generally. When people hung it, head of the birds would up-forward as do aerial view. While hole located in near back of animal, and head of animal is down-forward when hanging the jade. The difference of head direction is obviously allegoric.

We can also see human face shaped jade or animal face shaped jade. Some human shaped jade has horns on the head, two arms folding before chest, two legs squatting. Experts call such kind of jade as Titan jade. Those mysterious features drop a hint that ancestors believed their forefathers were some kind of animals with horns, such as cattle. Explained in a way, horns on the head and up to the air directly, which symbolized sovereign and the right and they can talk with heaven and god. Horn, also as weapon of protection, whether concern with power or not, it needs future analyze and research.

In conclusion, those different primogenitor sculpted articles show people's worship and reverence to their primogenitors and they wish blesses from their primogenitors.

The procreation totem was widely used in the Hongshan culture jade carving. Except some intuitionistic male and female genitalia shaped jade, most are shaped as animal, plant or geometrical. Those unique in shape, profoundly allegoric, realism or nonrepresentational style jade show visually or metaphorically physiological characteristics of man and woman, exposing mystery and social significance of reproduction. For example, the simplest ring jade or round flat piece jade symbolize female pudendum, while some tubal figure jade symbolize male genitals. More related details can be found in Collection of Aged Jade. In addition, cicada, silkworm, frog and rearhorse which have strong capabilities of multiplication were worshiped as nonesuch of propagation in Hongshan Culture.

There are some compound figure jade articles, either, in which most are flat, and others are three-dimensional statues. These abstractive works mostly compound with bird and beast which symbolize the combination of heaven and earth.

Hongshan-Culture jade is mainly animal shaped. These animals are dissimilar in shape and form, simple and unadorned in style, exquisite on workmanship and well polished, full of mystical feeling. The succinct highly broad artistic modeling has pushed the sculpture art to a forever peak.

Thanks to the different tribes, different living areas, different time and different jade textures, Hongshan-Culture jade has a few differences on style and processing. Therefore, we shouldn't deny any jade before we haven't seen it, because there are still a lot of jade under the earth. For instance, some experts didn't admit existence of human shaped jade, but it was found after two years. Moreover, some experts appraised a earthed jade ware as a sample, and identified following some clues. If there is a little difference between them, they would deny the appraisal one. As historical materialists, we should study and deal with problems objectively. We can't take it for object with arbitrary attitude, which will reflect mentality and working problem. Dead end will be induced by any captious, arbitrary, deliberately mystifying and hoity-toity attitude. In fact, genuine acknowledge come from practice, of course we can't ignore theories, especially on Hongshan-Culture jade study. We should analyze and summarize from practice continuously, but shouldn't be conducted by books completely. Some theories hadn't been identified by any practice, and they can't lead our practice, especially Jade identification.

Though styles of the jade changed a lot, but verve of the jade is the same. Verve, including texture, style, technics, and craftwork, is the unique sign of times. Verve composes visible and invisible beauty, reveals and connotes modality and expression, consciousness and concept.

Verse is soul and life of jade. Soul is formless; there is no criterion on it. We emphasize on verse here, but we also couldn't neglect the elements composing the verse. Verse is very important, but not absolute.

We say that verse is the life of Hongshan-Culture jade, because every jade object not only concern with god worship closely, but also profoundly allegoric. Ancestors mixed their own sub-consciousness with jade and expressed their own thoughts and wills through jade. Therefore we say every Hongshan-Culture jade had been given its own life. Hongshan-Culture jade displays not only the most primordial sculpture art and its shape, but also our ancestors' high productive capability.

We can understand the history and culture of five or six thousand years ago by analyzing and studying on shapes of Hongshan-Culture jade wares. For example, we couldn't find some jade pictured animals living in this world now, whether the animals really existed five or six thousand years ago and deracinate gradually? We found there is elephant shaped jade article, did this semi-tropical animal living in the north area in New Stone Age? Those provide veridical data for ancient aerography and biology study. And why most human sculptures fold the hands on their abdomen and two legs squatted? Why most of them have horns? These questions are significant for religion history study.

Through Hongshan-Culture jade we can know more about politics, economy, culture, religion and history of New Stone Age as well as developing history and civilization history of Chinese people.

图 20　块形玉兽（辽宁省文物商店在辽西地区征集）
尺寸：高 4.2cm
Picture20　Jade Coiled Animal(collecting at the Liaoning cultural relic shop in western area of Liaoning province)
Size: 4.2cm high

图 21　块形玉兽局部放大
Picture21　Jade Coiled Animal Partly enlarged

　　这件玉器曾被多位考古专家用以演示由块形玉兽到龙之演化过程。只是因为它与多数块形玉兽首、尾相连的形式，与伸展的"C"型玉龙形态有所不同，所以被作为承上启下中间演化环节。

　　红山文化玉器种类繁多，同类器物的造型也很难完全相同，都会存在一定差异。因此作者质疑红山文化在一千年延续时间里，在相同时期、相同环境下块形玉兽向玉龙的快速演化。考古专家的推论显然还缺少足够的科学依据。何况此器为民间征集所得。作者认为，块形玉兽与玉龙，两者不过所表现的动物不同而已。

　　我们的研究与鉴定工作，必须尊重科学。万不可仅凭想象，应鉴之有理、有证、有据，令人信服。

This jade ware have engaged in demonstration that the evolution course from jade coiled animal to dragon by many experts. Only because it is different with the form of "C"-type jade dragon on the form that majority of jade coiled animal's head and tail is linked together, so have been as intermediate evolution link to connect before and later.

There are numerous kinds of Hongshan culture jade wares, so the same kind of wears' modeling will not be completely identical, too. It would be certain discrepancy. Therefore the author suspect that for Hongshan culture lasting 1000 years, the jade coiled animal evolved to jade dragon so rapidly during the same period in the same environment. It obviously lacks enough scientific basis in the inference of expert yet, furthermore this ware is collected in non-governmental circles. The author thinks that the jade coiled animal and jade dragon just show two different animals.

Our studying and appraising work, must obey science. It cannot only rely on imagination, should appraise reasonably, certifiably and evidentially, so can make people to be convinced.

图 22 虎形佩
玉质：青玉
尺寸:高 12.4 cm 宽 3.4cm
（听雨堂珍藏）
Picture 22Name: tiger-shape jade pendant
Jade texture: blue-green jade
Size: 12.4 cm high   3.4cm wide
(Collection of "rain-hear hall")

图 23 虎形佩另面
Picture23 another side of tiger-shape jade pendant

同一种动物，因为地区、部落、制作时间等不同原因，其造型也不尽相同。

我们所见虎形佩，除此之外还见有直体的，器身打洼成阳线条纹，呈搓衣板状，极似虎身之斑纹。

在鉴定工作中，我们不要因器型的变化而给以否定。你所未见到的，不能说明此器客观不存在。

The same kind of animal for area, tribe, produce time etc, is different, so its modelling is also not identical.

The tiger-shape jade pendan that we see, besides there is straight body ware and its body carves convex line veins presenting scrubbing board shape, very like the tiger body's stripe.

In appraising work, we would not negate for the change of ware type. If you don't see it before, it would not explain tha the ware don't exist objectively.

图 24 虎形佩局部放大
Picture24 tiger-shape jade pendan partly enlarged

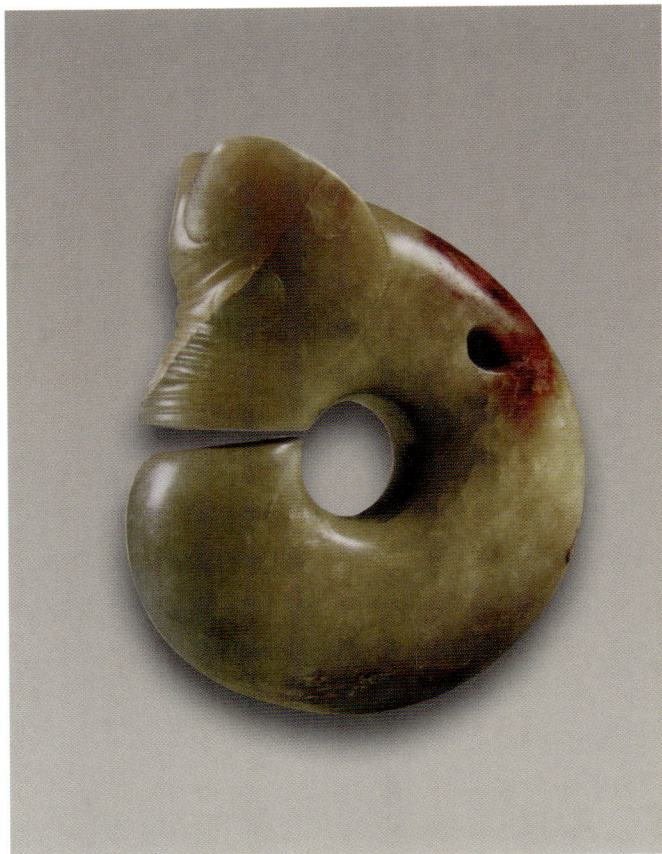

图25 玦形玉兽（牛河梁二号冢1号墓出土）
尺寸：高10.3cm
Picture25 Jade Coiled Animal(unearthed in the No.1 tomb from the No.2 stone mound of Niuheliang)
Size: 10.3cm high

图26 玦形玉兽局部放大
Picture26 Jade Coiled Animal Partly enlarged

　　玦形玉兽，属地母神器，在红山文化玉器群中较为多见。它独特的兽面、耸立的双耳、卷曲的身体、头尾相接处的切口，构成了玦形玉兽主要特征。

　　玦形玉兽额头处、鼻间、吻部皆刻画阴线纹，让玉兽更加鲜活而生动。

　　玉兽头部富有层次感的绺裂与兽背处灵动的铁锈沁斑及兽尾处的白化斑，多方面认证了此器的真实性。

Jade Coiled Animal, belongs to Earth mother supernatural ware. It is relatively common in Hongshan-culture jade ware. Its unique beast surface, erecting binaural, curl body and cut of head and tail's connective spot forms the major feature of jade coiled animal.

There is carved concave line veins on the forehead of jade coiled animal, between nose and on its mouth, which let jade animal more fresh and lively.

The rich sense of depth tuft split of Animal's head, the spot infiltrate by rust on animal's lively back and white spot on animal's tail certificate the actuality of this ware in various aspect.

图 27 马蹄形玉箍（牛河梁二号冢 1 号墓出土）
尺寸：高 18.6cm
Picture 27 hoof-shaped jade hoop (unearthed in the No.1
tomb from the No.2 stone mound from Niuheliang)
Size: 18.6cm high

图 28 马蹄形玉箍局部放大
Picture28 Jade hoof-shaped ornament Part is
enlarged

　　马蹄形玉箍，又被称作玉发冠、箍形器。某些人认为,因多发现在墓主头部，应为实用发冠。其实并不然。作者认为，此器当属祖先图腾崇拜器。先民们认为自己的祖先是由某种长角的动物演化而来。取角之一段，制成冠，用以与祖先灵魂相沟通。红山文化葬墓周围发现大量半面彩绘筒形器，其意义与象征性玉冠是相同的。

　　动物之角，直对蓝天，同时被认为至高无上，应与权力有关。桶形，腹腔中空，灵魂能入、能出。因此成为沟通天神的最好法器。

　　The hoof-shaped jade hoop is also called jade hair crest, hoof-shaped hoop. Some people think that it is practical hair crest for being on the head of grave owner. Actually on the contrary, the author thinks that this ware would belong to ancestors' totem worship ware. Late people think that their own ancestors were evoluted from the certain kind animal that grows angles. Taking a length of angles, they made into crest to link up with ancestors' soul. We discovered plenty of colored drawing can-shaped ware of half surface around Hongshan culture burying grave whose meaning and symbolization is identical.

　　The angles of animal are towards the blue sky directly, at the same time, have been thought that is paramount, it should be concerning with power. Barrel shape is empty inside abdominal cavity, so the soul can be in and out. Therefore it become the best ware of linking up with god.

图 29　马蹄形器图
尺寸：高 9.6 cm
玉质：青黄玉
（听雨堂珍藏）
Picture29hoof-sharped jade ware
Size: 9.6 cm high
Jade texture: blue-green jade
(Collection of "rain-hear hall")

图 30　马蹄形器局部放大
Picture 30 hoof-sharped jade ware partly enlarged

　　马蹄形器，筒状，又被称为玉发冠、筒形器等。看似造型比较简单但加工难度却很大。这种器型在红山文化玉器群中已见有多件。

　　The hoof-sharped jade ware, cylinder form, is also called jade hair crest、cylinder form ware etc. It seems more simple on modelling but its process is very difficult.
　　There have been a lot of this kind of ware type in the Hongshan culture jade ware crowd.

镯、环、玦、管、箍类红山文化玉器，皆属生殖图腾崇拜之神器。其造型形成特殊的规律性。镯，多外缘呈刃状，内缘两侧向内斜切，中间起棱线。箍，器面圆，两边呈刃状，内缘向外缓收，中间微突。

The hongshan-culture jade ware, such as Bracelet, loop, coiled and hoop, all belongs to supernatural ware of reproduction totem worship. Its modelling forms special regularity. Bracelet, besides much, reason is submited edge form, reason two side to oblique cut, from intermediate edge line. Hoop, ware surface is round, both sides are submited edge form, reason receive outward slowly, intermediate tiny suddenly.

图 31 玉镯（牛河梁五号冢 1 号墓出土）
尺寸：直径 8.5cm
Picture31 Jade bracelet (unearthed in No.1 tomb from No.5 stone mound of Niuheliang)
Size: diameter 8.5cm

这两件原本为淡青色玉质的玉器，由于长时期埋藏于地下，与各种元素相接触后，其质地已发生变化，已不再保持原本玉石颜色。因此我们现在所见红山文化玉器颜色，全部为玉器沁后颜色。

The texture of this two is light cyan jade formerly, since burying underground for a long time, after contacting with various elements, its texture has changed, and it have not maintained formerly jade color any more. Therefore, That we now see the colour of Hongshan-culture jade ware all is the colour after infiltration for jade ware.

图 32 玉箍（牛河梁五号冢 1 号墓出土）
尺寸：直径 5.75cm.
Picture 32 jade hoop (unearthed in No.1 tomb from No.5 stone mound of Niuheliang)
Size: diameter 5.75 cm

图 33 天地神佩
尺寸：高 5.8cm 宽 17.8cm
玉质：青玉
（听雨堂珍藏）
Picture33 Compound jade
baldric for heaven and earth
Size: 5.8cm high17.8 cm wide
Jade texture: blue-green jade
(Collection of "rain-hear hall")

图 34 天地神佩另面
Picture34 Compound jade
baldric for heaven and earth
partly enlarged

图 35 天地神佩局部放大
Picture35 another side of compound jade baldric for heaven and
earth

呈片状的天地神佩，多由鸟与兽复合
而成，象征着天地合一。

掌握红山文化玉器的造型，对于我们
的鉴定工作是十分必要的。

The compound jade baldric for heaven and
earth presents slice shape, majority of which is
compound by bird and beast, so it stands for
heaven and earth to join one body.

Grasping the modeling of Hongshan culture jade ware is necessary for our appraisal work.

图 36　双兽首璜形器
尺寸：长 18.5 cm
玉质：青玉
（听雨堂珍藏）
Picture 36 ancient jade-shape ware with double beast heads
Size : 18.5 cm long
Jade texture: blue-green jade
(Collection of "rain-hear hall")

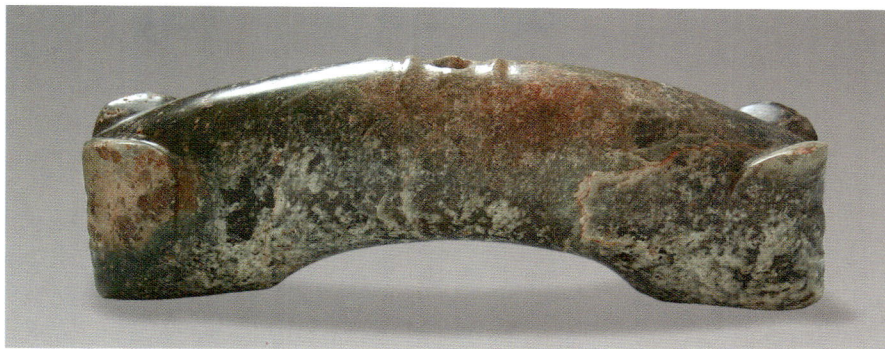

图 37 双兽首璜形器另面
Picture 37another side of ancient jade-shape ware with double beast heads

这件圆雕动物形玉器，不但生动的表现了动物的形态与神态，而且在造型上做了抽象化处理，因此更增强了神秘感与震撼力。

This round-carved and animal-shape jade ware, not only is lively to show the manner and form of animal, but also make abstract on modeling,therefore much more strengthened mysterious sense and shock force.

图 38 双兽首璜形器局部放大
Picture 38 ancient jade-shape ware with double beast heads partly enlarged

图 39 天地神佩
尺寸：高 16.3 cm
玉质：青玉
（听雨堂珍藏）
Picture 39 Compound jade baldric for heaven and earth
Size: 16.3 cm high
Jade texture: blue-green jade
(Collection of "rain-hear hall")

图 40 天地神佩另面
Picture 40 another side of compound jade baldric for heaven and earth

　　天地神佩，又被称为勾云形器。是由多个弯勾组合成器。
　　对这些弯勾进行分析，其形象多为鸟与兽复合而成，象征着天与地溶合为一体之神器。

Compound jade baldric for heaven and earth is also called hook-like cloud shape ware which is composed of many hooks.
　　Analysing these hooks, whose image is compounded with bird and beast, stand for the supernatural ware heaven and earth joining one body.

图 41 天地神佩局部沁象放大
Picture 41Compound jade baldric for heaven and earth infiltration phenomenon partly enlarged

图 42 玉龙
尺寸：高 23 cm
玉质：青玉
（听雨堂珍藏）

Picture 42 Jade dragon
Size: 23 cm high
Jade texture: blue-green jade
(Collection of "rain-hear hall")

图 43　玉龙另面
Picture 43 another side of jade dragon

　　圆雕玉龙要经过多道工序方能完成。观察龙体形象：伸曲有度，线条流畅，工艺精湛，温润亮泽，受沁变化真实自然。

　　Round-carved jade dragon must be through a lot of processes to finish. Observing the image of dragon body: having degree on stretch and bending, smooth line, consummate technology, moderate and moist bright, and its infiltration change true and natural.

图 44 玉龙局部放大
Picture 44 Jade dragon partly enlarged

图45 玉羊首
尺寸：宽11.5cm
玉质：青玉
（听雨堂珍藏）

Picture 45 Jade sheep head
Size: 11.5cm wide
Jade texture: blue-green jade
(Collection of "rain-hear hall")

图46 玉羊首另面
Picture 46 another side of jade sheep head

玉羊首以钻孔与线刻表现其面部形象，简练而生动。

从阴刻线条流畅程度来看，无专门工具，完全靠手工不能完成。

Jade sheep head expresses image of its face with drilling hole and carving line, and it is terse and lively.

From the smooth degree of concave-carved line, without special tool, and they only relied on handwork completely can not be completed.

图 47　玉鸟
尺寸：高 7.8 cm　宽 11cm
玉质：青玉
（听雨堂珍藏）

Size: 7.8 cm high　11cm wide
Jade texture: blue-green jade
(Collection of "rain-hear hall")

　　玉鸟造型朴拙而生动，器身多层次
变化，增强了鸟之动感与逼真。

　　红山文化玉器特殊的造型，明显有
别于其它年代玉器。

　　The modeling of Jade bird is simple,
clumsy and lively, and its body is much more
levels to change, which strengthen dynamic
and lifelike of bird.

　　The special modeling of Hongshan-
culture jade ware have obvious distinguish with
the jade ware of other age.

图 48　玉鸟另面
picture 48 another side of Jade bird

图 49 双兽首玉佩

尺寸：长 8.2 cm

玉质：青玉

（听雨堂珍藏）

picture49 Double animal heads jade pendant

Size: 8.2 cm long

Jade texture: blue-green jade

(Collection of "rain-hear hall")

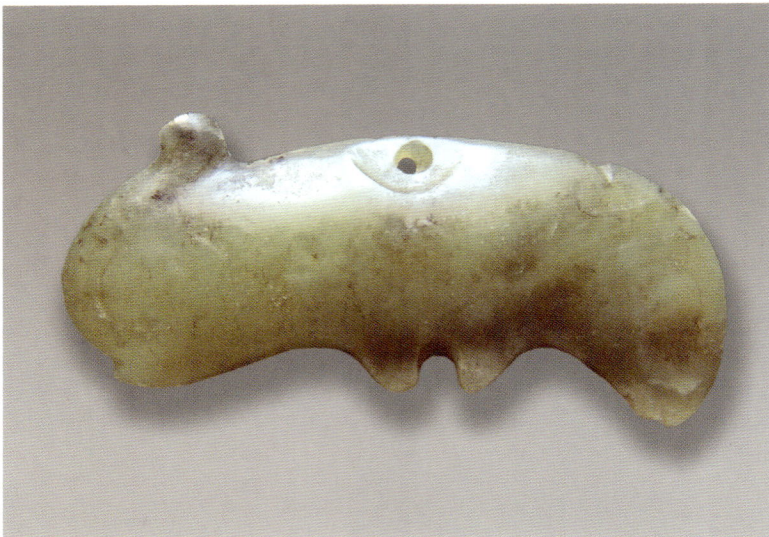

图 50 双兽首玉佩另面

picture50 another side of Double animal heads jade pendant

红山文化玉器，即使同类型也不完全相同。在鉴定工作中，我们不要固执的以出土器做为样本按图索骥，决定真赝。

Hongshan-culture jade ware, even if the same type is not completely identical. In appraising work, we would not be stubborn in ware as sample to decide real or fake.

图 51 玉蛙

尺寸：高 16cm　宽 8cm

玉质：青玉

（听雨堂珍藏）

Picture 51 Jade frog

Size: about 16cm long　about 8cm wide

Jade texture: blue-green jade

(Collection of "rain-hear hall")

　　玉蛙四肢连璧，为复合型器。造型简洁，寓意深刻。由此可见，以对称、和谐、图案形式表现方法由来已久。让我们从中感悟到，原始先民在创造文化艺术的同时，并在追求和企盼世间所有一切的平衡。

The four extremities of Jade frog are linked, which is compound type ware. Its modeling is succinct , and it has deep implied meaning. Thus it can be seen that the expression method symmetrical, harmonious, pattern form has come into being since a long time ago. And it let us experience that original late people created art culture and at the same time pursued and hoped all the balance in the world.

图 52 玉蛙局部放大

Picture52 Jade frog partly enlarged

图 53 勾云形大玉佩（牛河梁第二地点一号冢 27 号墓出土）

尺寸：长 28.6cm

Picture 53 Cloud-like Hook Large Jade Pendant (unearthed in the No.27 tomb from the No.1 stone mound at the No.2 location of Niuheliang)

Size: 28.6cm long

图 54 勾云形大玉佩局部放大

Picture 54 Cloud-like Hook Large Jade Pendant partly enlarged

勾云形玉佩，我称之为"天地神佩"，多由鸟与兽二者复合而成，象征着天地溶为一体，以企盼天、地合谐而永衡，希望人间永远的安定与一切生命物的健康。

天地神佩，属自然图腾崇拜神器。在造型上追求对称，对称即合谐，合谐则永衡。

此器为青玉制作，受沁后的器表可见复杂的沁象变化，真实而自然。

Cloud-like Hook Large Jade Pendant, which I call "Compound Jade Baldric for Heaven and Earth", and majority of it is compound by bird and beast, stand for Heaven and Earth blending into one body, so as to wish Heaven and Earth harmonious and eternal, and hope the world forever stable and health of all life things.

Compound Jade Baldric for Heaven and Earth, belongs to natural totem worship supernatural ware, pursuing symmetry on modeling. Symmetry is harmonious, and harmonious is eternal.

This ware is made of blue-green jade, and the surface of ware can be seen the complex change of infiltration after getting infiltration, true and natural.

红山文化玉器用材

Raw Materials of Hongshan—Culture Jade

红山文化玉器用材

关于红山文化玉器的原材料来源问题，多年来一直是人们探讨与研究的课题。大家普遍认为，由于历史的原因，交通运输工具的落后，恶劣的自然气候条件，原始先民只能就地或就近取材。

从目前我们所发现的红山文化分布情况来看，除已发掘的辽西牛河梁遗址外，并且在内蒙古的巴林左旗、巴林右旗、敖汉旗、翁牛特旗、奈曼旗、库伦旗、通辽地区及吉林的农安、黑龙江的依兰县，皆发现红山文化遗存。这些被正式发掘或发现的玉器无论器型或者制作工艺皆与红山文化相似。称其为红山前、红山后、前红山，后红山时期玉器。这些被通称为红山文化的玉器，分布面积极为广泛，除辽宁西部和内蒙古东部外，并跨越东北三省，连绵数千里。年代跨度约在距今4500——8000年。

如此大面积的红山文化分布区域，前后延续了3500年，这一时期的制玉材料究竟来自何处？围绕这一问题，我们的考古学家、地质学家，历史学家、古玉研究专家以及古玉收藏家都在潜心分析研究这一神秘而严肃的课题。专家们从红山文化玉器的玉质矿物构成、矿物成分、刻划硬度、玉石的色泽等诸多方面进行推论，在众说纷纭之后，大部分专家认为：红山文化玉器原材料来自于辽宁南部的岫岩，即我们所说的岫岩玉。

专家们这一结论是否正确？笔者在此不予妄加评论，就自己的认识略谈一二。

一、红山文化玉器的玉质

红山文化玉器的玉质，就我们较为普遍看到的，从矿物学的角度来说，主要为透闪石和蛇纹石两大类。透闪石类质地坚密，刻划硬度一般在4.5度——5度左右。蛇纹石类，质地较软，刻划硬度大多在3.5度——4度左右。由于两者矿物成分和玉理结构不同，其刻划硬度也各不相同。

需要明确指出的是，我们现在所测出的玉石硬度，是玉器受沁后的硬度，而并非受沁前玉石硬度。

我们完全可以领悟：当一件石器、铁器、铜器或其它物质，在土层下埋藏百年、千年以后，自然会受到土壤中各种元素的浸蚀，这种浸蚀与侵害由表及里逐渐深入。受侵害物体，不但外观形象有所改变，而且原有质地也会改变。玉器同其它物体一样，受沁后其质地已发生质的变化。这种质变，说明出土玉器已不再保持自己原有的坚密度和刻划硬度。如果我们今天仍然以受沁后的红山文化古玉器的刻划硬度与现今岫岩玉相比较。显然违背自然科学规律，因而其结论不能成立。

二、红山文化玉器的矿物成分

有人将红山文化玉器与现今岫岩玉矿物成分进行了分析比较，认定两者所含矿物成分基本相同，因此断定，红山文化玉器即岫岩玉制作。

我们知道，任何物质在正常条件下，自身特性都不会有较大的改变，这就是一定时期内的相对稳定性。比如透闪石类红山文化玉器，在其质地未遭受到破坏时，其所含有矿物成分自然与新玉无较大差异。而当玉质遭受到破坏时，各种金属元素与非金属元素随之侵入玉理，其矿物成分必然有所改变。因此，以现今岫岩玉与出土红山文化受沁玉器做矿物成分比较，显然缺乏科学性，因而其结论真实性受到质疑。

三、红山文化玉器的颜色

做学问，应该先研究而后结论，而结论必须注重科学依据。有人说，原有红山文化玉器用玉现已经绝迹。也有人说，红山文化玉器所见黄色玉又在岫岩细玉沟和瓦沟发现。如此种种论说，无外乎红山玉即岫岩玉已成定论。

我们目前所看到的红山文化玉器大致有以下几种颜色：深青色、青色、青白色、青黄色、黄色、绿色、鸡骨白色。凡玉器表面呈青色者，我们则统称为青玉。凡泛黄色者，我们统称为黄玉。要知道，这些不同颜色的玉，只是我们直观感觉表面现象，而并非玉之本质。

玉之本质颜色，当以原生玉固有颜色而定位。而并非完成器受沁后所呈显颜色。两者之间必须从根本上区别开来，否则我们势必进入误区。

红山文化玉器受沁后的颜色改变，取决于玉石本身的矿物成分，玉理的致密度，客观地理环境及土壤中所含有的元素等诸多方面条件。受沁玉器在颜色变化的同时玉石质地也在发生变化。发生质变的玉石无论受沁过程如何，都有其自身规律性。在通常情况下，当深青色玉受沁后其颜色会逐渐加深，按沁后颜色变化被我们称为苍玉。淡青色玉受沁后其颜色会逐渐变淡，或者呈黄色。被我们称为黄玉或青黄玉。颜色变深者，多为蛇纹石类玉器，由于其质地松软，易于浸入多种元素，加深颜色。而沁后呈黄玉者，多为透闪石类玉器，因其质地坚密，各种元素无法大量浸入，而土壤中微量元素透过玉表缓慢透进玉理所发生整体色变。

众多红山文化玉器受沁迹象表明：深色玉受沁后颜色会更深。浅色玉受沁后其颜色更浅。这就是我所总结出的：玉器受沁相向发展变化的"两极性"。

根据以上种种理由说明，以目前所见岫岩玉与红山文化玉器作颜色上的比较，以此确定红山玉即岫岩玉之理论当应该做重新考虑。

四、红山文化玉器的材料来源

红山文化玉器大部分为透闪石、蛇纹石制作，其中还有少量玛瑙、水晶、松石及其它杂石。松石的来源问题，还是来自于我国南方或者境外，有待于专门的科学研究。透闪石与蛇纹石目前还不能最终考定具体产地。其它石种皆产于辽宁西部和内蒙古东部地区。

关于红山文化玉器原材料来源问题，目前仍然存在着许多不解之谜。我们试想，假如红山时期先民大量从岫岩地区采集玉石材料，在恶劣的自然环境中，多变的气候条件下，生老病死，这是很正常的事情。做为物质交流或文化交流也当在情理之中。但迄今为止，在岫岩地区尚未发现一件红山文化时期玉器或其它遗存，这是值得我们认真思考的问题。

另外，根据史料记载医巫闾山产珣玗琪，珣玗琪即为玉石。有专家说，医巫闾即今天的岫岩。分析起来，这一说法似乎有些牵强。因为医巫闾山现今仍然存在，并且山名未改，它就在辽宁西部的北镇和义县一带，并已成为名胜风景区。但在现今医巫闾山又并未发现玉石矿遗迹。笔者始终认为，未发现的原因，或许矿藏已开发绝迹，或许仍旧未被发现。但史料白纸黑字不可能无中生有随意编造历史。

如果红山文化玉材产地果真在现今医巫闾山地区，这将大大缩短了玉石运输路程，也更符合就地就近取材的客观条件和规律。因此说，研究红山文化玉器，确定玉材来源，我们必须持慎重态度。要尊重历史，提倡科学，注重证据。对悬而未决的问题，尤其作为权威专家，还是不要轻易下结论的好。

红山文化正在研究之中，甚至是刚刚开始，单凭主观想象而妄加断言势必将我们的研究工作引入歧途，后果是误国误民。

Raw Materials of Hongshan–Culture Jade

Raw materials of Hongshan-Culture jade are problems that has been studied and researched for many years. It's widely believed that because of some historical reasons, transport tool backwardness and tough living circumstances, raw materials were only quarried nearby.

Hongshan Culture articles scattering in thousand miles in three north provinces of China, mainly founded at Niuheliang site, Balinzuoqi, Balinyouqi, Aohanqi, Wengniuteqi, Naimanqi, Kulunqi, Tongliao of Inner Mongolia, Nongǎn of Jilin province and Yilan county of Helongjiang province. Those findings have similar style in many aspects, thus named all of them as Hongshan-Culture jade. According to the shape, processing and unearthed situation, those jades were divided into pre-Hongshan Culture period, early Hongshan Culture period, late Hongshan Culture period and post-Hongshan Culture period as mentioned above.

Where is the origin place of raw materials in that extensive area? Archaeologists, geologists, historians, ancient jade experts and ancient jade collectors try to answer this serious and mystic question. According to jade texture, mineral components, hardness, color and luster, most of experts think raw stones come from Xiuyan, south of Liaoning province, which is so called Xiuyan Jade.

Is this answer right or not? I'd like to talk some personal opinions here.

I Texture of Hongshan–Culture Jade

Textures of most Hongshan-Culture gems, as we see, are generally tremolite and serpentine. Tremolite is hard and dense; the hardness is from 4.5 to 5 degrees. While serpentine is softer comparatively, and the hardness is about 3.5 to 4 degrees. Different mineral components and texture result in different hardness.

What we should point out is that hardness tested here is not the hardness of jade itself, but the hardness of jade which had been infiltrated.

We can easily speculate that stone ware, ironware, bronze ware or any other object would be infiltrated and invaded by all kinds of elements in soil when it is under the earth more than thousand years; the surface as well as the structure of the object would be changed slowly.Jade ware is the same as other object whose density and hardness would be changed by infiltration, either. It would be unscientific if we still compare the changed jade with modern Xiuyan jade.

II Mineral components of Hongshan–Culture Jade

Some people compared Hongshan-Culture jade mineral components with Xiuyan jade, confirmed that the two are basically the same, then drew the conclusion that Hongshan-Culture jade was made by Xiuyan jade stone. We know that object almost wouldn't change itself under normal conditions. This is called relative stability. For instance, if aged tremolite is not eroded seriously, the mineral components almost seem with the new quarried. But if the texture of jade was penetrated by many metal or nonmetal elements, mineral components would change too. Therefore, comparing the entreated jade with the new one is questionable.

III Color and Luster of Hongshan–Culture Jade

Many people write books or articles demonstrating that raw materials of Hongshan-Culture jade come from Xiuyan. Some said the materials had vanished; some others said yellow Hongshan-Culture jade was found at Xiyugou and Wagou of Xiuyan. From all sorts of above dissertations, as if the conclusion that Hongshan-Culture jade is Xiuyan jade is undisputed.

We saw until now the following colors: dark cyan, cyan, bluish white, bluish yellow, yellow, green and chicken bone white. We call all cyan color jade as cyan jade, and yellow color as yellow jade. Those colors are from presentational impression, but not original colors of the jade. So we should distinguish differences between the two, otherwise we would make dogmatic mistakes.

Jade color change depends on jade mineral component and density, environment, elements in soil and many other aspects. Color change has its own regularity regardless that the jade was infiltrated by which way. Generally speaking, dark cyan jade would be penetrated darker until dark green which we accordingly called dark green jade. While light cyan jade would become lighter and lighter until yellow, we call it yellow jade. The dark green jade is generally serpentine, while yellow jade is normally tremolite.

Those changes indicate that dark color would change darker while light color would be lighter and lighter with infiltration. I call such phenomena as Two-Poles Extremity.

According to the above reasons, it's obviously unscientific that Hongshan-Culture was made by Xiuyan jade as comparing the color of Hongshan-Culture jade with that of the new Xiuyan jade. So this theory should be reconsidered cautiously.

IV Origin Place of the Raw Materials

Besides tremolite and serpentine, Hongshan-Culture jade materials also include agate, quartz, turquoise and other kinds of stones. Though producing place of tremolite and serpentine is still not finally confirmed, we are sure that turquoise is not rich in north of China, but other materials mentioned above were abundant in west of Liaoning province and east of Inner Mongolia.

Where dose the tremolite and serpentine come from? This question keeps confusing us in these years.

But we still haven't found any Hongshan-Culture jade ware or other remains until now in Xiuyan; this is a question we should think about.

Moreover, according to recordation in some history book, Yiwulv Mountain produces jade stone. Some experts said Yiwulv Mountain is today's Xiuyan. But this conclusion is not exact. Because there is named Yiwulv Mountain nowadays located near Heyi County, west of Liaoning province, which has been developed to beauty spot. Some people said there is no sign of jade stone and historical remains in this Yiwulv Mountain, but I think that's might because jade stone was run out or still haven't been discovered. Recordation of history book wouldn't be made out by imagination.

Suppose that Hongshan-Culture jade producing area is today's Yiwulv Mountain, journey of transport would shorten greatly. That also conforms to detachment conditions and rule of nearby material select. One should be cautious on jade source identification with deference of history and evidence, don't draw conclusion on suspending issues rashly.

图 55 双联玉璧（牛河梁第二地点一号冢21号墓出土）

尺寸：（左）高5.5cm（右）高6.1cm

Picture 55 Double-joined jade(a doughnut-shaped piece of flat jade with the hole's diameter shorter than the width of the rim)(unearthed in the No.21 tomb from the No.1 stone mound at the No.2 location of Niuheliang)

Size: 5.5cm high (left) 6.1cm high (right)

图 56 环形佩

尺寸：高 10cm

玉质：青玉

（听雨堂珍藏）

Picture 56 Annular-shape jade pendant

Size: 10cm high

Jade texture: blue-green jade

(Collection of "rain-hear hall")

　　这种透闪石类玉质玉器，因质地坚密，在较为干燥的沙土层中，受沁变化不是很大，常常完好如新。

This kind of tremolite texture jade ware, as its texture is hard, in the relative dry sandy soil layer it doesn't get obvious change on infiltration, and often intacts as new.

图 57 玉蝗
尺寸：长 5.7cm
玉质：青玉
（听雨堂珍藏）

Picture 57 Jade locust
Size: about 8cm long
Jade texture: blue-green jade
(Collection of "rain-hear hall")

图 58 玉蚕
尺寸：长 6cm
玉质：青玉
（听雨堂珍藏）

Picture 58 Jade silkworm
Size: about 6cm long
Jade texture: blue-green jade
(Collection of "rain-hear hall")

图 59 玉蜘蛛
尺寸：高 7.8cm
玉质：青玉
（听雨堂珍藏）

Picture 59 Jade spider
Size: 7.8 cm high
Jade texture: blue-green jade
(Collection of "rain-hear hall")

　　同种类玉质玉器，在客观环境与条件基本相同情况下，受沁变化基本无较大改变。

　　The same kind of texture of jade ware has not so big change on infiltration in the same objective environment and condition.

图 60 玉凤
尺寸：高 3.3cm 宽 6cm
玉质：青玉
（听雨堂珍藏）

Picture 60 The jade phoenix
Size: 3.3cm high   6cm wide
Jade texture: blue-green jade
(Collection of "rain-hear hall")

图 61 玉蝉
尺寸：高 4.7cm
玉质：青玉
（听雨堂珍藏）

Picture 61 Jade cicada
Size: 4.7cm high
Jade texture: blue-green jade
(Collection of "rain-hear hall")

很多红山文化出土玉器，因质地坚密，常常不见沁色、绺斑、孔洞等沁后特征。

A lot of uneathed Hongshan-culture jade ware, as jade texture is hard, often do not see the colour of infiltration, tuft crack spot, and hole etc. that the feature after getting infiltration.

图62 竹节形玉珠（高3.8cm）勾云形玉佩（长8.8cm）
（均为牛河梁二号冢1号墓出土）
Picture62 bamboo joints-shaped Jade Beads (3.8cm high)
Hoop Cloud-like Jade pendant (8.8cm long)
(both unearthed in the No.1 tomb from No2 stone mound of Niuheliang)

这种呈黄绿颜色的玉器在红山文化玉器群中较为多见，属透闪石类玉质，质地比较坚密，刻划硬度一般在4.5度左右。尽管玉器表面刀不能入，但经过数千年的浸蚀，仍然在玉器坚硬的表面留下明显的沁后不同特征，成为我们鉴定玉器真伪的重要科学依据。

This kind of jade ware that arises yellow green color is relatively more in the Hongshan-culture jade ware crowd, and it belongs to tremolite texture jade, its texture is hard and dense relatively, which carving hardness is general in 45 degrees. Though the surface of the jade ware can not be destroyed by knife, through the etch of thousands of years, it still leaves the different feature in the hard surface of the jade ware after obvious infiltration, which becomes the important scientific basis to appraise jade ware real or fake.

图64 玉龟（辽宁省阜新县胡头沟墓地1号墓出土）
尺寸：高4.8cm
Picture64 Jade Turtles(unearthed in the No. 1 tomb in Hutou ditch graveyard at Fuxin county of Liaoning province)
Size: 4.8cm high

图 65　　形玉兽　Picture 65　Jade coiled animal
尺寸：高 16 cm　Size:16cm high
玉质：青玉　Jade texture: blue-green jade
（听雨堂珍藏）　（Collection of "rain-hear hall"）

图 66　　形玉兽另面
Picture 66 another side of Jade coiled animal

图 67 玉璧（牛河梁
第二地点一号冢 7
号墓出土）
尺寸：直径 11.3cm
玉质：青玉

Picture67 one kind of Jade(a doughnut-shaped piece of flat jade with the hole's diameter shorter than the width of the rim)
Size: diameter 11.3cm
Jade texture: blue-green jade

蛋青色玉，是由于玉器受沁而改变了其原本颜色。

此类玉石因自身所含矿物成分、元素与众不同，因而受到浸蚀后器表多出现点状与蚕食状麻斑。

Egg blue-green jade, as to get infiltration in jade ware, so it have changed it formerly color.

As the mineral composition and element that this kind of jade itself contains different, So after geting corrosion, the ware surface appears speck and nibble shape spot.

图 68 天地神佩
尺寸：高 23.2 cm
玉质：青玉
（听雨堂珍藏）

Picture 68 Compound jade baldric for heaven and earth
Size: 23.2cm high
Jade texture: blue-green jade
(Collection of "rain-hear hall")

图 69 祖先神
尺寸：高 25.9 cm
玉质：青玉
（听雨堂珍藏）

picture 69 ancestors numen
size :25.9cm high
Jade texture: blue-green jade
(Collection of "rain-hear hall")

这种青中泛白呈鸭蛋青色的玉石，刻划硬度比较高，而且沁象明显与其它质地、颜色玉石有所不同，形成了它自身的沁后特征。

This kind of white in blue-green and presenting blue-green of duck's egg of jade stone that carving hardness is higher, and its infiltration is obviously different with other jade of texture and color, which formed infiltration feature of itself.

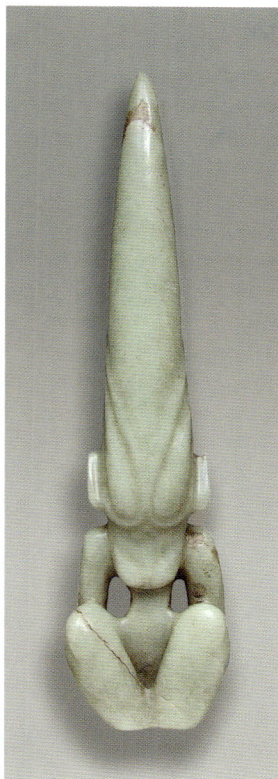

图70 天地神佩局部放大可见点状麻斑与孔洞
Picture 70 Compound jade baldric for heaven and earth partly enlarged can see drop-shaped spot and hole.

图 71 玉鸟
尺寸：高 7.8cm
玉质：青玉
（听雨堂珍藏）
Picture 71Jade bird
Size: 7.8cm high
Jade texture: blue-green jade
(Collection of "rain-hear hall")

图 72　玉鸟器背
Picture 72The back of jade bird

图 73 玉蛾　　Picture 73　Jade moth
尺寸：高 9.1cm　　Size: 9.1cm high
玉质：青玉　　Jade texture: blue-green jade
（听雨堂珍藏）　　(Collection of "rain-hear hall")

玉质决定沁象。玉石所含有的矿物成分，玉石的坚密度，决定着玉器的受沁变化。一般质地较松软玉器受沁较重。

Jade texture decides infiltration.The mineral composition and the hard level of jade decide the infiltration change of jade ware. Generally, the jade of soft texture is more deep on infiltration.

图74 七孔刀形玉鸟

尺寸：高 10.05cm　宽 34.3cm

玉质：青玉

（听雨堂珍藏）

Picture 74 knife-shaped of seven holes jade bird

Size: 10.05cm high　34.3cm wide

Jade texture: blue-green jade

(Collection of "rain-hear hall")

　　青玉，是红山文化玉器的用材主流。青玉中又分为淡青、深青、苍青。呈不同青色的玉器，受沁后皆已改变其原来本色，颜色的改变向两极转化：淡青变黄、深青变暗，苍青近黑。

　　The blue-green jade, is the main material of Hongshan-culture jade ware. The blue-green jade is also made up of light cyan, dark cyan and pale green. Presenting different blue-green of the jade ware, after infiltration, have changed it original ture colors, The change of color transforms to the two poles: light cyan changes into yellow, dark cyan changes into dark, and pale green is near dark.

图75 七孔刀形玉鸟局部放大，沁象真实自然

Picture 75 knife-shaped of seven holes jade bird partly enlarged, infiltration true and natural

图 76　斧形鹿神祖
尺寸：高 13.4 cm
玉质：青玉
（听雨堂珍藏）

Picture 76　Axe-shaped deer numen
Size: 13.4cm high
Jade texture: blue-green jade
(Collection of "rain-hear hall")

图 77　斧形鹿神祖头部放大
Picture 77　Axe-shaped deer numen head enlarged

　　这种深青色的玉石，在红山文化玉器中较为多用。属透闪石类玉质，质地比较坚密，因此受浸蚀不是很严重。

　　This kind of dark cyan jade is being multi-purpose in Hongshan-culture jade ware. It belongs to tremolite texture jade type, and its texture is very hard and dense, therefore its corrosion is not very serious.

图 78 玉龙
尺寸：高 18.7 cm
玉质：青玉
（听雨堂珍藏）

Picture 78 Jade dragon

Size: 18.7cm high

Jade texture: blue-green jade

(Collection of "rain-hear hall")

图 79 玉龙另面

Picture 79 another side of Jade dragon

青色最重者，人们称为苍玉。

苍玉特有的矿物成分、结构，使其有效抵御了各种元素对它所造成的侵害。

It is called pale green jade that its blue-green is most heavy.

The peculiar mineral composition and structure of pale green jade let it resiste hurt effectively by various elements.

图 80 锥形器
尺寸：高约 12cm
玉质：青玉
（听雨堂珍藏）

Picture80 cone ware

Size: about 12cm high

Jade texture: blue-green jade

(Collection of "rain-hear hall")

图 81 玉神面
尺寸：高 3.7cm
玉质：青白玉
（听雨堂珍藏）
Picture 81 Jade god face
Size: 3.7cm high
Jade texture: blue-green white jade
(Collection of "rain-hear hall")

图 82 玉神面器背
Picture 82 The back of jade god face

图 83 玉蝉
尺寸：长 3.9cm
玉质：青白玉
（听雨堂珍藏）

Picture 83 Jade cicada
Size: 3.9cm long
Jade texture: blue-green white jade
(Collection of "rain-hear hall")

在相同环境与相同客观条件下，同类玉质的玉器其沁象有许多相似之处。这与它们自身所含有的矿物元素有关。

In the same environment and objective condition, the infiltration of the same texture jade ware has a lot of similar places. This is concerning with their mineral element that itself contains.

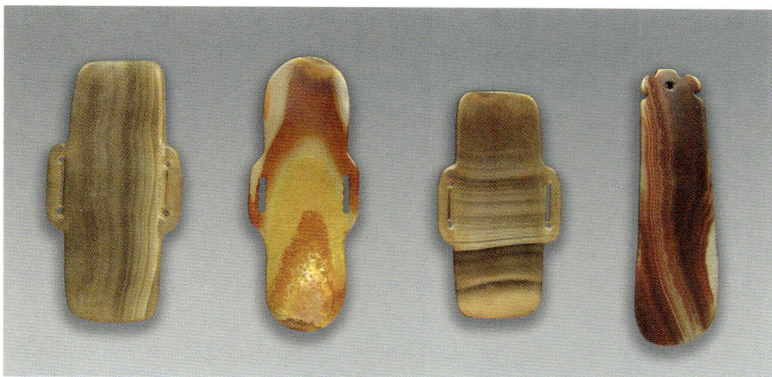

图 84 鞋拔形器
尺寸：高 7.6—9.8cm 宽 3.4—4.3cm
玉质：玛瑙
（听雨堂珍藏）

Picture 84　shoehorn-shaped ware

Size: 7.6—9.8cm high　3.4—4.3cm wide

Jade texture: agate

(Collection of "rain-hear hall")

红山文化玉器用材品种较多。这是以玛瑙制作成的玉器。

It is more material kind of Hongshan-culture jade ware. This jade ware is made of agate.

图 85 玉鸟
尺寸：高 6.5cm
玉质：黄晶
（听雨堂珍藏）

Picture 85 Jade bird

Size: 6.5cm high

Jade texture: citrine

(Collection of "rain-hear hall")

图 86 玉鸟
尺寸：高 6.6cm 宽 5.6cm
玉质：黄晶
（听雨堂珍藏）

Picture 86 Jade bird

Size: 6.5cm high　5.6cm wide

Jade texture: citrine

(Collection of "rain-hear hall")

这是以黄晶所制作成的玉器。黄晶硬度很高，五千年前原始先民能够制作出如此精美的玉器，实在令人惊叹。

This jade ware is made of citrine. The hardness of citrine is very high. 5000 years before, original late people can make out so exquisite jade ware as this, really surprising everyone.

图 87 玉鸮
辽宁省喀左县东山嘴遗址出土。
尺寸：高 2.5cm
玉质：绿松石
Picture 87 Jade eagle
(unearthed at dongshanzui site in Kazuo country of Liaoning province)
Size: 2.5cm high
Jade texture: turquoise

古人云："石之美者为玉"。在红山文化玉器群中，以玛瑙、水晶、松石等材料所制之器，广义皆称作玉器。

有人认为，红山文化绿松石并非国内所产，应来自阿富汗。对这一问题，有待国家文物研究部门进一步考证。

The ancient says: "The beautiful stone is jade." In the Hongshan-culture jade ware crowd, with the materials such as agate, crystal and turquoise making ware, which is generalizedly called jade ware.

Somebody thinks that Hongshan-culture turquoise is not domestic produce, and it would come from Afghanistan. For this problem, it would be investigated and verified further by the national research department of cultural relic.

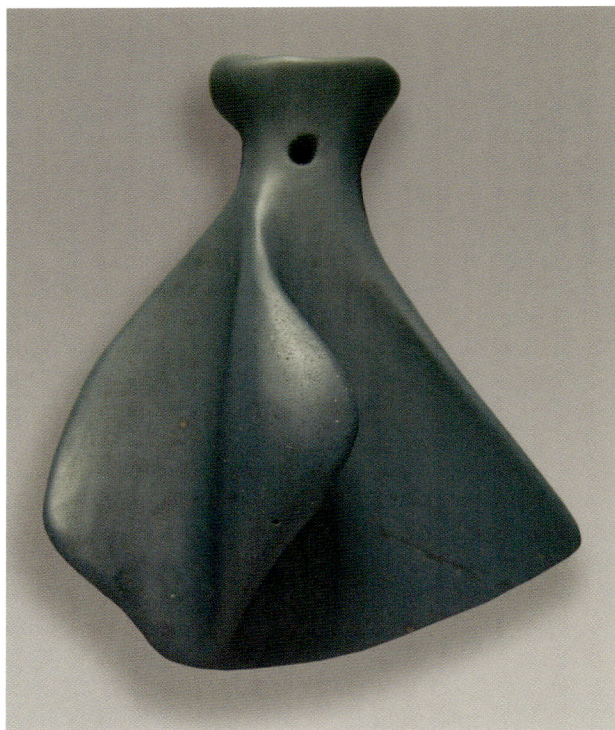

图 88 骨形器

Picture 88 Bone-shaped ware

尺寸：高 7.1cm 宽 6cm

Size: 7.1cm high 6cm wide

玉质：绿松石

Jade texture: Turquoise

（听雨堂珍藏）

(Collection of "rain-hear hall")

图 89 绿松石鱼形耳坠（辽宁省
阜新县胡头沟墓地 3 号墓出土）
尺寸：（左）高 2.7cm （右）高 2.5cm
玉质：绿松石

Picture 89 Turquoise fish-shaped
earrings(unearthed in the No.3 tomb
at Hutou ditch graveyard in Fuxin
county of Liaoning province)

Size: (left) 2.7cm high (right)2.5cm
high

Jade texture: Turquoise

图 90 玉鸟
尺寸：高 3.6cm
玉质：绿松石
（听雨堂珍藏）

Picture 90 Jade bird

Size: 3.6cm high

Jade texture: Turquoise

(Collection of "rain-hear hall")

图 91 玦形玉兽
尺寸：高 4.5cm
玉质：绿松石
（听雨堂珍藏）

Picture 91 Jade coiled animal

Size: 4.5cm high

Jade texture: Turquoise

(Collection of "rain-hear hall")

　　以绿松石制成的红山文化器物，在考古发掘中已出土数件。关于材料来源问题有待于进一步分析研究。绿松石在红山文化玉器群中的出现，很可能打破红山人就近取材的理论观念。

　　Several wares have been uneathed in archaeology excavate that are made into Hongshan-culture wares by turquoise. About material source problem, we need further analysis and research. Turquoise appearing in the Hongshan culture jade ware crowd may break the theoretical idea of Hongshan people that the material was drawed nearby.

图 92 玉鸟
尺寸：高 12.5cm 宽 16cm
玉质：鸡肝玛瑙
（听雨堂珍藏）

Picture 92 Jade bird
Size: 12.5cm high 16cm wide
Jade texture: chicken liver-shaped agate
(Collection of "rain-hear hall")

图 93 玉鸟局部放大
Picture 93 Jade bird partly enlarged

在正式考古发掘中，尚未见鸡肝玛瑙红山文化玉器。但在民间收藏中已有多件。从此器造型、加工工艺、沁象等方面特征看，其真实性不容置疑。

In formal archaeology excavate, we have not seen chicken-liver shaped agate of Hongshan-culture jade ware. But there have been a lot of wares in non-governmental circles collections.From modeling, processing technology and infiltration ect. feature of this ware, its actuality needn't to doubt.

图 94 玉斧

尺寸：高约 5 cm

玉质：墨玉

（听雨堂珍藏）

Picture 94 Jade axe

Size : about 5 cm high

Jade texture: black jade

(Collection of "rain-hear hall")

图 95 玦形玉兽

尺寸：高 19.4 cm

玉质：墨玉

（听雨堂珍藏）

Picture 95 Jade coiled animal

Size: 19.4cm high

Jade texture: black jade

(Collection of "rain-hear hall")

新石器不同历史时期，墨玉被广泛应用于制作玉器上。

凡出土墨玉制器，品相皆比较完好，受沁后变化不是很大。墨玉之所以抵御浸蚀能力较强，这与自身所含有矿物成分与结构有关。

During the different historical period of Neolithic, black jade has been applied extensively in producing jade ware.

All the unearthed ink colour jade makes into the wares whose appearance is intact, the change is not so grate after geting infiltration. So the ability of ink colour jade to resist corrosion is much stronger, just as it is relevant with mineral ingredients and instuct itself contains.

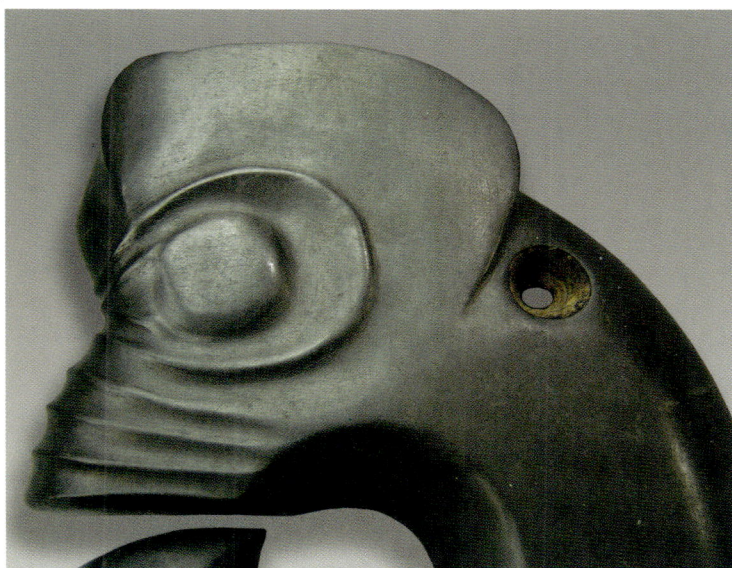

图 96 玦形玉兽局部放大

Picture 96 Jade coiled animal partly enlarged

图 97　天地神佩

尺寸：高 16.5 cm 宽 7.8cm

玉质：墨玉

（听雨堂珍藏）

Picture 97　Compound jade baldric for heaven and earth

Size: 16.5cm high　7.8cm wide

Jade texture: black jade

(Collection of "rain-hear hall")

　　以墨玉制作的红山文化片状玉器，边缘处大多出现钙化，较少看到沁后其它特征，然而包浆却依旧明朗。

　　Producing the Hongshan-culture slice form jade ware by the ink colour jade, whose edge mostly arises calcification, and we see much less other feature after infiltration, However its Baojiang is still obvious.

图 98 天地神佩

尺寸：高 8.5cm
　　　宽 17.3 cm

玉质：墨玉

（听雨堂珍藏）

Picture 98 Compound jade baldric for heaven and earth

Size: 8.5cm high　17.3cm wide

Jade texture: black jade

(Collection of "rain-hear hall")

图 99 天地神佩局部放大

Picture 99 Compound jade baldric for heaven and earth partly enlarged

红山文化玉器制作工艺

Process of Hongshan-Culture Jade Production

红山文化玉器制作工艺

红山文化玉器始终被一些人错误的认为，是在没有任何专门设备和工具条件下，完全靠手工制作出来的。并因此相信，制作一件玉器需要花费数年时间才能完成。更有某些专家说，红山文化玉器的开片，即对原石的切割是以牛筋或皮条制成的绳锯加解玉砂所完成，甚至故弄玄虚到解玉砂中必须加入动物的鲜血方可切割开来。当然，也有人认为石轮锯是玉器开片的主要工具。

对以上种种说法，只是一些人的片面主观臆断或凭空想象，并没有足够的说服力和充分的科学依据。实际在客观上否定了原始先民的创造力，低估了先民们的聪明才智，抹杀了中华民族最早进入人类文明时代的佐证。

我们提倡对一切事物必须以历史唯物主义的观点，客观分析问题和认识问题。任何不负责任的胡编乱造不仅给那些不学无术的人制造了理论根据，更给红山文化研究工作设下重重障碍。尤其奉劝那些专门从事红山文化考古和古玉研究工作的专家们，不要动辄以太上皇和绝对权威的架势惟我独尊。学海无涯，应以理智而谦逊的态度进行学术研究，要学会随时纠正自己的错误。红山文化研究工作才刚刚开始，学术研究的序幕也才只拉开一角，真正的论争还在后面。

通过对新石器时期中国古代史的研究及对红山文化玉器更深入的分析认为，这一时期已经产生以部落或部族为单位的专门制玉的队伍和机构，发明并制造了专门用于加工玉器的设备和工具，形成了手工业作坊生产模式。

专门的制玉队伍和机构是根据社会需要而产生的。首先我们从原始人类的崇玉观念说起，从科学考古发掘发现的中国古代玉器说明，早在八千至一万年人们便发现了质地坚密、温润而亮泽的玉石，并称之为"石之美者"，进而升华"玉集天地之灵气而生成"之说。从爱玉到崇玉，人们相信以玉所制成的器物具有护身、辟邪功能，能够与神相通的灵性宝物。因此玉被赋予更深意义的宗教涵义。

随着原始宗教意识的产生，无论部落中的上层权贵还是平民百姓，对神灵的崇拜都是相同的。每个人都渴望得到神灵的保护。因此，以玉制成的神器并不受等级观念的约束，只是两者所拥有的品种、数量、质量不同而已。

从辽西牛河梁积石冢发掘我们可以看到，普通墓中有玉器一二件，而中心大墓多达二十件。没有发现葬有玉器的很少，由此可见其普遍性。

由于做为神器的玉器大量需求和加工难度，一支专门制作玉神器的队伍应运而生。这些能工巧匠，在历史上被称为"玉人"，就是专门从事设计制作玉器的专门技术人员。与此同时，相应的管理机制和机构必然随之而出现，这应当被认为那些能够与神灵对话的巫、或者部落首领。专门的制玉设备是根据社会对玉器的大量需求而产生，并在实际工作中得到不断的改进、完善和发展。完全靠手工打磨出玉器，无论从质量或者数量上已远远不能满足社会群体的需求。这时，一个以木制为主体框架的、以木轮为传动方式的、以脚踏或手摇为动力的、能够使其快速旋转的专门用于制玉的设备不但出现，而且已经被"玉人"们熟练掌握。这种设备应该相似于宋应星《天工开物》制玉图中的水凳。

我们从同时期所出土的红山文化陶器制作痕迹中，已经可以明显看出，它的制坯工艺完全是机械旋转出来的。也就是说，红山文化时期已经有了可以使其旋转的机械加工设备，这是不可否认的历史事实。手工与机械是先进与落后的历史分水岭，并成为研究古代历史和社会生产力发展的重要依据，同时对于我们研究红山文化玉器制作至关重要。

由此可以说明，处于同一历史时期的、用于制陶工艺半机械化的、可以使之快速旋转的设备必然同时用于制玉工艺上。而制玉设备较之制陶设备更复杂，并具有多重功能。因为制作玉器需要开片、制坯、琢磨、抛光等多道生产工序方能完成。

当我们能够以充分理由说明和论证红山文化玉器完全以机械加工后，对于我们研究红山文化玉器的工艺特征，对于分析判断红山文化玉器的真正存世数量等诸多长期疑惑和困扰我们的问题，必将逐一揭开谜底。

在以机械旋转为动力制玉设备出现的同时，需要配置专门工具，从而彻底告别完全靠手工制作玉器的落后局面。应该说这是人类历史的一大进步，同时可以完全印证人类已步入文明时代。根据史料记载，我国在新石器晚期已经初步掌握了青铜冶炼技术，并发现这一时期的青铜制品遗存。然而在青铜时代之前还存在红铜时代。由此说明，我国在新石器时代中晚期已经有金属器问世。

从红山文化较大型玉器的开片和小件玉器切口的切割痕来看，所用工具薄至以毫米计，这是绳锯或者石轮锯所根本不能完成的。经过充分分析，惟一一种可能，就是以金属制作的片状工具带动解玉砂切割而成。除此之外，任何其他材料制作的工具都达不到如此精密程度。

另从一些玉器的切割口看，边缘平齐、锐利、切割面坦直，由此进一步说明除金属制作工具，其它材质工具皆不能为。笔者为此曾做过多种实验：当以皮条做的弓锯加最粗的金刚砂，在玉石上进行切割时，当拉动三万余次时，皮条由于金刚砂的磨擦，五次拉断。由于水对皮条的浸泡，在拉动二千次时变软、变形。玉石切割处呈现较浅磨痕，类似于抛光，无法更深进入。尽管切割处两边固定的木条以防跑线，但切割处圆滑，不能出现锐利边缘线。由此可以说明，绳锯不能完成红山文化玉器特征的切割工艺。

试想石轮锯的切割。首先，石质较软、制成片状而极薄的工具不但难度大，费工费时，而且又很容易破碎，即便制成，在实用过程中稍有不慎则前功尽弃。如以较坚硬石质制成工具，没有相应的特别工具，单就其薄度其艰难可想而知。另外，从一些较大型红山文化玉器的开片来看，大而薄的石质工具根本无法完成玉器的制作。

当以上两点被彻底否定以后，那么惟一一种可能就只有金属器才能够完成对红山文化玉器的加工。

为什么我们至今尚未发现红山文化时期玉器加工金属器呢？笔者认为这不难理解，因为较薄的红铜或青铜极易被腐蚀而烂掉。而且到目前为止，考古中尚未发现红山文化时期专门制作玉器的遗址和遗存，也许有一天会证明这一切。

由于红山先民对神灵崇拜的普遍性，其需求量越来越大，随着特别的机械制玉设备和专门制玉工具的出现，生产力得到大大提升。这支以制作玉神器为职业的专门队伍得到不断发展壮大，其制玉技能得到飞快提升，并已发展到手工业作坊的生产形式。这些"玉人"们各自有明确的分工，专门从事玉石的采集、运输、划线、开片、设计、制作、抛光等各项工作。因为从已见的大型红山文化玉器分析，这些器物并非一人所能完成，而必须要两个人以上方能进行有效加工。

专门生产玉神器手工业作坊的出现，会根据社会需要源源不断的将这些以玉制作的神器提供给宗庙、祭坛、家庭及那些希望得到神灵保护的人们。一些较大型器，用于供奉或祭祀活动，小型器用于佩带。因为这些玉神器绝大多数皆有系挂或系佩孔。

在我们对红山文化玉器制作程序和制作工艺进行分析后认为，一件玉器的制作，需要以下工作程序完成：开片、划线、制坯、琢磨、钻孔、抛光、浸油。

1、开片：

开片即对玉石原材料的切割。根据用途和需要、玉器的形状或大小将玉石分切开，以制作成器。这是玉器制作的首道工序。切割时，首先将玉石固定，然后在切割线处落锯，让锯片带入解玉砂，从而进行切割。切割时要不间断地往锯口处注水，用以活动解玉砂和降温，以免受热后玉质受到损害。从我们所见到过的红山文化玉器"中华第一龙"来说，其高度为26厘米，如果单面进刀，轮锯片直径最小要达到30厘米以上。如果双向两面进刀，轮锯片的最小直径也要在16厘米以上。无论从龙体的平整度、匀衡度，还是龙鬣处的对称度和精确度来看，其技术要求都达到尽善尽美程度。再从红山文化玉器中常见的呈薄片状的天地神佩来分析；这些片状玉器薄及1—3厘米，从开片时遗留痕迹看，切割锯片当薄及0.3—0.6厘米，而最大误差只在1—3毫米之间，将这些玉器平置时，几乎无任何翘动感，极其平整。

无论青铜还是红铜，以此制作成薄片状切割工具较之其它材料制作工具相对要容易些。可将溶点较低的铜溶化后，将铜水浇铸在事先做成的沙模中，待其成形后，再以粗糙石制工具磨薄、磨光。为更好解决其平整度，还可以在石板上敲打，从而使其达到严格的技术要求。当锯片完成以后，再在其刃部磨出等距凹槽，这些凹槽可存入解玉砂，当锯片运动时，解玉砂即对玉石进行有效的磨切。

解玉砂取之于河道，不同河道里的沙石其硬度不尽相同，这要视其所含矿物体及成份。

一般要求其硬度要高于玉石硬度，如玛瑙、石英、水晶及其他矿物晶体所构成的细砂。对这些取之于河道里的细沙要进行多次淘洗，以根据不同加工工序而区别使用。切割大块玉原石时一般采用较粗解玉砂，粗砂磨削速度相对较细砂要快，但精细程度不及细砂。

根据同形状玉器存在两件以上情况分析，作坊式生产很可能形成根据需要的批量生产。比如同一品种、同一大小型号的玉器同时下料。这样可以更有效的提高工作效率。

2、划线：

划线即设计。就是在切割后准备制作圆雕的、板状的或片状的玉材表面画出玉器的形状，然后依据划线纹样进行再加工。专门从事划线的"玉人"相当于我们今天的工艺设计师。从某种意义上讲，应该是倍受人们尊重的"神的使者"，或称为"巫"的人来完成。因为从作为能够与神灵相沟通的神器来说，绝不是任何人都可以随意而为的，它特有的严肃性和神圣性决定了玉器的设计工作被授于更深涵义。

3、制坯：

制坯，就是按照划线的基本轮廓，去除多余部分，制成毛坯。制坯是玉器粗加工阶段，一些较大去除部分仍然由锯片进行分段切割。一些较小边角等去除部分，则由圆锥形、呈螺旋状、表面较粗糙的特制工具进行刮磨。为提高工作效率，刮磨时所用解玉砂一般颗粒较粗。从一些较大型玉器表面，仍可见到刮磨时留下的印痕，印痕无一定方向性，按加工部位需要随意而为。对印痕放大来看，多呈沟槽形，沟槽中呈现横向丝纹，类似于木螺丝旋纹。以此分析，这种圆锥形刮磨工具是被固定在特制的旋转机械上，机械的快速转动带动工具对玉器表面进行刮磨加工。

制坯是一件玉器造型的基础，是骨架、是整体形象的初现。同时它决定着玉器最终所要达到的整体艺术效果的关键。

4、琢磨：

当玉器完成制坯工序后，还需要进一步对其进行精细加工，我们称此为琢磨。琢磨之前仍要在玉器表面划线，或可称为绘线。需要详尽绘制出玉器所有细部具体形象，依照线样决定保留或去除。

红山文化玉器的主要工艺特征为"压地隐起法"，也有人称此为"打洼法"。就是按玉器造型设计要求，让玉器表面以缓坡形式平稳过渡，突起与凹进相交点若隐若现，自然而柔和。有些过渡面甚至肉眼都难以觉察，只有用手触摸方能感觉到。如此精妙的工艺，完全靠制玉工人自我感觉和娴熟的高超技艺方能完成。"压地隐起法"工艺，不但完美表现了玉器的整体形象和细部特征，更达到了形态准确生动、神态出神入化的最高艺术境界。

根据对红山文化玉器的综合分析认为，"压地隐起法"工艺是这样具体实施的：将锥形的、表面粗糙而呈螺纹状的磨削工具固定在旋车上，旋车带动锥形工具在玉器表面进行刮磨。

大件则放置于旋车特制的平台上，可随意翻动，小型物件则以手持之。

呈螺旋纹的锥形工具可带入解玉砂，从而进行刮磨。此时所用解玉砂颗粒相对都比较细，但仍然可以从红山文化玉器所留印痕分析出，在加工过程中最少需使用两种不同型号颗粒解玉砂完成。比如，红山文化玉器中玉鸟的双翅，是以打洼出阳线纹表现其动感与美感的。当我们仔细观察后就会发现，其沟槽处经常留下螺丝状横线纹，这些横向线纹有的十分明显，有些需要借助放大镜才能隐约断续呈现，还有一些玉器压地处甚至根本看不到这种工艺特征。经分析认为：这一工艺是由两道工序所完成的。就是先以较粗解玉砂在玉器表面纵向趟出沟槽，然后在精细加工时以较细解玉砂顺向平掉沟槽中的印痕。从一些制作完成的红山文化玉器表面，时常发现这种现象。尤其一些较大型玉器，其表面有的留下很明显断续刮磨痕，有些较小精致玉器就较难发现这种特征，这是因为作为玉器精品在加工时进行了多次重复磨制。

我们在认定红山文化玉器的真伪时，不能片面以印痕特征存在与否作为惟一依据，还要对全器进行多方面综合分析后方可最后认定。玉器表面沟槽中横向丝纹的存在与玉器的大小，所选用的玉材、所要求的精细度有很大关系。相对较大或玉质硬度较差些的蛇纹石类玉器，在器表非重点部位出现这一痕迹者较多。而小型玉质较好玉器出现这一特征相对较少。但以放大镜仔细搜寻沟槽，仍会偶尔发现一些所遗留蛛丝马迹。

红山文化玉器的"压地隐起法"制作工艺，完全有别于其他年代玉器工艺特征，所以也才更具有很强的时代特殊个性。它朴拙、简洁、浑厚、神秘而精美。它特别的加工工艺、质朴的形象、神秘的内涵，可谓形神兼备，出神入化，将造型艺术与神灵崇拜有机融为一体，因此将中国的雕塑艺术推向了颠峰，在世界文化史上创造了奇迹。

红山文化玉器很少见繁琐的装饰性纹线。目前我们只是在龙形及部分兽形玉器的额上或下颌处发现网状纹，这些线纹多数以较细棒状工具刮磨而成，因此可见明显螺丝状横线纹。也有一些经过二次精加工，无此印痕。这时直线横断面多呈三角形，纵向印痕长而直。经分析，显然以特制工具加极细解玉砂对沟槽进行过重新平整。

5、钻孔：

红山文化玉器绝大多数皆有孔，只有极少数圆雕玉器可坐立而无孔。对红山文化玉器加工程序进行分析，玉器的钻孔一般在最后阶段完成。玉器的孔可分为造型孔和实用孔两种。造型孔，即根据玉器造型的需要，在玉器上镂空成不同形状较大的孔。这些孔具有一定规律性，如块形玉兽和璧类玉器的中孔，玉神祖双臂及两腿间的镂空孔，皆两面对钻而成，而且其位置基本无较大改变，尤其讲求对称和均衡。实用孔，则属于功能性孔。如较大器型的系挂孔，是为穿绳悬挂祭拜所用。小型玉器的系佩孔，用以随身佩带穿绳。无论系挂孔还是系佩孔皆有一定规律性，这些孔大都以玉器的特殊功能钻在玉器的上端或器背偏上处，而且多数对钻，极少单面钻孔。

从红山文化玉器钻孔特征分析，所用工具为圆锥形，表面较粗糙，前端钝尖，中后端渐粗。所钻出的孔内小外扩，象马蹄，所以又被称为马蹄形孔。无论是系挂孔还是系佩孔皆以锥形钻加较粗解玉砂向内偏斜对钻相通，形如象鼻，因此被称为象鼻孔或牛鼻孔。

因考虑孔的实用性和为提高工作效率，不仅所用工具表面粗糙，而且解玉砂颗粒相对较粗，所以常在孔壁处留下较明显丝扣状旋纹。造型孔直接关系到玉器整体形象，所以在一次钻孔成型后，再进行反复修整，因而孔壁处极少留下印痕。

片状玉器因其较薄，钻孔时极易破损，故采取正反两面大坡度斜向对钻，所钻出的孔壁呈斜坡形，孔的相交点薄而锐利，有刺手感。

红山文化玉器的孔周一般比较圆滑，无刺手感。这不是因为原始先民长期佩、挂磨损所形成的，而是在钻孔时由于钻具缺乏稳定性而自然形成。孔的边缘处过于锐利，极易磨断系挂绳，因此也不排除在钻孔时故意而为之。

目前我们所见到的红山文化玉器仿制品，其孔沿处多锋利，有明显刺手感。这是因为现代钻具转动较快，无法让孔沿处更圆滑。为达到与真品更接近，只能在原钻孔基础上，换更大一号钻头采用"划窝"法扩大孔沿，这时我们可明显看出一次钻孔和二次扩孔之间形成微小台痕。

6、抛光：

玉器制作的最后一道工序，即对雕琢后的玉器进行全面抛光处理，以增加玉器表面的光亮度，更充分表现玉之温润亮泽之本质，使玉器更熠熠生辉，光彩照人。所以说，抛光这一工序对于玉器的最终形象至关重要。

玉器抛光，分为粗抛光和精抛光。一般情况下，这两种方法同时使用在一件玉器上，粗抛光为去除玉器表面细小印痕，此时所用解玉砂颗粒较粗。精抛光以提高玉器表面光亮度，此时所用解玉砂颗粒较细。

对红山文化玉器抛光后器表所显现微小印痕分析；所使用抛光工具，当为根据用途以木制成的不同形状专门工具。在这些棒状工具上面缠裹棉麻或兽皮再蘸抹微粒解玉砂从而对玉器进行全面抛光处理。在放大镜下仔细观察，器表所留微小印痕无明显规律性。因此判断，红山文化玉器抛光应该手工和机械同时并用。

7、浸油：

当玉器抛光后则对其进行浸油处理。浸油的目的是为了使玉器更光亮，并可起到一定防腐作用。尤其葬墓中出土玉器，在系挂孔处常发现较厚污垢，试着用竹刀刮下，在放大镜下观察，这些污垢呈白色腊状，在白纸上涂抹后可见油性污染。

因此让我们联想到，为什么红山文化玉器深藏地下数千年有些仍然光亮鉴人。为什么一些玉器表面完好如初，而内部腐朽严重。这当与玉器的浸油防腐处理有关。

分析和了解红山文化玉器的制作工艺，对于我们签定玉器的真伪十分重要。分析，必须是理性的，客观的，符合科学规律的。了解，是为了更深层次的进一步研究。

在学术研究方面，要相信，没有绝对的权威。他或许是考古学家、历史学家、矿物学专家但他不一定是古玉鉴定专家。古玉鉴定不但需要掌握多学科的知识，更需要科学的头脑、敏锐的思维、深邃的洞察力。学无止境，为此，我们永远需要进行不懈的努力。

Process of Hongshan–Culture Jade production

Hongshan-Culture jade has been erroneously considered entirely handmade without any specialized equipment and tools, and therefore the production of one piece of jade need to spend several years to complete. Some experts said that jade cutting was completed by ox tendon or leathern strips in combination with corundum or even under the help of animals' blood. Some people also believe that stone disk cutter is the main tool for cutting. I think the above points are just subjective judgments or come from imagination. These statements objectively deny the creativity and underestimate ingenuity of the ancient settlers and obliterate evidences that Chinese is the first nation to enter the era of human civilization. We need to advocate historical materialistic view to all things and analyze issues objectively. Any irresponsible boasting not only created a theoretical basis to those ignorant and incompetent people, but also set obstacles to Hongshan cultural research.

Through studies on The Neolithic Period history and analysis on Hongshan-Culture jade, we believe that in this period specialized systems and teams devoted to jade production, the equipments and tools for jade processing had been invented and applied, and handicrafts workshops also emerged.

Specialized jade teams filled social requires. Archaeological excavation prove that as early as eight thousand years ago, people have found high compactness, mild and vivid jade, calling it as the most beautiful stone with nimbus of earth and air. They loved jade, adored jade and believed jade wares can communicate with gods and protect themselves from evil. Thus jade was given deeper religious meanings. With the development of the original religious sense, the worship of the gods prevailed from the top tribal officials to the civilians. Everyone desired gods' protection. Two grades were in possession of different numbers of jade.

Niuheliang sites tell us that there are one or two pieces of jade in common tomb, and as many as 20 pieces of jade in center tomb. Jade as mortuary object was universal in ancient times. Because jade was largely demanded as divine utensil and its difficulty of processing, specialized teams of jade production came into being. Those skilled craftsmen known as the jade men dedicated to jade design and production. Meanwhile, witches, who were supposed to be able to talk with gods directly, inevitably corresponded to the production management.

Special equipments were created according to social require, and been improved in practice. Both quality and quantity of hand-made jade were far beyond social needs. Then, the equipment with a wooden main framework, round wood as transmission, foot or hand-driven, enabling it to rapid spinning was not only invented, but also mastered by the jade men. That equipment is similar as the water bench in Tian Gong Kai Wu, which was written by Ying-Xing Song.

The unearthed Hongshan-culture pottery wares show clearly that the flans was spun out by mechanic entirely. In other words, it is an undeniable historical fact that Hongshan-Cultural period rotary mechanical processing equipment has appeared. Man-made technology or machine-made technology is historical watershed of the backward and the advanced, which is also an important basis for studying ancient history and the development of social productivity. Moreover, it's also essential for the study of Hongshan-Culture jade production. It's certain that the semi-mechanized factory processes that enable rapid spinning of the equipment must also be used for contemporaneous jade processes. And the Jade equipments would be more complicated and multi-functional since producing a piece of jade needs cutting, blanking, grinding, and other aspects of the production process to complete.

The judgment that Hongshan-Culture jade was entirely by mechanical processing could help us study the process features and reveal the number problems and many doubts and questions that were confusing us for a long time.

Emergence of Rotary-driven mechanical equipments facilitated the development and innovation of many things in various fields in this period. At the same time, jade equipment required deploying specialized tools to complete farewell to handmade situation. It should be said that this is not only a big progress in human history, but also an important symbol of mankind going into the civilization age. According to historical records, mastery of bronze smelting technology and bronze products remains were found in the New Stone Age in our country. However, before the era there was Red Copper Age. This shows that in the late Neolithic Age, metal objects have been developed in our country.

View from cutting and incision of the large and small pieces of Hongshan-Culture jade, the tool wouldn't be rope saw or stone disc saw since the incision counted by millimeter is very thin. The only possibility is the metal cutting tools bring along naxium (corundum) to cut the jade. Any other the tools can not achieve such sophistic level. Incision edge of some other jade is even, sharp, and surface of incision is flat and smooth, which further proved the mechanical process. I have tested many times: when jade was cut by bow saw with hide strip driven the largest naxium grains, the strip broke off five times during 30,000 times of pulling because of the attrition of naxium. When I pull the strip 2000 times, it softened and distorted by water and couldn't cut jade deeper, while mark of incision is very shallow, like being polished. Though two battens were fixed on both sides of the cutting place (in case the line runs off), the cutting line is not sharp but arc shaped, which indicated that those saws were unable to complete the cutting processes of Hongsahn-Culture jade.

Try to Imagine Shek round saw cutting. First, stone's texture is softer and more friable, thus it is extremely difficult to be made into laminose tools. Even if it's produced, in the practical course the tools would easily broke with slight carelessness. While if the stone is hard, it's also very difficult to be made into laminose tools. Besides, from the cutting of some larger pieces of jade we can see that large and thin stone tools can't made cutting. Thus the only processing tool for jade is made of metal since the above points were denied.

Why haven't we found metal devices yet until now? I think this is not difficult to explain: because thin red copper or bronze is easily rotten to corrosion. And there are no sites and remains of jade producing so far until now.

Ancestors' demanding of jade kept growing thanks to the universality of worship of the gods, with special mechanical equipment and specialized jade making tools, productivity has been greatly enhanced. Workers' skills were improved quickly, members of the teams were constantly developed, and systems had been developed into handicraft workshop patterns. Analyzing the large Hongshan-Culture jade, we can say that jade item was not completed by one man, but by two or more effective processing. Those "jade men" have their own clear division of labor, specializing in jade collection, transport, line, cutting, design, production, polishing, and other work.

The craft workshops not only increased productivity, but also according to social needs, supplied continuingly those jade productions as divine utensil to the ancestral temple, altar, families and those who wanted blessing. Some larger jade objects were for worship or worship activities, while the smaller one for wear. That's why most of gems have a hole.

Once the prevailing mode of the production of that time is nailed down, then it's easy to study the processes one by one. A jade production basically was completed by the following procedures: cutting, designing, blanking, burnishing, drilling, and polishing.

1、Cutting

Jade is cut according to uses or needs and shape of raw material. This is the first process. First, jade is fixed at the location of slitting wheel. Then, imposing impetus for disk-grinding slitting wheel bringing along naxium; water should be added continuingly to the wheel to keep naxium active and low temperature, avoiding jade quality compromised because of heat. For example, the diameter of Hongshan-Culture jade ware "the first China Dragon" is 26 cm. If we cut totally on one side, the diameter of the slitting wheel should be 30 cm at least; if we cut both two sides, the smallest diameter should be 16 cm. It is perfect for many aspects, such as plainness and balance of dragon's body, or symmetry and precision of dragon's mane. Then let us analyze slice jade baldric of heaven and earth, thickness of the jade is only 1 to 3 cm, from the cutting sign we speculate that the thickness of disk wheel is 0.3 to 0.6 cm. The maximum error is only between 1 to 3 mm. The jade is so level that it wouldn't hold up when we put it flat. Both bronze and red copper are relatively easier to be made to disk wheel cutting tools. The melted copper could be cast into the sand mould then polished by rough stones after it shaped. The ancestors would also beat the wheel on flagstone to make it flatter to meet the strict technical requirements. Then isometry grooves were made on the edge of the disk cutting wheel. Naxium could be deposited in those grooves and grind and cut the jade stone when the disk wheel running. Naxium is fetched from river, and the hardness of naxium varies depending on naxium's component. Generally, naxium is required harder than jade, so agate, quartz, crystal, and other mineral crystals can be used as naxium. Those sands must be elutriated many times and divided in accordance with different manufacturing processes. Larger particles, whose grinding speed is faster than smaller ones, were used to large jade cutting, but not as fine as the later.

After the objective analysis, we think batch producing was likely to be practiced in a workshop to fill the needs. For example, the same species, the same size and type of material of jade were produced at one time. This will effectively increase production volume, and form a clear division of work functions.

2、Design

Design is drawing initial shape. Those "jade men" should be messenger of god, or so-called witch since jade, as divine object which has its own special solemnness and holiness, couldn't be made by everyone liberally. But technically they are equal to designers today.

3、Blanking

According to the drawing line, cutting off the useless parts. The bigger scraps were rid off by disk cutting tool, and the smaller ones were scratched and grinded off by a special coniform spiral fashioned rough tool. Larger grains were used to improve efficiency, so in some larger jade surface we still can see the non-fixed direction moulage according to the process needs. Watching moulage under magnifier, we can see hairline transverse striate similar to the wooden spiral stripes. Thus we judge that the coniform tool was fixed on rotating mechanical equipment and bring about rapid speed to scrape and skive the jade surface.

Blanking is the foundation of jade figure and its framework as well as primary integrated imagination of the jade. It's also critical to ultimate overall artistry.

4、Bruting

Jade needs further fine processing after blanking. We call this procedure as bruting. Before it, all details should be drawn on the surface of jade, and then decide which part should remain and which should be off. The main carving technique is Shallow Relief. According to jade shape designing requirements, burnishing gentle slope surface to form a smooth transition, intersection of sticking up and sinking is natural and gentle. Even some transitional faces are invisible, and they can only be felt by hand touch. Therefore, meticulous process relies entirely on the self-perception and superb skills of workers.

Shallow Relief not only perfectly performed the overall image and detailed features of jade, but also shows vivid patterns, reaching the artistic superb state.

Based on the comprehensive analysis of Hongshan-Culture jade, we think that the Shallow

Relief is implemented specifically by the fallowing: the taper shaped, tough and whorl grinding tool was fixed and driven by a rolling machine to cut and grind. Large piece of jade is put on a special flat roof, which can be turn over randomly, while the smaller one is held by hand to grind.

The whorl grinding tool can bring along the naxium to burnishing. This time the naxium should be at least two types of the fine grain. For instance, we found that veins on striates of two wings of the jade bird are transversal. Some such veins are obvious, but some could be seen under magnifier, even some don't exist. We presume that result in two processes: first producing longitudinal striates with larger naxium, and then using fine naxium to cover those striates. In addition, we can see there are intermittent grinding signs on the surface of some larger jade wares while there is no such sign on the smaller ones.

Therefore we conclude that the reality of Hongshan-Cututre jade shouldn't only be judged by the moulage, but also by comprehensive analyses of all aspects. The horizontal vein existence depends on size of jade and sophisticated gradation. Generally, those veins appear on larger jade, softer texture jade such as serpentine or unimportant part of jade. Occasionally such traces would be found either under loupe on the surface of small jade.

The Shallow Relief process is distinct from other craft features, concise, simple and honest, mysterious and beautiful, with unity of form and spirit, integration of plastic arts and god worship, which therefore, will push the peak of ancient sculpture art, and even let us feel far behind to the ancestors.

We rarely see multifarious ornamental chevee on Hongshan-Culture jade. Currently we only found retiary chevee on forehead or underjaw of jade dragon and jade animal. Those reticulations were made by thin taper tool, thus obvious perverse screw thread appears. Some jade wares were re-processed, so veins on transverse section are not perverse screw thread but triangle, and the length-ways trace is long and straight. Obviously the striates were retreated by special tool and fine naxium.

5、Drilling

Most jade wares have a hole, only few three-dimensional statues jade haven't holes. After analyzing production procedure of Hongshan-Culture jade, we believe that drilling is the last stage of procedure. Hole can be divided into two forms: ornamental hole and practical hole. There is rule of ornamental hole. For example, holes of c-shaped jade animal, jade ring, jade disc or holes be-tween two arms or two legs of jade Numen were drilled with both sides of jade. Holes were emphasized on symmetry and balance. Practical hole is functional, for fastening by rope as cult device or as pendant. Those holes generally locate on the head or on the back of jade, being drilled on both sides, rarely on one side.

The analysis of holes implies that drilling tool should be taper-like with crude surface and blunt sharp head, thicker gradually until the end. The inner hole is small while the border is broader;

the whole hole is as horse's hoof, or as U-shape-like. Hole of the practice jade was drilled on both sides slanting like trunk, which called trunk hole or cattle nostril hole.

Because of practicability of practical hole and to enhance the work efficiency, not only wooden tools are relatively rough, but also naxium is relatively big; so more obvious gyroidal veins were often left. But ornamental hole is directly related to the image of the surface, so it is repeatingly polished until it is very smooth.

Holes of sheet jade are highly split while drilling. Therefore taking plunge drilling methods, thus it's slope-shaped, and intersection of hole is thin, sharp and barbed.

6、Burnishing

Burnishing is the last procedure of jade production to increase luster and brightness of jade surface, to show better elegant luminous texture. Therefore, the process of polishing jade is critical to final image.

Jade polishing can be divided into rough polishing and precise polishing. Normally, both methods are simultaneously used in the same jade piece: roughly polishing the surface to remove small jade moulage and naxium rough sand particles were used. Refined polishing is to enhance brightness of jade surface, when naxium particles are smaller.

We can see from the tiny scratch mark that the polishing tool is wooden and specialized one. Diablement fort or animal skins are wrapped on the wooden tool dip in naxium particulate and then comprehensive polishing was performed.

Careful observation under magnifier indicates the remaining small scratching without apparent regularity. Therefore, Hongshan-Culture jade polishing should be fully completed by hand.

7、Anticorrosive treatment

Jade would attach oil processing after polishing. The use of oil is supposed to make jade more bright, which plays a certain role in anti-corrosion. Thick dirt is often found in holes of Chinese jade unearthed in mass graves.After strickling it by bamboo knife and put it under magnifier to observe, the dirt is like white wax, and the greasiness pollution appeared when daubing on White paper.

That's why some Hongshan-Culture jade wares still bright buried in the ground for thousand years, why some jade surface is fine but the internal decays seriously. That's related to oil anti-corrosive treatment.

Analysis and understanding of the jade production processes is of great importance for the identification of jade. Analysis must be rational and objective, in keeping with the laws of science. Understanding is for further study.

In academic research, we should believe that there is no absolute authority. He is probably an archaeologist, historian, or mineralogist, but not a connoisseur on ancient jade. We should not only master various disciplines of knowledge, but also have keen insight. We must make great effort for this.

图 100 牛河梁第二地点附近出土之字纹陶钵
尺寸：高 7.5cm
Picture100 word-shaped stripe pottery bowl (unearthed near the No.2 location of Niuheliang)
Size: 7.5cm high

图 101 之字纹陶钵局部放大
Picture 101 word-shaped stripe pottery bowl partly enlarged

　　陶钵口沿下装饰线纹。对线纹进行观察分析：线纹连贯，无中断处。由较硬物体所刻划，深浅有度。如果手工刻划线纹，因为分段，中间当有断续处，自然连贯性较差。由此认为此器属机械制坯，线纹是在快速旋转陶坯时刻划而成。

　　从陶钵的装饰线纹，认证了在红山文化时期玉器的制作已进入陶车机械加工的可能性与可信性。

The mouth of pottery bowl is along the veins of decorative thread. As observing and analysing the line veins that links up and has not suspending place. It carves stroke by more hard object and has suit degree on depth. If carving the veins on handwork, as divided into sections, so it may have intermittent place in intermediate, and its continuity is lacked comparatively. Therefore we think that this ware belongs to mechanical-made semifinished product, the line veins come into being on carved by revolving pottery semifinished product rapidly.

　　From the veins of decorative thread of pottery bowl certificating that during Hongshan-culture period the produce of jade ware have entered pottery vehicle credibleness and the possibility of machining.

图 102 牛河梁二号冢出土彩陶瓮

通高 40.4cm

Picture 102 Painted pottery urn (unearthed in the No.2 stone mound of Niuheliang)

40.4cm high

图 103 牛河梁第十六地点下层积石冢

彩陶筒形器 高约 35cm

Picture 103 the underground stone mound at the No.16 location of Niuheliang

Painted pottery cylinder-shaped ware about 35cm high

此器造型生动而端庄。无论器身与瓮盖做工极为规范，线条自然流畅。

从陶瓮外观分析，应为轮制法制作。决非泥条盘筑法、捏塑法或模制成器，显然应用了动力旋转技术制坯。

在牛河梁四号冢石墙内侧立有成排的彩陶筒形器。

从这些大量的筒形器外观形象来看：收、放有度，线条流畅，规矩严谨。除旋转制坯工艺外，别无其它方法能达到如此精密程度。

以次可以认定，与其处于同时期的红山文化玉器加工，已经采用以人之四肢为动力的、以木制框架结构的、可以使之快速旋转的加工机械。

The modelling of this ware is lively and dignified. No matter what the ware body or the cover of urn's workmanship is very standard, and its line is nature and smooth.

Analysing the appearance of pottery urn, it should be made by turn facture not mud strip building, kneading or mould made into ware, obviously they have applied power revolving technical system to make semifinished product.

There are rows of painted pottery cylinder-shaped ware on the inner side of wall at the No.4 stone mound of Niuheliang.

Observing these appearance images of plent of cylinder-shaped wares: having suit degree to gather and send, smooth line and strict rules. Except revolving producing technology of making semifinished product, there is no other method to reach so precise level.

This can be found that the producing of Hongshan-culture jade ware have adopt the process machine that is with human's arms power, with wooden frame structure, and can make it fast revolving.

图 104 玉璧 （牛河梁二号冢 1 号墓出土） Picture 104 a kind of Jade (a doughnut-shaped piece of flat jade with
尺寸：直径 12cm the hole's diameter shorter than the width of the rim) (unearthed in the
No.1 tomb from the No.2 stone mound of Niuheliang)
Size: diameter 12cm

图 105 玉璧局部放大
Picture 105 Jade partly enlarged

　　在红山文化玉器群中，璧、环、瑗、镯 玉器为多见器物，这些看似造型简单的玉器，其内涵却十
分深邃，并具有非常重要的研究价值。

　　In Hongshan-culture jade ware crowd，jade, ring, coiled, bracelet jade ware is usual wares. Its intension is
very deep, though the modeling of these jade wares seem simple，and has very important research value。

图 106 大玉璧 （牛河梁二号冢1号墓出土）
尺寸：直径 14.7cm

Picture 106 Large Jade (a doughnut-shaped piece of flat jade with the hole's diameter shorter than the width of the rim) (uneathed in the No.1 tomb from The No.2 stone mound of Niuheliang)

Size: 14.7cm in diameter

图 107 大玉璧局部放大
Picture 107 large Jade partly enlarged

　　这件片状的大玉璧，直径达 14.7 厘米。很难想象，此玉器的开片工具应为何种材料所制，如何进行有效切割？对这些问题需要我们进行全面科学分析与论证。以得出正确答案。

　　The diameter of this slice-shaped Large Jade is 14.7cm. It is impossible to imagine that cut tool of this jade ware should be what kind of material, and how to cut efficiently? For these problems, we need to carry out all-sidedly scientific analysis and demonstration. So we can get correct answer.

图 108 玦形玉兽（辽宁省建平县征集）

尺寸：高 15cm

Picture 108 Jade Coiled Animal(collected at Jianping country in Liaoning province)

Size: 15cm high

图 109 玦形玉兽局部放大

Picture 109 Jade Coiled Animal partly enlarged

　　此器完美的造型，精湛的琢磨工艺，实在令人叹服。人们想象不出五、六千年前原始人类是如何创造了这样的奇迹。因此许多人在猜想，并妄下着各种不同结论：有人说，玉器的开片是以石轮锯完成的。也有人说，玉石的切割是绳锯带动解玉砂，甚至注入动物的鲜血所完成。

　　很多人相信了这些观点和结论，并相信原始先民完全靠手工制作了这些玉器，认为一件玉器的完成需要数年，甚至几十年时间。

　　作者做了很多种实验，事实证明：石轮锯与绳锯切割玉石皆不能出现我们所观察到的红山文化玉器加工工艺特征，因此说玉器的加工并非完全手工所完成。

　　我们从玦形玉兽头、尾处切割口可见看到：切割面平齐，收刀处尖锐，口沿处呈直角，为两刀切割而成。这一特征除较薄金属器能够做到外，其它皆不能完成。

　　The perfect modeling of this ware and consummate polishing technology makes people admire really. People can't imagine that 5000–6000 years ago, the original mankind is how to create such miracle. Therefore a lot of people are guessing, and drawing various different conclusions: Somebody says that the cut of jade ware is completed with stone wheel saw. Somebody also says , jade cut is rope saw driving to untie jade sand, even to pour into the blood of animal to finish.

　　Many people have believed these viewpoint and conclusion, and believe original late people reled on handwork completely to make these jade wares, and think that the completion of a jade ware need several years, even tens of years time.

　　The author makes various experiments, the fact prooved: The stone wheel and rope saw cut jade all can not arise we have observed the processing technology feature of Hongshan–culture jade ware, therefore the processing of jade wares is not complete handwork to finish.

　　We can see from the head of Jade Coiled Animal and its tail cut: The flat of cut is orderly and the end of knife cut is sharp, the mouth along it is right angle, which is cut for two knives. This feature can accomplish only with thin metal ware and others can not complete..

图 110 块形玉兽（牛河梁一带地区出土）

尺寸：高15cm

Picture 110 Jade Coiled Animal(unearthed near the area of Niuheliang)

Size: 15 cm. high

图 111 块形三兽局部放大

Picture 111 Jade Coiled Animal partly enlarged

我们在不能准确认定玉器具体制作时间，按照工艺特征相同，统称为红山文化时期的玉器。尤其中晚期阶段，其制作工艺虽然有微小区别，但可以排除一点的是，并非完全手工制作。

这件块形玉兽面部的阴刻线，入刀与出刀处锐尖，线条坚挺有力，弯曲有度，决非手工刻划能完成，而具有明显铊刻特征。

以此我们可以断定，当时红山文化玉器加工已进入施用专门设备与工具作坊式生产。

厚重的包浆、明显的绺裂、密集的麻斑、过渡而完整的沁色，这些自然而真实的沁象，皆有力证明这件玉器的真实性。

We are can not be accurate to decide the specificly produce time of jade ware，according to identical technology feature, unified called jade ware of Hongshan-culture period. Especially in middle and late period, its produce technology although has a little distinguish, but what can remove is not complete handwork producing.

The head surface of this Jade Coiled Animal concave carved line. Its in-knife and out-knife place is sharp, line is strong and right curved, which is not only by handwork carving to be completed, and have obvious thallium carved feature.

So as this we can conclude that the processing Hongshan-culture jade ware has entered to use special equipment and tool in workshop to produce.

Massive baojiang, obvious tuft crack pattern, dense numb spot, and transition and complete infiltration colour that these natural and actual infiltration are strong to prove the actuality of this jade ware.

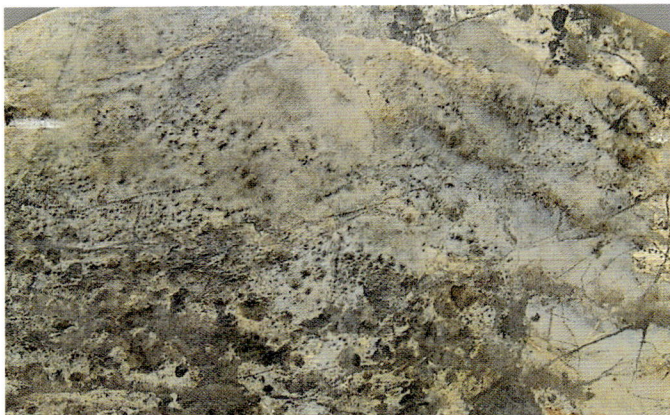

图 112 双鸟首玉佩

尺寸：高 10.2cm 宽 21cm

玉质：青玉

(听雨堂珍藏)

Picture 112 jade pendant of double bird heads

Size: 10.2cm high　21cm wide

Jade texture: blue-green jade

(Collection of "rain-hear hall")

图 113 双鸟首玉佩局部放大

Picture 113　jade pendant of double bird heads partly enlarged

无论动用任何高科技手段，人们都永远无法逼真仿制的沁象。

逆光下我们可以清楚看到被平除的切割痕。

No matter what kind of high-tech method, people can not modelled on lifelike infiltration forever.

Under countrary light we can see having been leveled cut trace clearly.

图 114 双鸟首玉佩局部放大

Picture 114　jade pendant of double bird heads partly enlarged

图 115 双鸟首玉佩另面
Picture 115 another side of jade pendant of double bird heads

图 116 双鸟首玉佩切割痕逐步放大
Picture 116 the cut trace of jade pendant of double bird heads enlarged step by step

图 117 双鸟首玉佩切割痕逐步放大
Picture 117 the cut trace of jade pendant of double bird heads enlarged step by step

很多人错误的认为，红山文化时期玉石的切割是以绳锯完成的。从此器切割痕看：线条笔直，双向对切衔接交点误差只有毫米，不但可见原始先民当时的计算精确程度，而且绳锯根本无法做到和出现这样的切割特征。

根据多方面对红山文化玉器切割痕分析，诸多特征说明，此时原始先民已初步掌握了红铜或青铜冶炼技术，并制造出专门应用于玉石切割的片状金属工具。

Many people wrong think that the jade cut of Hongshan-culture period is with rope to complete. Since seeing from the ware cut trace: Line is straight, the join intersection error from both sides cutting is only millimeter, we can see not only the calculate accurate degree, but also with rope saw this kind of cut feature cant't be made or appeared.

According to analyse many aspects on cut trace of Hongshan-culture jade ware, a lot of feature can explain that at that time original late people has grasped smelting technology of red copper or bronze, and made out the slice-shaped metal tools applied specially in cutting jade.

图 118 玉蝙蝠
尺寸：高 16cm 宽 23.7cm
玉质：青玉
（听雨堂珍藏）

Picture 118 Jade bat
Size: 16cm high   23.7cm wide
Jade texture: blue-green jade
(Collection of "rain-hear hall")

图 119 玉蝙蝠另面
Picture 119 another side of Jade bat

图 120 玉蝙蝠局部放大
Picture 120 Jade bat partly enlarged

　　玉蝙蝠呈片状，在如此薄的器面上进行双面雕琢，而且压地隐起阳线纹纤细流畅，镂空对接准确，实在令今天的人们感到惊讶和不可思议。

　　但事实就是这样。先民们的聪明才智和伟大的创造力在某些方面已远远超越现代人的想象。

　　远古人类所创造的历史神话，对我们应该有所启迪和更深刻的认识。改变思维方式，去除头脑中始终对祖先存疑的固执和偏见。

Jade bat presents slice shape, on so thin ware surface to carry out two-sided carving, the protruding line veins of pressing and latent is fine and smooth, and the hollow-out joint is accurate, which make people of today feel surprised and unimaginable.

　　But the fact is such. The great creativity and wisdom of late people are over the imagination of modern person in some aspects.

　　The historical mythology that ancient mankind creates, which should be enlightenment and more deep cognition for us. We should change the way of thought, exclude suspect stubborn and prejudice for ancestors all along in our brains.

图 121 天地神佩

尺寸：高 5.9cm　宽 16.7cm

玉质：青玉

（听雨堂珍藏）

Picture 121 Compound jade baldric for heaven and earth

Size: 5.9cm high　16.7cm wide

Jade texture: blue-green jade

(Collection of "rain-hear hall")

"压地隐起法"琢磨工艺，又被称为"打洼法"。即在完成雏形的玉器器表以棒状工具进行刮削，趟出沟槽，这时沟槽中常留下横向螺丝状刮削痕。为消除这些印痕，让打洼处更光滑顺畅，再二次以细砂顺沟槽精磨，以达到更完美艺术效果。

The "gentle slope shape" carve and polish technology, is also called "dig hollow method". That is scraping with stick-shaped tools on the surface of complete embryo jade ware and made cannelure on it,in which often left screw-shaped scrape trace. In order to eliminate these traces, and let hollow place more smooth, then they again used sand along the cannelure grinding precisely to get more perfect art effect.

图　122　鸟翅形玉佩

尺寸：高 5cm

玉质：青玉

（听雨堂珍藏）

Picture 122 Bird wing-shaped jade pendant

Size:5cm high

Jade texture: blue-green jade

(Collection of "rain-hear hall")

图 123 玉神祖
玉质：青玉
尺寸：高 16.4 cm
（听雨堂珍藏）
Picture 123 Jade numen
Jade texture: blue-green jade
Size: 16.4cm high
（Collection of "rain-hear hall"）

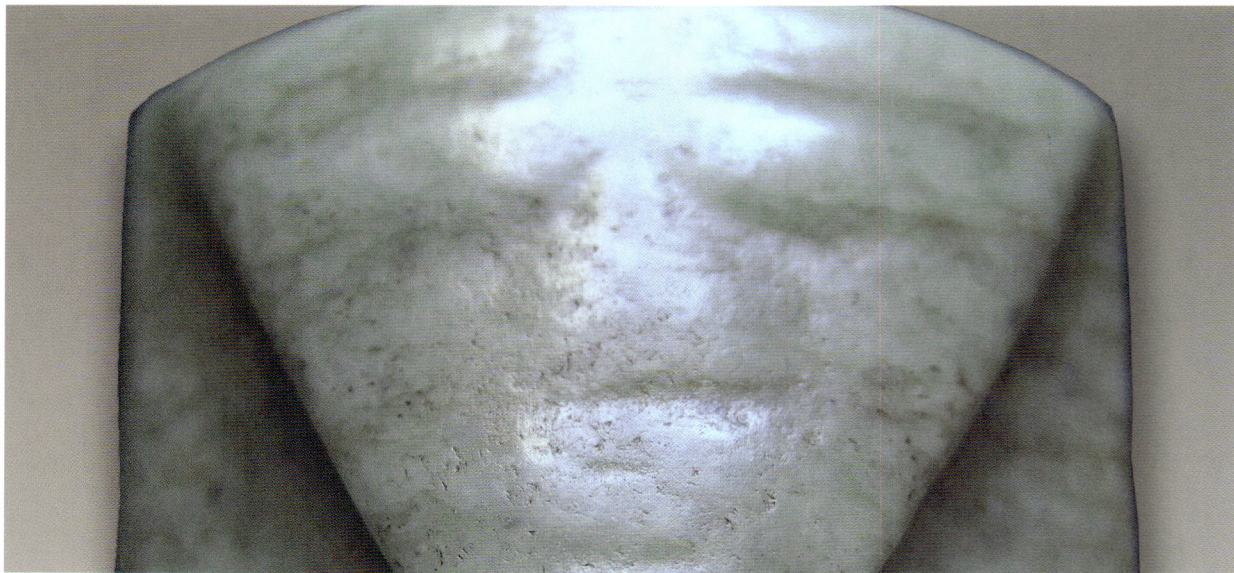

图 124 玉神祖头部放大
Picture 124 The head of jade numen partly enlarged

图 125 玉神祖系挂孔处放大
Picture 125 the head of Jade numen partly enlarged

玉神祖头部压地隐起呈朦胧状态，五官若隐若现，更具神秘感。

系挂孔内可见镙丝状旋纹，这是红山文化玉器钻孔一大特征。

The "gentle slope shape" of Jade numen head presents dim state, and the facial features tappear indistinctly, so it more have mysterious feeling.

In hole place we can see screw-shaped spiral aeins, which is a big feature for drilling hole of the Hongshan-culture jade ware.

图 126 玉神祖器背
Picture 126 the back of Jade numen

图 127 玉鸟

尺寸：高 7.6cm 宽 11.1cm

玉质：青玉

（听雨堂珍藏）

Picture 127 Jade bird

Size: 7.6cm high　11.1cm wide

Jade texture: blue-green jade

(Collection of "rain-hear hall")

图 128 玉鸟器背

Picture 128 The back of jade bird

图 129 玉鸟系佩孔

Picture 129 jade bird hanging hole

原本和谐对称鸟之双翅与尾，右侧因为钙化严重而出现明显萎缩。

红山文化玉器皆由内向外逐渐收敛，玉器边缘厚度减薄或呈刃状。

系佩孔沿圆滑，无刺手感。孔壁可见解玉砂磨削螺旋纹。

Originally symmetrical bird's tail and the two wings, as right side serious calcification to appear significant atrophy.

Hongshan-culture jade wares are all from inside to outside gradually convergence, and the jade border's thickness reduce thin and present blade shape.

The hanging hole's edge is smooth and without thorn feeling. The wall of hole can see grinding spiral veins of cutting jade sand.

图 130 玉鸮（辽宁省阜新县胡头沟墓地1号墓出土）

尺寸：宽3.8cm

Picture130　Jade bird (unearthed in the No.1 tomb from Hutou ditch graveyard at Fuxin county in Liaoning province)

Size: 3.8cm wide

图131 玉鸮局部放大

Picture131　Jade bird partly enlarged

"压地隐起法"是红山文化玉器制作的主要工艺特征。此器制作工艺明显较为粗糙，尤其鸮的双翅，只用刮削法趟出沟槽，并没有再进一步平沟缓慢隐起阳地。尽管这一工艺特征在红山文化玉器加工中并不多见，但客观确实存在这一特殊情况。

这件几乎完全被石化了的玉鸮，沁象真实自然。因此我们在红山文化玉器鉴定工作中，一定要进行综合分析，不能因一点之差而给予全盘否定。

The "gentle slope shape" method is the major technology feature of Hongshan-culture jade ware produce. This ware produce technology is rough obviously, especially the two wings of bird, only to scrape cannelure, and do not level the slope with slow ditch again. Though this technology feature is not not seen in Hongshan-culture jade ware technology, it is objective and definite to have this special condition.

This nearly complete infiltration of jade bird is true and natural. Therefore we must carry out integration analysis in appraising work of Hongshan-culture jade wares, and can not negate completely for a little difference.

红山文化玉器沁象

Presentation Infiltration of Hongshan—Culture Jade

红山文化玉器沁象

距今 5000 — 6000 年的红山文化，绝少有未曾入土的传世器。凡出土的古玉器，因与土壤长时期相接触，无不受到土中所含各种元素不同程度的浸蚀，这些由于浸蚀所形成的诸方面特征，是真古玉器永不消逝的时代与时间烙印。

沁象，即玉石受自然界各种客观因素影响，所产生由表及里的玉理质地与颜色变化。这种直观形态变化，我谓之沁象。

沁象能够客观解释玉石受沁的自然变化过程和原因，同时也是我们鉴定玉器是否达到年代标准要求、真与伪的重要科学依据。

一、玉器的受沁原因和条件

1.玉石的中空现象

由于地壳的运动变化，地层受到挤压溶动形成含有不同矿物质的玉石。玉石在缓慢形成的过程中，由于受各种客观因素所影响，玉理会出现不同形态变化，或紧密、或松软、或晶莹透沏、或混浊着包裹体。不但玉石的颜色不尽相同，而且其质地也各不相同。无论仔料还是山料，无论何种玉质，当在高倍放大镜下观察时，其内理皆或多或少含有云雾状、棉絮状、条纹状生态特征，通常我们所称为棉、绺、璺、瑕。对此，我称之为玉石中空现象。

玉石的中空现象，应该说是玉石的自然缺陷。而真正完全达到"完美无瑕"者极少。正是玉石这些微小的中空缝隙，给土壤中各种元素的浸入以可乘之机。这些最薄弱点难以抵御各种元素的强烈攻击，最终土壤中的微量金属元素与其他非金属元素会乘虚而入，并因此造成对玉石的侵害，我们称作玉石的"受沁"。

玉石的中空现象，成为玉石受沁的主要条件。受沁后的玉石，不但会改变其原有颜色，而且质地也会发生根本变化。可能造成原本深色的玉受沁后颜色变淡，质地坚密的玉因受沁而脆弱，受沁严重者甚至腐朽为泥土。因此我们说：受沁，即各种元素对玉石质地的侵害和破坏。

玉石器受沁必须具备以下几方面条件：

2.湿度：

湿度是玉器受沁的条件之一。没有相对湿度，玉器就不能够受沁。"沁"，实为"浸"。浸，则离不开水，无水或者无一定湿度，无论沁色、包浆、蚀斑、蛀孔、络裂等沁象就不会产生。各种元素都是在相对湿度条件下而浸入玉理之中。如果将一件新制作玉器放置于封闭的干燥箱内，无论与任何物体和元素相接触，都不会发生颜色和质地变化。

3.温度：

根据"热涨冷缩"物理原理，温度的变化能够促使玉质发生变化，从而产生沁象。在温度骤高骤低，在冷冻和化解情况下，由于玉器内、外温度的反差，造成了膨胀系数的差异和波动。在长期的"涨"与"缩"过程中，玉理遭受破坏则会出现绺裂纹。裸露的伤痕给各种有害物质的浸入创造了可乘之机。同时，温度的变化又促使受到伤害玉器产生内分泌，自然形成自我保护，并因此也会产生其他各种不同的沁象。

4．空气：

深入地层的葬墓在完全封闭状态下，在尚未与空气接触前，玉器的玉理内部结构完全呈开放状态，质地相对较为松软，此时正是玉器受沁的最佳时机。当出土玉器与空气相接触后，在数分钟内开放的气孔逐渐关闭，使玉质坚硬起来或者因风化而破裂。因此我们说，玉器在出土前与出土后当有着明显差别。由于空气作用，玉器的质地与颜色都会有所改变。

考古证明，葬墓中一些本来完好的丝织品，因为保护不当，在与空气相接触后，在短时间内可以化为灰烬。淤集于土层中的瓷器在未见空气前，以铁制利器可以戳出残洞。古人道，片状玉器在墓穴中由于摆放不平，能够使之变形。

"近朱者赤，近墨者黑"。近，并非物体实际接触，而只是相近。当玉器与铜、铁、铅、锌等有色金属元素或含有碳、酸、碱、钙等化学物质相邻近时，由于空气的作用，玉器即会被所邻近金属及非金属元素染色，甚至质地受到破坏。因此说，空气中的多种气体也是传播和导致玉器受沁的重要途径之一。

5．玉石的特性：

红山文化玉器的用材除极少数松石、玛瑙、水晶外，绝大多数为常见软玉。从分类看，主要为透闪石和蛇纹石。透闪石类玉器，致密度较高，玉理结构坚密，绺、棉、瑕相对较少，因此可以有效抵御来自土壤中各种微量元素的浸蚀，让有害物质无孔可入。所以这类质地玉器沁象不十分明显，而且沁色多浮于器表，不易深入玉理之中。蛇纹石类玉器，由于玉理结构松散，坚密度较差，自我保护能力远不及透闪石，所以有害物质可以长驱直入，迅速漫延玉器全身。因沁象较为明显，并因此给我们留下了很多鉴定依据。

6．玉石的矿物成份：

不同质地的玉石含有不同的矿物成份。这些含有不同矿物成份的玉石受到浸蚀后，沁象各有所不同。

在红山文化葬墓中我们发现这样一种情况：同一葬墓中葬有多件玉器，在相同条件下，有的亮丽如新，有的则受沁严重，甚至完全钙化或石化。这是为什么？经分析研究认为，这是因为除玉器自身器形、工艺等诸多外部因素，更重要的是与它们所含有的矿物成份有关。这些钙化或石化了的玉器因其所含有的矿物成份恰与葬墓石灰岩质砌筑石板成分极易融合和吸收，并因此产生化学反应与变化。

由此我们可以说明，在同样条件下，不同质地的玉器受沁情况不能够完全相同，而是因矿物成份不同各有所异。

二、玉器受沁的特别规律

我们所说红山文化玉器的沁象，是指玉器在完成制作后，整体与土壤相接触所发生的浸蚀变化。也就是说，凡长时期与土壤中任何一种物质或金属元素相接触皆有可能使玉理发生变化，出现沁象。而且这种沁象必须保证相对的完整与统一。为此，我们需要进一步强调玉器沁象的规律性、完整性、过渡性和真实性。

1. 规律性：

我们分析和研究红山文化玉器的沁象，必须首先了解和掌握这一历史时期的诸多方面史实。例如，社会背景、地理环境、气候条件、葬墓特征、土壤成份、玉器材料及工艺特征等。这些客观因素，都有利于我们从中把握玉器受沁变化，并从中找出它的规律性。

红山文化地处我国北方地区，它特有的自然气候条件和四季气温变化，决定着玉器受沁后的诸多方面特征。尤其骤冷骤热的较大温差变化，玉器极易出现物理变化，象我们所看到的绺裂和包浆，就是在这种特殊条件下所形成的。

从已发现的红山文化遗址看，大都依山傍河，而且葬墓多在山坡被称为"台地"处，这应与当时丧葬习俗有关。这些地方多以沙土为主，水土流失严重，葬墓中不易存水。所以在此环境下出土玉器多干爽洁净，绝少有水沁痕迹或较大酸蚀麻斑。偶见有水沁痕迹者，经分析这些器物当放置于墓中陶罐因积水所沁成。

红山文化葬墓多以石灰岩质石材砌筑。长不过 2 米，宽约 1 米，墓内无木棺。当我们了解这些情况后，就容易分析和解释红山文化玉器的诸多方面沁象特征。

红山文化古玉出土地区不同，土壤中所含成份也有所不同。或酸碱性较大、或金属元素复杂、受沁后的变化都有着明显的区别。因为这其中蕴含着错纵复杂的多种因素。但同一地域、同一玉质、相同土壤所出土的玉器受沁情况又有许多相同之处。因同一地域土壤成分除相接近处，地域性气候条件基本无大变化。因此，从客观上讲，红山文化玉器的沁象具有明显的统一性。

尊重历史，尊重科学。根据中国古代史分析，红山人的衣着仍然局限于兽皮和简单的麻类织物，假如有人认为玉器中艳丽的红、绿沁为寿衣染色浸成，显然是错误的。红山人的就地就近取材制作玉器是历史客观事实，远离红山文化地域的其它玉种所制作的红山文化玉器难免让人存疑。因为从我们所掌握的红山文化所用玉材，从品种、玉质、颜色等方面来看，最多也不超过十几种，仍然具有一定的局限性。

红山文化玉器特殊的艺术造型和独特的制作工艺，给玉器受沁留下了许多较为明显的沁象特征。比如，我们经常看到的板状和片状玉器，其边缘处多呈刀状。圆雕玉器也是中间处较厚而突起，玉器周边缓收。这些玉器的边缘处或较薄处与土壤接触面较广大，受沁也就更严重。因此形成由最薄处向厚处，由边缘向中间，由表面向内理延伸的自然受沁过程。这就是规律性。并因此让我们能够从玉器自然受沁规律性中正确判断玉器真伪。

我们所说的规律性，是玉器受沁的自然科学规律，这一规律是永恒不变的。违背客观规律性则脱离历史现实，脱离科学轨道。对于这一问题我们万不可忽视。

2．完整性：

这里所说古玉器沁象的完整性，并非玉器沁象通体绝对的完整与统一。而是玉器受沁后，发生某些细微变化的沁象整体相对的完整。

红山文化历经数千年，由于墓穴简易、透水、距地表较浅等客观原因，决定了玉器被土壤埋没的可能性与长期性。这些长期被埋入土下或裸露于地表的玉器，无论自身的移动或者土壤的流动，皆能够造成对玉器的全面侵害。因此，玉器的沁象应该是完整的。在完整的沁象中包含着它的统一性和连续性特征。并从这些特征中看到玉器表面所呈现出的轻重、深浅颜色之变化。

具体说来，沁象的完整性即在同一特定环境与土壤中，受沁玉器的正面、背面、侧面、甚至镂空处和系挂孔内，其沁象都应该保持总体上的相对一致。纵观全器，在玉器制作加工后的低洼处不能与突起处之间出现"断沁"现象。

举例来说，以一块已受沁的老玉仿制真古玉器，它就必须进行再加工。在加工过程中，其原生沁即遭到破坏，去除部分与保留部分沁色不能和谐衔接，甚至出现中断现象。我们较常见以原生沁河漠玉加工的玉器，因为它要从大块玉石表面剥离下来，所以加工出的玉器不但会出现断沁现象，而且玉器的正面和背面，沁象会出现许多明显的差异，因而玉器整体受沁的和谐过渡和完整性即遭受破坏。

3．过渡性：

古玉的受沁是经过日复一日，年复一年逐渐完成的，而并非在一日之间骤然发生之奇迹。因此我们说，古玉是岁月的沉淀，是历史的见证。

在漫长的风霜雪雨中，由于受自然界多种因素所影响，玉器则发生缓慢质的变化。尤其多种元素的浸入，给受沁后的玉器留下诸多特征。由于沁象的发生与发展是缓慢进行的，因此沁象则出现过渡性和层次感。

具有过渡性的沁，我称之为活沁。活沁；生动、活泼、自然，有流动感。缺乏过渡性的沁，我称之为死沁。死沁；生硬、僵滞、呆板、缺乏生机。

活沁，为自然形成。死沁，为人工所为。

比如，一件边缘呈刃状的板状青玉质红山文化玉器，它受沁最重处应该是最簿的边缘部分，当边缘处呈鸡骨白色时，这时它的变化顺序是这样排列的：已钙化了的白色－－灰白色－－浅糖色－－糖色－－青白色－－青色。各颜色之间平和过渡，无明显分界线，犹如喷绘一般。这就是沁象的过渡性和层次感。真正的玉器沁后特征，做伪者永远无法模仿。

再比如，一件全部呈鸡骨白色的红山文化玉器，它的受沁过程也是逐步完成的。首先，在白化前它同时还要受到土壤中的其他元素所浸蚀，而生石灰可能是其白化的主要成分和原因。这些白化了的玉器应该不是单一的纯白色，其中还夹杂着灰暗的其它色斑。这些色斑的客观存在，同样能够说明，白化了的玉器存在先后受沁顺序和两者之间所形成的过渡性。反之，这件鸡骨白色玉器就值得产生怀疑，因为它违背了自然科学规律。

4．真实性：

红山文化因为年代久远，每件玉器都会通过器表将沁象反映出来。鉴定红山文化玉器的真伪，沁象将起70%决定作用。因此，分辨和认定沁象的真实性，对于我们来说至关重要。

何为真实性？其一，符合客观自然规律。其二，人为永远无法仿制。说起来就这么简单。

大自然造化万物，同时也造化了古代玉器的沁象。大自然的刀斧神工使今天的人们采取任何高科技手段都望尘莫及。所以我们说，沁象为上天和大地所创造，因为它没有丝毫的做作和虚伪。

毛主席曾说过："要想知道梨子的滋味，就必须自己去亲口尝一尝。"这是唯物辩证法。他告诉我们，实践出真知。要充分掌握玉器沁象的真实性，就必须深入实地考察和了解红山文化遗址的地理环境，葬墓特征等诸方面客观情况。就必须有针对性的深入市场了解各种作伪动态。就必须亲自动手做各种实验。通过调查研究，我们可以掌握大量与玉器鉴定有关信息。通过实验，我们才能够了解古代玉器的加工手段;自然沁与化学沁的不同;自然沁孔洞与人工做伪孔洞之差异;自然形成绺裂与做伪绺裂之区分;自然包浆与人工抛光之区别，哪些沁象人为可以模仿，哪些永远不能够逼真模仿。只有做到知己知彼，方才不致于产生盲目性，也才能够在玉器鉴定工作中做到有的放矢。

真实性，是玉器的灵魂，没有灵魂的玉器只不过是一件现代工艺品。

三、玉器的沁后特征

当我们了解和掌握了玉器受沁的多种因素之后，还要进一步分析玉器各种沁象形成的原因及其主要特征。因为这对于我们正确认识和鉴定玉器非常重要。

1.古玉的包浆：

凡出土玉器，皆有包浆。包浆，就是玉器表面所呈现一种温润而亮丽的光泽。这种光泽，光感柔和，温而不火，润而不燥，无强烈耀眼感觉。当我们逆光观察玉器表面时，你会发现之所以光感柔和，是因为玉器表面布满许多微小的麻坑，正是这些麻坑将光吸收和分散。微小的麻坑是由于玉器长期与土壤相接触,被土壤中多种元素侵蚀而成。

包浆的生成与玉器所处客观环境与气候条件有着密切的关系。从科学发掘情况看，红山文化庙、冢、坛多分布于山坡台地。这里的土壤多沙化，不易存水，由于通风和干燥，所出土玉器皆包浆明显。尤其北方地区的气候条件，四季分明，温差变化较大，这都为玉器包浆的生成创造了条件。在气温骤然升高和降低的情况下，处在正常温度状态下的玉器不能立即适应突然间的温度变化，就会出现"发汗"现象，在玉器表面泛出一层密集的水雾，并聚集成微小的"露珠"。"露珠"生成的同时，包含着玉石自身的内分泌。在所分泌的"汗水"中，玉石所含有的微量矿物元素随之被排出体外。当玉器恢复到正常温度时，这些"汗水"便被晾干凝结在玉器表面上，仿佛为玉器镀了一层保护膜。年复一年，周而复始，这层亮膜越积越厚。由于亮膜中含有微量矿物元素，因此也增加了玉器表面的亮度与硬度，使一些有害元素无法侵入，从而起到自身保护作用。

在红山文化出土玉器中常发现这样一种情况：一件外表完好无损、光泽亮丽的玉器，当破开外表时，内腐十分严重。这是因为玉器表面某一点空隙或小的残破渗入有害元素所造成。之所以没能从外至内全部腐朽，除抛光因素外，玉器外部紧密的包浆犹如一层丝滑的外衣，使土不能粘附，元素不能进入。自身抵御作用十分明显。

红山文化真古玉器，受沁后无论石化、钙化或残破到如何程度，皆可见有明显包浆。这种罩于器表的包浆是经过漫长岁月自然形成的，而并非文盘或者武盘人为所能盘化出的。不管是早期出土传世还是刚刚出土玉器，你只要用棉布稍加擦拭则光泽照人，宝光四溢，充分显现一种蒸煮熟透了的感觉。

凡无包浆红山文化玉器，皆不能认定为真古玉器。包浆的存在与否，是鉴定红山文化玉器的重要条件。

2．古玉的沁色：

沁色，即在特殊条件下，各种元素通过玉石之瑕疵而浸入玉理之中所呈现出的不同颜色。沁色的形成，必需具备玉器所处环境的湿度、温度、元素及玉石所存在可进入沁色的薄弱点等四个主要条件，这样沁色才能够浸入玉器玉理之中。否则，沁色则不能深入，只能形成表面浮沁。

凡土壤中的有机物、无机物、矿物质、金属元素，在一定条件下皆能对玉器浸染，形成沁色。

通过对红山文化玉器沁色的分类，我们已知的大概有这样几种沁：土沁、石灰沁、酸碱沁、水银沁、铁锈沁、水沁、炭黑沁、其它金属元素沁。

土沁：受土沁者大部分为蛇纹石类玉器，严重者出现大面积石化斑，甚至整器石化。沁象呈淡赭石色，与土壤颜色十分接近。这种颜色看起来质朴、温和、自然而真实。这是因为土壤中微量元素和土浆同时浸入玉器之内并逐渐漫延而成。受沁玉器大部分先行钙化，当质地变软之后，土色随之渗入玉理并凝固。因这种沁色极难仿造，所以目前尚未发现人为制作土沁玉器进入市场。

石灰沁：沁象呈白色，成斑块状，点状，或玉器整体白化。俗称"鸡骨白"或"象牙白"。红山文化葬墓多以砂岩和硅质石灰岩石材构筑，所以玉器常被生石灰所沁。尤其颜色艳绿者玉器受沁更为严重。分析认为，此种玉石所含矿物元素，应该恰与生石灰起了化合反应。

酸碱沁：酸与碱对玉器的危害性和破坏性都绞大。受酸碱浸蚀严重者可出现麻斑和蚀孔。从来自众多不同地区出土玉器沁象看，目前尚未发现含有较高酸碱性土壤的侵蚀特征，而且在科学发掘时也并未发现大麻斑沁象玉器。因此，凡具有泛白灰大麻斑玉皮特征的玉器，目前已被普遍认为人工强酸碱浸蚀作伪玉器。

水银沁：土壤中常含有微量水银，有些微小的水银颗粒我们的肉眼很难观察到。由于玉石特殊的矿物成份和特征，水银对玉有着极强的附着力和穿透力。因此，古人们认为水银遇玉而凝固。在汉代，为防尸体腐烂，常在尸身内注入水银，并以玉塞七窍，以防水银外溢。水银沁，呈黑色。浸入玉器玉理后呈凝固状，但在一定温度下会产生流动感，并能够从玉理中慢慢渗出。玉器被水银所沁，轻者呈丝状、蚁状，颜色较浅淡。重者连成片，色如黑漆。玉器全部被水银浸染者，被人们称作"黑漆古"。

铁锈沁：红山文化时期，铁器尚未问世。我们所见到的玉器铁锈沁，是土壤中含有的铁元素氧化后对其产生的浸染。铁锈沁，呈暗红色。深入玉理多成片相连，侵入点处呈暗黑色。沁色较扎实、稳定、无轻浮感。在红山文化出土玉器中，铁锈沁并不多见。目前市场所见红色沁红山文化玉器，多为化学原料高温浸染所成，看起来无定律，漂浮或过于艳丽。

水沁：因红山文化特殊的地理环境和特殊的墓葬形式，玉器受水沁者较少。偶见水沁玉器，多在河道改变后，距水源较近的沙土中。受水沁玉器，颜色灰白，犹如在玉器表面加纱或镀膜，呈朦胧状。严重者，可见水渍凝结玉表，但不甚牢固，稍用力即崩散。也有水沁完全钙化的玉器。

炭黑沁：在红山文化葬墓中时常发现有黑色木炭粉灰，或撒于地面、或与玉器一同装入墓中陶罐。由于这些玉器长期与炭黑相接触，因而被浸染成黑色。被浸染严重者大都为质地松软的蛇纹石类玉器。当以强光照射时，玉器较薄处仍可看出青色玉质。被炭黑所沁玉器，其色较灰暗，无亮丽漆光，与水银沁有明显区别，但包浆明显。

其他金属元素沁：由于土壤中含有微量铜、铁、铅、锌、锡等有色金属元素，这些元素皆能造成对玉器的侵害，并产生不同的沁色。但一些沁后特征，目前我们还没有完全掌握，尚有待以科学手段进一步分析和研究。

无论任何元素的产生，任何颜色对玉器的浸染，必有其进入点。无进入点者，被视为无本之木，无源之水。凡自然浸入玉理之颜色，在玉器表面必有"露头"现象，这就是沁色所以进入的瑕疵处。凡内含玉理无头沁色，皆为玉石原生包裹体颜色。

古人云："真沁必深入玉骨，伪沁则浮于器表。"此话虽说无大错，但却不是绝对的。从大量红山文化出土玉器来看，有些并无明显沁色，甚至完好如新。这是因为玉器的质地非常坚密和缺少受沁条件。但是从中仍可以发现许多沁后特征。因此我们在验定玉器的沁色时，一定要对客观事物进行客观分析，万不可贸然决断。

3．绺裂：

在红山文化玉器的表面，我们时常见到绺裂。轻微者，裂隙较浅，层叠分布。严重者，起层脱落，造成破损。

绺裂，是因为温度变化，玉器自身不能进行有效调解平衡，在热涨冷缩原理下所产生的炸裂。

在北方气候条件下，骤冷乍暖的天气变化，时常将饱含水分的玉器突然间强行冷冻，玉器甚至会出现结冰现象。当天气变暖时，冰冻的玉器开始得到缓解，在缓解过程中，由于玉器的表、里温差变化所产生的澎涨系数明显不同，因而玉器表面出现炸裂。对这种炸裂现象我们称之为绺裂。

自然形成之绺裂，以玉理形成层面为走向，有明显的层次感，并不深入。看起来真实自然。绺裂严重者，成片脱离玉器表面，所留残痕边缘参差不齐、深浅不一。

人为制造绺裂，多在冰箱或雪地冷冻，然后放入热水中，在骤冷骤热中使玉理产生炸裂。作伪者多利用炸裂纹对玉器浸色。以此法作出的绺裂，因冷热变化突然，裂纹多向玉理纵深走，且走向无序、杂乱生硬、无起层感。

以原生绺裂玉石仿制高古玉器，极具欺骗性，但仔细观察，你会发现，这种绺裂只在玉器单面，并因此无法保证绺裂的完整性。

因为真古玉器绺裂人为无法逼真仿制，所以成为红山文化玉器真伪鉴定的重要依据。

4．孔洞：

孔洞又称蛀孔。是指由玉器表面向玉理纵深浸蚀而形成似虫蛀样小孔。这些小孔或单一，或成片分布于玉器表面，无规律性。小的孔洞象针刺，并有一定深度。大的孔洞由许多较小孔洞相连扩大而成，边缘处参差不齐，呈腐烂状。

孔洞的形成，是由于玉器长时期与酸碱接触浸蚀成。玉石所含棉、绺之簿弱点给酸碱提供了可浸入点，正是以这一点为突破口，大量有害玉石元素乘机侵入玉理，造成对玉器的全面伤害。酸碱的腐蚀性很强，有时我们只在玉器表面看到极小蛀孔，而玉器内里却有可能被全部蛀空，造成内腐。严重者玉质似粘合的沙土，其重量远低于同等体积末受沁玉器。孔洞在形成之前，先出现局部钙化斑，钙化斑逐渐扩大面积甚至全器钙化或石化。这时最先浸入点则成蛀孔。自然浸蚀蛀孔人为不易仿制。

5．蚀斑：

蚀斑，是玉器表面绺裂玉皮脱落，或跌打形成的疤状残破。这些残破处呈凹坑形。在温度变化下，玉器自身分泌和产生的水雾聚集成水珠存积于凹坑内，久而久之则形成蚀斑。蚀斑呈赭石色，凡蚀斑皆有色。人为制造蚀斑无色，且缺乏真实感。

6．牛毛纹：

是指玉器受沁后表面所出现的细若游丝线状沁纹，尤其钙化了的玉器多见牛毛纹。因钙化了的玉质已丧失原有硬度，当钙化程度不够深透自身内外温度不能平衡时，热涨冷缩原理使其出现密细裂隙。具有较细和一定方向性裂隙是牛毛纹的主要特征。以高温烧烤人工伪造牛毛纹，不但无方向性，而且裂隙较宽，被称为火劫纹，两者之间有明显区别。

7．钙化、白化、石化：

三者皆因与土壤中某种或多种元素与玉器相接触或接近受浸后而发生的质变现象。其色为乳白、亮白和土黄。对三者人们广意通称钙化。其实三者受沁因素各不相同，应有所区分。

钙化，应认为玉器受土壤中炭酸钙类或碱性物质浸蚀而成。

白化，即某种单一元素恰与玉石中所含矿物质成份相融合而发生化合反应所出现的质变。

石化，为土壤中多种微量元素，伴以土浆为主要浸入颜色，将呈微透明状态的玉质改变成不透明的石质。被石化了的玉器，不但质地被彻底改变，而且常出现萎缩痕，形状有时也会被改变。

无论钙化、白化或者石化，因玉石质变原因，质地已不再坚实，玉理结构遭受严重破坏，从而变的疏松和脆弱。

综上所述，可见红山文化玉器的沁象对于我们鉴定工作非常重要。只有在我们充分了解和掌握古玉受沁变化的原因、条件、规律、特征后，方能给我们所要鉴定的玉器一个公正而又合理的结论。以科学理论指导实践做好文物鉴定是我们今后工作的惟一准则。

Presentation Infiltration of Hongshan-Culture Jade

There isn't Hongshan-Culture jade (5000-6000 years ago) that hadn't been buried under the earth. The unearthed ancient jade, as long as contact with the soil, contained varying degrees of infiltration (erosion, also called encrustation) which result in penetration of various elements in soil; erosion is the brand of time.

Presentation of infiltration is intuitional exhibition of texture and color changes from jade surface to inner of jade.

Presentation of infiltration as an objective interpretation of natural course and cause of infiltration is an important scientific basis of the identify authenticity of jade.

Jade produced from different minerals combination with lithosphere movement and changes. Various jade with different color and quality formed during the process. Some kind of jade structures are close, others are loose. Likewise some kinds of jade glistening, while some turbid mixture with impurity. No matter what kind of jade, observing under high-powered magnifier, hollowness exist within jade more or less, which the patterns look like cloud, batting or striation. I call these hollows as Mian, Luo and Wen according with their shapes.

Hollow is defect of jade when it generated. Only little jade can achieve "perfect". It is because of these tiny gaps, all kinds of elements can get into jade, this phenomena is called infiltration. Not only color but also texture would be changed after the jade infiltrated. Deep color would become lighter and lighter while hard texture becomes more fragile even collapse to sand. Thus infiltration is aggrieve and damage to jade. Infiltration requires the conditions as follows:

1、 Humidity.

Humidity is one of important conditions of infiltration. Dry or non-relative humidity would prevent color changing, eroded speckles, moth-eaten holes and cracks to be occured. Without relative humidity various elements which can not get into jade.

If placed a new production of jade in a closed drying oven, regardless of contact with any object, there would no a great colour and texture change.

2、 Temperature.

According to the physical principles of subject, it would expand when hot and shrink when cold, temperature changes can result jade qualitative changes which is infiltration. When temperature changing, the expanding coefficient obviously different between the exterior and interior of jade that might produce amination cracks on the surface of jade. That gave opportunities to all kind of injurant elements to invade the jade. At the same time, as a protection of itself from the temperature changes, jade also made internal secretion that also provide various presentations of infiltration.

3、Air texture

of jade should be more soft in strata when the mass graves have not been permeates with abundant of fresh air; this is the best time for infiltration since an opening state of internal structure. When the tomb of Chinese jade contact with the air a few minutes, open cells then closed, thus jade would harder or cracked by weathering. So we can say there is much difference of the artifacts between buried in the earth and after unearthed. Archaeologist found proof that silk would become ash in the air in short time if the protection is improper. Unearthed porcelain can be stabbed a hole by sharp metal tool, Our forefathers said, slice jade would be distorted if it's been put on an uneven place in the graves.

One who stays near vermilion gets stained red and one who stays near ink get stained black. Nearby, but needn't contact. Jade would be dyed and eroded by the nearby copper, iron, lead, zinc and other metals, or contain elements carbon, acids, alkalis, phosphorus material. Air circulation is also one of the important ways lead to the infiltration of jade.

4、except turquoise

agate, crystal, normally raw material of Hongshan-Culture jade is nephrite which mainly consist of tremolite and serpentine. Density of Tremolite is comparatively higher, so outside elements gnaw into it easily, thus not only inner of jade has fewer flaws such as Luo, Mian and Xua but also we can only found presentation of infiltration on the surface. While nephrite is softer and looser, so particulates can penetrate into jade faster and roundlier. Thus the presentation of infiltration is obvious, leave us a lot of appraisal evidence.

5、Mineral composition

Different jade contains different minerals ingredients. Different jade produce different infiltration representation.

We found a phenomenon that in a same grave same conditions, some jade wares as light as new, while some penetrated seriously, even become Chick Bone jade (appearance is look like white chick bone). What causes that? Except texture of jade, mineral ingredients also related with infiltration. The inherent mineral elements of these calcified jade or whiten Jade easily integrate and absorb the components of the burial tomb limestone, thus occurring chemical changes.

So we can see, in the same conditions, infiltration representations of different quality of jade are not same, because of the different contains of jade.

We say infiltration here is erodes changes of the whole jade body contacted with soil. In another words, any jade contacting with any kind of elements or tantalum of earth would appear infiltration presentations, which integrative and unified comparatively. Therefore, we need further emphasize regularity, integrity, ransition and authenticity of jade infiltration.

1、Integrity

Analyzing and studying the Hongshan-culture jade infiltration presentations, we must understand and grasp many Aspects of this historical period first. For example, the social background, the geographical environment, the climatic conditions, the grave

characteristic, soil ingredient, the jade material category and the craft characteristic and so on. The entire objective factors can grasp the jade infiltration representations, and discover its regularity.

Hongshan culture is situated in the northern area of our country, its unique natural climatic conditions and the temperature four seasons change decided many jade changing characteristics. The jade qualitative change easily that happened under temperature sudden changes, cracks and a Baojiang formed under such special condition too. Most Hongshan culture ruins located near hill and river, and most the graves were on sandy soil hillside places according with the local customs. Jade is dry and pure under this environment. Only few jade wares have water infiltration and speckles. After analyzing we believe these utensils lie in the earthenware jar with water.

Most the Hongshan graves were built by lime stones. Charcoal and white calx was found at the bottom of the graves. And there is no wooden coffin in the graves. This situation easily explained that why some jade wares were whiten or darken.

Hongshan culture scattered in different areas, which soil contains result in complicated and various infiltration vestige. But jade wares unearthed from the same spot have similar infiltration traces. Therefore, because the identical region soil ingredient and climates, Hongshan culture jade infiltration has the obvious unity.

Respect history means respect science. According to the historical analysis, the Hongshan people's attire still limited to the animal skin and the simple hemp fabric, universal application printing technology was not grasped yet at that time, so it's wrong that some people thought that red, green infiltration representations were produced by the shrouds.

Hongshan culture jade is special carving art modeling and the unique manufacture craft, create many obvious infiltration characteristic. For instance, edge of ban jade or slice jade is often blade shaped, while three-dimensional statue jade is also thick at center while thin on edge. Thin parts would be penetrated more easily which result in rule that infiltration representations of the surface of edge is the most obvious and serious, then gradually reduced to the thicker parts and inner of the jade. This rule can help us on jade appraisal.

We said the regularity is the jade infiltration natural sciences rule, which eternal invariable. Who violates the regularity is deviate from the historical reality and the scientific track. This is a question that shouldn't be neglected.

2、Integrality

We say infiltration integrality here not mean absolute and uniform integrity but relative the whole integrity with small differences of infiltration presentations.

Speaking in detail, in contain circumstances, integrity of the face, back, side, even hole of the jade should remain relatively consistent, there wouldn't drop off infiltration trace between the low-lying and the hump place.

For example, if we reproduce an aged jade to Hongshan-Culture jade, part of the original infiltration would must be reduced during the processing, thus would cause infiltration presentations couldn't link up harmoniously even interrupt. We often see fake Hongshan-Culture jade made by aged Hemo Jade, because the surface of the Hemo jade was peeled off, infiltration is not only break but also very different between the two sides, without harmony and integrality.

3、transition

infiltration was produced not in one day but after thousands years, so we say it's the deposition of time and symbol of history.

During the weather changes for a long time, because changes of the jade occurred very slowly, infiltration presentations are gradational and transitional.

We call the transitional infiltration as live infiltration, which is natural, vivid and flowing while dead infiltration charactering as stiff and incondite. Live infiltration is made by nature, dead infiltration is man made.

For a green slab Hongshan-Culture jade, the most eroded part is the blade shaped edge. When edge was infiltrated as white-chicken-bone color, and the color changed from the edge to center which looks like white calcification, grey iron, shallow soy-and-sugar shallow, soy-and-sugar bluish white and green. The various colors gently transferred and no obvious boundary, just like spurts draws. That's transition and layer of infiltration can't be imitated forever.

Another example: An entirely whiten jade ware was infiltrated step by step too. While it was penetrated by calx mainly and eroded by other elements at the same time. So the colors of whiten jade is not pure but lard with murky splashes. Those splashes shows that whiten jade still? conform to infiltration order and transition rules. Otherwise, this whiten jade is doubtable.

4、Authenticity

Because of the remote age, infiltration can be reflected on the surface. 70 percent of appraisal was decided by infiltration presentations. So identify authenticity of infiltration is a critical issue.

What is authenticity? It's not very complicated, conform to nature rule at first, then never made by man.

Nature creates the world including infiltration of jade. People in nowadays still can not catch up with the extremely excellent craftsmanship of nature.

Chairman Mao said that who wants to know the pear the taste, he must taste it personally. This is the materialistic dialectics. He told us, true knowledge come from practices. One who wants to master the infiltration of jade, he must not only do on-the-spot investigation and review of the local geographical environment and the grave characters, but also go down the market to understand all kinds of imitation tendency and do each kind of experiment personally. Through the investigation and study, we may grasp the massive information. Through the experiment, we can know difference between the natural infiltrations with the chemistry ones, natural penetrated holes with artificial holes, natural cracks with cracks of aged jade, natural Bao Jiang with man made polishing light. We also can know which kind of infiltrations can be copied, while what kind of infiltration can't be imitated completely forever. Only one knows himself and the counterparts, he can shoot the arrow at the target without blindness.

Authenticity is soul of jade, a jade ware which without soul is only a modern handicraft article.

After knowing various elements of infiltration, we still need further analyses reasons and main characteristic of each kind infiltration. Because this is very important for the correct appraisal.

1、Bao Jiang

very unearthed jade has Bao Jiang. Bao jiang is the good luster which jade contained. The resinous luster is gentle but not dazzling, moist is not dry and warm but urgent. When we observe jade surface in back light, you can discover that surface of the jade covers many very small pockmarks, which make the light absorption and the disperser, so we feel the luster is very gentle. Those small pockmarks caused by the long time soil-erosion of jade.

Bao Jiang creation related local environment and the climatic conditions. science excavating indicate that, the Hongshan culture temple, graves and altars generally built on the hillside where ventilated and dry, in addition the sand soil lose water easily, created conditions for Bao Jiang formation. The north distinct seasons and resilient weather also contributed to Bao Jiang formation. Occupied under the normal temperature condition, jade does not adapt to the temperature change immediately and suddenly, created "the perspiration" the phenomenon, spilled over crowded mist in the jade surface, then the mist gathered to small "the dewdrop". The micro mineral element is discharged along with the "sweat" secretes. When the jade restores to the normal temperature, the air-dried "sweat" then congealed in the jade carving surface, as if plated a bright membrane for the jade, to come full circle, this bright membrane was more and more thick. The micro mineral elements that bright membrane contains also increased the jade surface degree of hardness and prevent some harmful elements invade to protect itself.

Often discovers this kind of kind of situation in the Hongshan culture unearthed jade: A semblance perfect gloss jade, when breaks the semblance, the inner eroded very serious. This occurred when the harmful elements permeated from small cracks or brokenness on the surface, but the jade exterior thick Bao Jiang just like a silk slippery coat, prevent soil and elements enter. Own resistance function is obvious.

Every Hongshan-culture ancient jade has Bao Jiang, no matter how seriously it damaged. This kind of Bao Jiang formed naturally through long time, but couldn't form by Pan (to banish foreign matter by all kinds of methods which mainly rubbing jade surface by hands or by white cloth). No matter the unearthed jade or that early time unearthed and handed down for generations, if you wiped the jade slightly with the cotton fabric, then the gloss illuminated brightness, fully demonstrate its age feeling.

We cannot recognize a jade ware as the real if it is not with Bao Jiang. The existence of Bao Jiang is one of important conditions of appraisal.

2、Infiltration color

Infiltration color namely is under the special condition, various colors presented on the surface after kinds of elements penetrated jade. The infiltration color formation need four conditions: environmental humidity, temperature, foreign elements and exists of the weakness jade. Otherwise, infiltrated colors could only floats on the surface, but cannot penetrated into inner of jade.

In soil organic matter, the inorganic substance, the mineral substance, the metallic element, all can form infiltration color under a certain condition.

We knew normally the following kinds of infiltrations: soil infiltration, the lime infiltration, the acid and alkali infiltration, the mercury infiltration, the rust infiltration, water infiltration, the black carbon seeps and other metallic element infiltration.

Soil infiltration: serpentine is easier penetrated by earth, seriously infiltrated jade even present petrification spots, even entire petrification. Color of this infiltration is pale ocher color likely and closely with the soil color. This color looks like plain, temperate, natural and real. Because this kind color infiltration extremely difficult to be copied, therefore at present the artificial earth infiltration jade not discovered yet in the market.

The lime infiltration. It appears white color and speckles or entire whiten. The popular name is chicken bone or ivory white. The Hongshan culture graves are limestone material construction, while quick-lime covers the bottom, therefore the jade often penetrated by the quick-lime. The bright green jade especially penetrated seriously.

The acid and alkali infiltration: The acid and the alkali are all hazardous and destructiveness to jade. Speckles and eroded holes would occur if it was penetrated seriously. At present the high acid-base soil not discovered yet in Hongshan-Culture area. Only few light acid-base lands were found in the local area. Nomads choose this environment to live because high acid-base soil is not suitable for the forage grass growth and the animal lives. Moreover there is no jade that large speckle on surface in science findings. Therefore, jade has the thick white speckles skin at present is the artificial one which eroded by strong acid and alkali.

The mercury infiltration: soil contains mercury elements, some mercury pellets are too small that our naked eye is very difficult to observe. Because the special mineral ingredients and the characteristic, mercury can attach and penetrate the jade very easily.

Thus ancient people thought mercury would freeze encounter jade. In Han dynasty, mercury was often injected in the body for prevent it rotten, and plug the seven apertures in the human head with jade to prevent mercury from flowing outwards. The mercury infiltration is black color and coagulation shape, but can flow under certain temperature, even can seep out slowly from the jade. If the jade was penetrated seriously, the presentation is like thread and ant, the color is light. While the penetration is fragmental, and the color is like black lacquer. The whole penetrated jade is called black lacquer jade.

The rust infiltration: in the Hongshan culture time, the iron hardware hadn't yet produced. We saw the garnet jade rust infiltration was made by iron elements in soil and stretches. The color is solid, stable, the not frivolous. There are no many rust infiltration jade wares in the Hongshan culture unearthed findings. At present in market the red rust infiltration jade is contaminated by chemistry raw material and high temperature, looks frivolous and too gorgeous.

Water infiltration. Water infiltration jade is seldom found in the unearthed jade. Only when river change it way and near the jade buried spot, jade could penetrated by water. Such kind of infiltration is grey which like voile or membrane cover on the jade surface. If the jade penetrated seriously, we can see water blot cohere on the surface, but can get rid off by slight force.

The black carbon infiltration with black charcoal power was often found in graves; the power normally scattered on the ground, or put into gallipots with jade. So jade dyed to black by the carbon. This kind of infiltration is generally happened on serpentine, we still can see cyan texture on thin part when put jade under strong light. Color of carbon infiltration is gloom, no lacquer light, though still has obvious Bao Jiang.

Other metal elements of infiltration. Many metal elements, such as copper, iron, lead, zinc, tin and other metal elements can penetrated in jade, and produce different infiltration color. But some features we have not yet fully grasp yet which need scientific means of further analysis and research.

No matter what kind of colors changes, there must be the entry point. If there is no entry points, the color is original color of the jade contains, or the jade is not the real one.

Cracks we often can see cracks on surface of jade which caused by maladjustment of temperature changes. Some cracks are shallow and cascade, while some cracks fall of the jade and cause disrepair.

The nature form cracks trends along the stratification plane of jade, is lays but not very deep, which looks very natural and aged. Some cracks, Large off the jade surface, keeps the remnant edge to be irregular.

The artificial cracks produced by the following process: freeze jade in the refrigerator or the snowy area, then puts jade in the hot water, the sudden temperature result in cracks. Imitators often use crack to dye the jade. , because the cold hot change suddenly, the crack is depth; also moving direction is disorder and stiff, non-aliquation feeling.

The fake Hongshan-Culture jade made by aged jade with cracks, but observes carefully, you can discover, this kind cracks only one-side, therefore unable to guarantee crack integrity.

Because the real ancient jade cracks to be unable to imitate, therefore which becomes the important basis of Hongshan culture jade appraisal the.

Hole: Also calls the worm hole. It refers erosion holes of the jade from surface to the jade depth, which destroyed by insects the type eyelet. These eyelets are sole or large disorder distribution in jade surface. The small hole is like puncture, and has certain depth. The big hole becomes by many small hole connected expansions, the edge is irregular, assumes the rotten shape. The hole formation, is because the jade contact long time acid and alkali. The jade contained the cotton and kapok shaped hollows weakness provide possible spots to the acid and alkali, the massive harmful elements seized the opportunity to invade the jade, created comprehensive injury. The serious jade nature resembles the agglutination of the sandy soil, its weight is much lighter than same bulk but unfiltrated jade. Hole before formation, appears the partial petrified spot first, the petrified spot expands the area even entire petrification gradually. By now first plunged becomes the worm hole. The natural erosion worm hole is not easy to imitate.

5、Eclipse spot

The eclipse spot is the scar shape or broken on surface of jade made by cracks off surface, or the injury forms. These broken places are pit shaped under the temperature changed, jade secretion and the mist gather the water drop in store in the pit, gradually forms the eclipse spot. The eclipse spot is ocher color; every eclipse spot is colored. The artificial eclipse spot is colorless, which lack of the third dimension.

6、hair grain

hair grain refers to the gossamer striation on the surface of jade. Calcification jade carving saw the hair grain especially. Because the calcification jade nature has lost the natural hardness, when inside and outside temperature cannot balance, the heat rises the contraction principle namely to its react, appears the dense thin crevasse and has certain direction are the two main characters of hair grains. The man made hair grains not only out of order, but the cranny is also wider which called Huo Jie vein.

7、Calcification

albinism, petrification: All the three qualitative change phenomenon caused by contacts or approach with elements soil. The colors respectively are creamy white, the transparent white and sienna. The above three phenomenon generally called thcalcification. Actually reasons of the three infiltrations are different, should be discriminated.

The calcification should caused by the calcium carbonate class or the alkaline matter erosion.

The albinism, namely some kind of sole element chemical combination with the jade, thus appears qualitative change.

The petrification, many kinds of trace elements accompany with soil changes the subtranslucent jade to opaque stone. Color of the petrification infiltration is like earth. Petrified jade not only the quality of material is completely changed, sometimes moreover often appears the atrophy mark, the shape also changed.

Regardless of the calcification, the albinism or the petrification, the jade qualitative changed, the texture is no longer solid but suffers the serious destruction, become loose and frails.

图 132 牛河梁第十六地点 4 号墓

红山文化时期葬墓多距地表 1—3 米左右，以石灰岩质页岩砌筑墓穴四壁、铺底与封顶。这一特殊葬墓特点和形式，为我们客观分析玉器的沁象发生原因，提供了重要的鉴定玉器科学依据。

Picture 132 The No.4 tomb at the No.16 location of Niuheliang

The grave of Hongshan culture period is more from the surface of land about 1–3 metre, with limestone shale building the walls of tomb and paving bottom and top. This special tomb characteristic and form have offered important scientific basis of appraisal jade ware for our objective analysis infiltration of jade ware.

图 133 牛河梁第十六地点 4 号墓细部

葬墓中不同玉质、形状玉器的放置形式与位置，其受沁变化各不相同。对每一件需要进行鉴定的玉器必须进行客观的分析和研究。

当我们面对这些历经数千年的白骨和神圣的古玉器时，你首先应该想到的是：应该具备良好的职业道德，较高的业务素质与严肃认真的工作态度。

Picture 133 The No.4 tomb details at the No.16 location of Niuheliang

The infiltration change is different from one another in putting form and location of diferent texture and shape jade ware in graves. For each jade ware that need appraise must carry out objective analysis and research.

When we face these previous white bones and sacred ancient jade wares through thousands of years, what you first think of that: We should have good professional morals, higher business quality and serious and conscientious working attitude.

图 134 牛河梁第二地点一号冢 4 号墓玉器出土情况

Picture 134 the unearthed circumstances of Jade ware in the No.4 tomb from the No. 1 stone mound at the No.2 location of Niuheliang

处于同一葬墓中的玉器，受沁也有所不同。这与玉质、环境、条件有直接关系。这两件相邻的玦形玉兽，一件明显呈钙化状，而另一件则青色依旧。仔细观察你会发现：上方钙化玉器直接摆放在石块上。而下方这件玉器处于泥土中。与石灰岩质石块相接触，是造成上方这件玉器钙化的主要原因。

The infiltration is not the same of jade ware though in the same grave. It has direct relation with jade texture, environment and condition. This two adjacent Jade coiled animal, one present calcification form obviously, and another present cyan as before. Observing carefully you can discover: Its upside calcification jade ware is directly put on the stone. And downside jade ware is under soil. It contacted with limestone stone, which is the major reason that causes upside calcification of this jade ware.

图 135 天地神佩
尺寸：高 5.5cm 宽 9.1cm
玉质：青玉
（听雨堂珍藏）

Picture 135 Compound jade baldric for heaven and earth
Size: 5.5cm high 9.1cm wide
Jade texture: blue-green jade
(Collection of "rain-hear hall")

图 136 天地神佩另面
Picture 136 another side of compound jade baldric for heaven and earth

凡红山文化真古玉器皆有包浆。因此说，包浆是玉器的灵魂。凡无包浆玉器皆不能认定为真古玉器。包浆，给人以玉器被充分蒸煮熟透、器面油光外泄之感觉。具有强烈的年代感。

All Hongshan cultural real ancient jade ware has baojiang. Therefore we can say that baojiang is the soul of jade ware. If there is no baojiang in jade ware it doesn't regard as real ancient jade ware.

Baojiang, presents the feeling that the jade ware have been steamed and ripe fully, the gloss of ware surface rushes outside. It have strong time sense.

图 137 玉龟
尺寸：长 5.3cm
玉质：青玉
（牛河梁第二地点一号冢 21 号墓
出土）
Picture137 Jade tortoise
Size: 5.3cm long
Jade texture: blue-green jade
(unearthed in the No.21 tomb from
the No.1 stone mound at the No.2
location of Nuheliang)

图 138 玉龟
尺寸：高 8.1cm 玉质：青玉
（听雨堂珍藏）
Picture138 Jade tortoise
Size: 8.1cm high
Jade texture: blue-green jade
(Collection of "rain-hear hall")

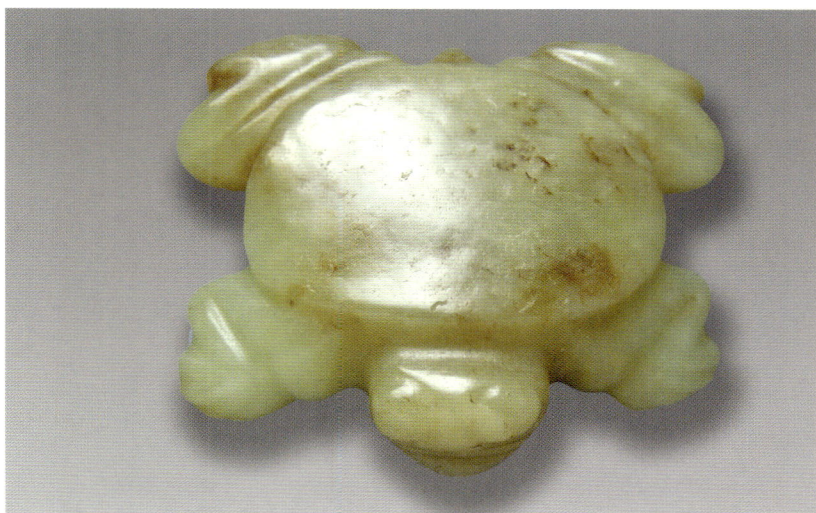

相同玉质的玉器，由于自然
环境、葬墓条件、土壤成分等客
观因素，玉器的受沁变化各不相
同。但有一个共同特征：包浆非
常明显，温润剔透。

The infiltration of identical
texture jade ware is different from
one another due to natural
environment, grave condition, soil
composition etc. the objective
factors. But there is a common
feature: baojiang is very obvious,
moist and hyaline.

图 139 玉龟器背
Picture139 The back of jade tortoise

图 140 虎形佩图
尺寸：高 12.4cm 玉质：青玉
（辽宁省文物商店征集）
Picture140 Tiger-shaped jade pendant
Size: 12.4cm high Jade texture: blue-green jade
(collected in the relic shop of Liaoning province)

141 兽形佩
尺寸：高 5.8cm 玉质：青玉
（听雨堂珍藏）
Picture141 Beast-shaped jade pendant
Size: 5.8cm high
Jade texture: blue-green jade
(Collection of "rain-hear hall")

透闪石类玉器质地非常坚密。但历经数千年，由于各种元素的逐渐浸蚀，在玉器的表面仍可见到沁后所形成微小的麻斑,并且显露出厚重包浆。

The texture of tremolite type jade is very dense. But through thousands of years, as various elements corroded gradually, there is still small spot on the surface of jade wares after infiltration and show massiness baojiang.

图 142 动物形玉佩 Picture142 animal-shaped jade pendant
尺寸：长 7.2cm Size: 7.2cm high
玉质：青玉 Jade texture: blue-green jade
（听雨堂珍藏） (Collection of "rain-hear hall")

图 143 三联玉璧
尺寸：高 6.4cm
玉质：青玉
（辽宁省阜新县胡头沟墓地 3 号墓出土）
Picture 143 Three joined jade(a doughnut-shaped piece of flat jade with the hole☐ diameter shorter than the width of the rim)
Size: 6.4cm high
Jade texture: blue-green jade
(unearthed in the No.3 tomb from Hutou ditch graveyard at Fuxin country of Liaoning province)

图 144 刀形佩
尺寸：长 5.3cm
玉质：青玉
（听雨堂珍藏）
Picture 144 knife-shaped pendant
Size: 5.3cm long
Jade texture: blue-green jade
(Collection of "rain-hear hall")

　　红色沁，为氧化铁元素浸染而成，古人称之为血沁。其实并不然。
　　颜色进入器体必有可进入点。进入点即玉石的微小缝隙，此处颜色明显较深。由一点再向周边慢慢晕散，自然形成沁色的过渡性。

　　Red color infiltration is contaminated by the element of ferric oxide, so the ancients called it as blood infiltration. Actually not.

　　It will be the access Point that color enters ware body. It is the small chink of jade, and the color of this place is obvious comparative deep. From one point again to periphery slowly breaking up, it can naturally form the transition of infiltration colour.

图 145 刀形佩局部放大
Picture 145 knife-shaped pendant partly enlarged

119

图 146 双联璧
尺寸：高 6.6cm 宽 3.5cm
玉质：青玉
（听雨堂珍藏）
Picture146 Double joined jade
Size: 6.6cm high 3.5cm wide
Jade texture: blue-green jade
(Collection of "rain-hear hall")

图 147 双联璧另面
Picture147 another side of double joined jade

这件原本为青色玉质的双联璧，受沁后先变为糖色，然后出现局部钙化斑。糖色和白色在无特殊原因下不能变为青色，尤其玉器自然受沁这种可能出现机率极小。因此，从沁色自然变化可以认定此器为青玉质红山文化玉器真品。

This is Double-bi-shaped jade pendants of cyan Jade texture formerly, after infiltration, it is sugar colour to change first, Then arise local calcification spot. Sugar colour and white colour can not become cyan without very special reason,Under geting infiltration condition naturally, this kind of possible rate is very little. Therefore from infiltration colour natural change, can believe that this ware is tasted really for the green Hongshan cultural jade ware of jade texture.

图 148 玉鸟
尺寸：高 17.3cm 宽 21cm
玉质：青玉
（听雨堂珍藏）
Picture 148 Jade bird
Size:17.3cm high　21cm wide
Jade texture: blue-green jade
（Collection of "rain-hear hall"）

图 149 玉鸟局部放大
Picture 149 Jade bird partly enlarged

　　红山文化大件玉器同小件玉器一样，较薄处和周边受沁明显重于器中。这一客观自然规律使受沁玉器的沁色具明显过渡感和层次感。因这一沁象无法仿制，所以确定此器为真品无疑。

　　The large Hongshan-culture jade ware is the same as little, whose thin place and periphery is more obvious in infiltration than inside. This objective natural regular makes the infiltration colour of jade ware have obvious transition and level sense. Since this infiltration can not be copied, so we can determine this ware is real one undoubtedly.

图 150 玉鸟器背
Picture 150 The back of jade bird

图 151 玉鸟
尺寸：高 5.6 cm 宽 7cm
玉质：青玉
（听雨堂珍藏）
Picture 151 Jade bird
Size: 5.6 cm high 7cm wide
Jade texture: blue—green jade
(Collection of "rain—hear hall")

图 152 玉鸟器背
Picture 152 The back of jade bird

　　由于各方面因素，同玉质玉器受沁后所呈现颜色不尽相同。
　　鉴定玉器，一定要从整体到局部认真分析受沁后的细微变化，从中找出能够充分证明其真伪的科学答案。

For the factor of each aspect, after the same texture jade ware got infiltration, their colour is not so identical.

Appraising jade ware must analyse the subtle change carefully from whole to part after infiltration, from it we can find out to fully prove it real or fake the scientific answer.

图 153 天地神佩
尺寸：高 4.3cm 宽 9.1cm
玉质：青玉
（听雨堂珍藏）

Picture153 Compound jade baldric for heaven and earth
Size: 4.3cm high   9.1 cm wide
Jade texture: blue-green jade
(Collection of "rain-hear hall")

图 154 天地神佩另面
Picture154 another side of compound jade baldric for heaven and earth

　　古玉鉴定尤其要讲求科学性，要以科学态度和道理分析介释玉器的受沁变化及其特征。
　　这件天地神佩的受沁变化之所以看起来真实，因为它以客观规律形成从边缘到中间，从薄处到厚处的自然受沁变化过程和沁后应有特征。

Ancient jade appraisal must especially be scientific, with scientific attitude and reason, we analyse and explain infiltration change and its feature of jade ware.

The infiltration change of this compound jade baldric for heaven and earth looks real, because it forms with objective regular since edge to the intermediate, that from thick tothin place nature infiltration change course and feature it should have after infiltration.

我们需要科学鉴定玉器。除仪器鉴定外，鉴定专家必须以科学的思维方式，科学的态度指导和寻找能够证实玉器真实与非真实的科学依据。

此二器，沁象真实自然，包浆明显，沁色过渡有致，从多方面认证了它所具备的真实性特征。

We need to appraise jade ware scientifically. Except instrument appraisal, appraising expert must use scientific thought way, scientific attitude to guide and seek the scientific basis that can confirm jade ware real or false.

The infiltration of this two wares is true and natural, its baojiang is obvious, and its infiltration colour transit regularly, which certificate from various espects the actuality feature it has.

图 156 蜂形佩　　Picture 156 bee-shaped pendant
尺寸：高 7.2 cm　Size: 7.2 cm high
玉质：青玉　　　Jade texture: blue-green jade
（听雨堂珍藏）　(Collection of "rain-hear hall")

图 157 玉龟
尺寸：高 7.4cm 宽 7.2cm
玉质：青玉
（听雨堂珍藏）

Picture 157 Jade tortoise
Size: 7.4 cm high   7.2cm wide
Jade texture: blue-green jade
(Collection of "rain-hear hall")

相同的玉质，由于不相同的多种因素和客观条件，其沁象各不相同。
玉龟器身黑色蚁状斑，是在玉质发生白化后，由于质地松软微量水银随之而浸入。

The infiltration is different from one another in identical jade texture, for various factor and external condition different.

The ware body of Jade tortoise has black ant-shaped spot, which is after jade texture occur white calcification, since its texture is soft, trace mercury soak in.

图 158 玉蝉
尺寸：高 7cm
玉质：青玉
（听雨堂珍藏）
Picture 158 Jade cicada
Size: 7cm high
Jade texture: blue-green jade
(Collection of "rain-hear hall")

图 159 蜂形佩
尺寸：高 7.2 cm
玉质：青玉
（听雨堂珍藏）
Picture 159 bee-shaped pendant
Size:7.2 cm high
Jade texture: blue-green jade
(Collection of "rain-hear hall")

图 160 玉人
尺寸：8 高 cm
玉质：青玉
（听雨堂珍藏）
Picture 160 jade person
Size: 8cm high
Jade texture: blue-green jade
(Collection of "rain-hear hall")

图 161 玉人器背
Picture 161 The back of jade person

此二器皆受土壤中所含微量水银所沁，器表可见蚁状黑斑入肌理。

This two wares all received infiltration from soil that contains trace mercury, whose surface can see ant-shaped black spot enters skin.

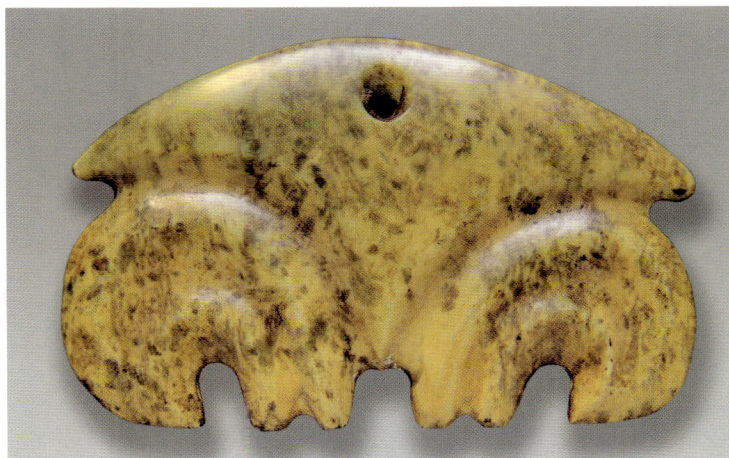

图 162 龟形佩
尺寸：高 6.4cm 宽 10.3cm
玉质：青玉
（听雨堂珍藏）

Picture 162 Tortoise-shaped jade pendant
Size: 6.4cm high   10.3cm wide
Jade texture: blue-green jade
(Collection of "rain-hear hall")

图 163 马蹄形器

尺寸：高 15.6cm

玉质：青玉

（听雨堂珍藏）

Picture 163 Jade clevis hoop

Size: 15.6cm high

Jade texture: blue-green jade

(Collection of "rain-hear hall")

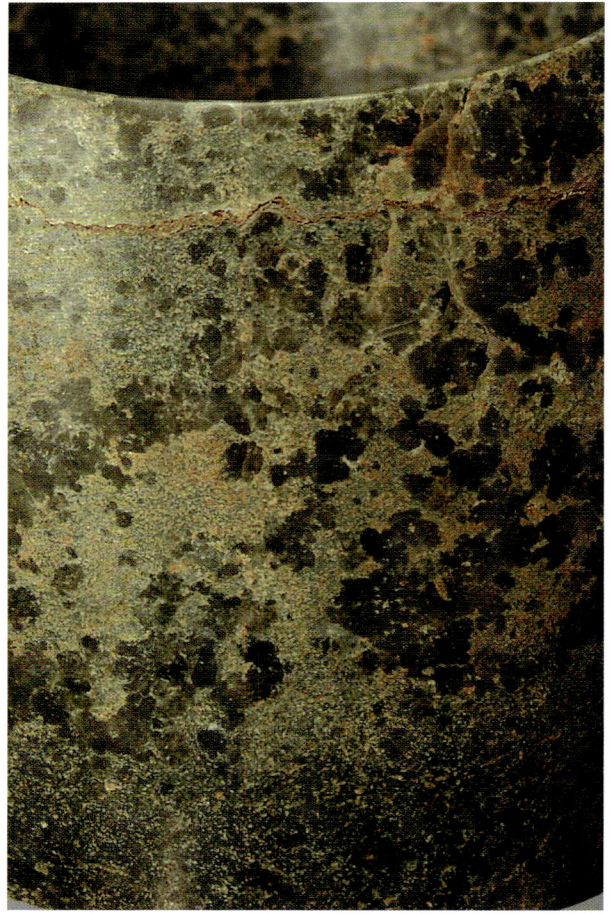

图 164 马蹄形器局部放大

Picture 164 Jade clevis hoop partly enlarged

此器被泥沙所沁。泥沙中的酸碱与水渍对玉器表面浸蚀后，所以才会出现分布不匀的白色钙化花斑。

This ware received infiltration by silt. After the soda and acid that contains in silt are corroded for the surface of jade ware, so it arise uneven distribution of white calcification spot.

图 165 块形玉兽
尺寸：高 14.7cm
玉质：青玉
（听雨堂珍藏）

Picture 165 Jade coiled animal
Size：14.7cm high
Jade texture: blue-green jade
（Collection of "rain-hear hall"）

图 166 块形玉兽局部放大
Picture 166 Jade coiled animal partly
enlarged

图 167 块形玉兽局部放大
Picture 167 Jade coiled animal partly
enlarged

　　此器被河沙所沁。因沙土中含有微量酸碱，当河沙粘附玉器表面以后，酸碱便对其进行浸蚀。并由于颗粒状河沙粘附不实，因而出现钙化花斑。

　　This ware received infiltration by river sand. For sandy soil contains trace acid and soda, when the river sand adhered the surface of jade ware, soda and acid would erode it. And since the particle river sand adhesion was not strong, thus it arised calcification spot.

图 168 勾云形玉佩（牛河梁五号冢一号墓出土）

尺寸：长 20.9cm

Picture 168 Cloudlike-shaped Jade pendant(unearthed in the No.1 tomb from the No.5 stone mound of Niuheliang)

Size: 20.9cm long

  自然生成之绺裂，目前人为无法逼真仿制。尤其玉器的正、背或多方位皆出现呈起层状绺裂，更让仿红山文化古玉者望尘莫及。因此，绺裂成为鉴定红山文化玉器真伪的重要依据。

  现在市场所见人为制造绺裂，多对玉器进行烧烤，然后放入冷水使其炸裂，其目的为了通过炸裂纹往玉器内里做色。

  这件玉器通体遍布绺裂的原因，经分析认为玉石的切割恰在玉石的生长水平面上，因此而产生大面积绺裂。

  Naturally generating tuft crack pattern, which at present hasn't be copied lifelikely by artificial. Especially in the main and back or other side of jade ware all appear layer-formed tuft crack pattern, which let the copier of Hongshan-culture ancient jade can not be compared. Therefore tuft crack pattern become the important basis for appraising Hongshan-culture jade ware real or fake.

  Now the artificial tuft crack pattern seen in the market is all roasting on jade ware, and then put it into cold water to make it explode split, whose purpose is through split veins to make colour in it.

  The reason of the jade ware all over is spreaded tuft crack pattern is that the cut of the jade just is on the growth horizontal surface by analysis, therefore producing tuft crack pattern of large area.

图 169 玉鸟

尺寸：高 7cm 宽 8.4cm

玉质：青玉

（听雨堂珍藏）

Picture 169 Jade bird

Size: 7 cm high   8.4 cm wide

Jade texture: blue-green jade

(Collection of "rain-hear hall")

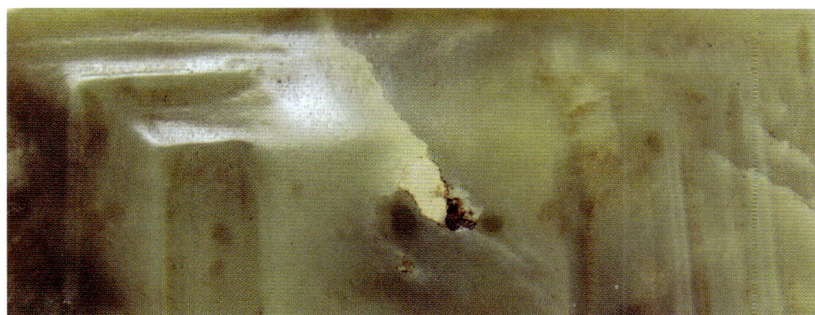

图 170 玉鸟局部放大

Picture 170 Jade bird partly enlarged

玉器绺裂的形成，是由于温差变化。玉器表里温度不能平衡，在热胀冷缩过程中缓慢完成。它的主要特征是较浮浅，呈起层状。

绺裂缝隙处，一边与器体扎实结合，一边呈现过渡性起层泛白。

The form of Jade ware tuft crack pattern is because of the change of difference in temperature. It can't be balanced in temperature between inside and outside of the jade ware, it slowly complete in expanding when hot and shrinking when cold. It's major feature is more shallow and present layer shape.

The place of tuft crack pattern, one side combine with ware body strongly, one side is transitional layer to arise white colour.

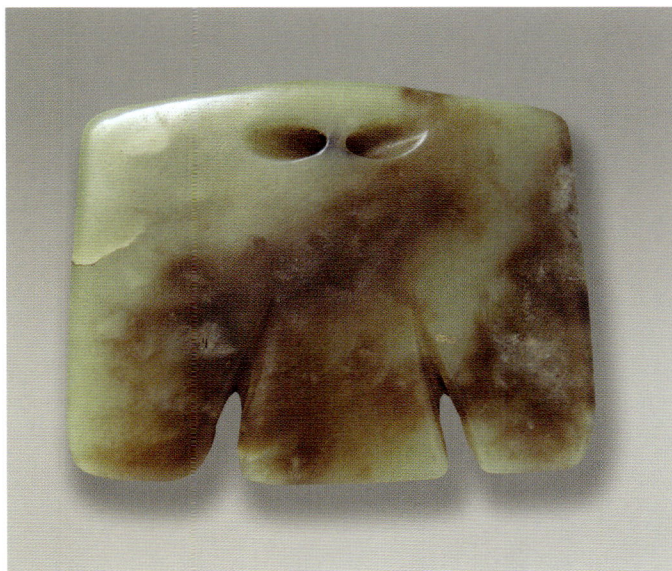

图 171 玉鸟器背

Picture 171 The back of jade bird

图 172 玉凤（牛河梁 16 号墓出土）
尺寸：长 19.5cm
Picture 172 jade phoenix (unearthed in the No 16 tomb of Niuheliang)
Size: 19.5cm long

当玉器深藏地下，土壤中的水分渗入玉理当中时，由于气温的变化，时而被冷冻，时而又缓解。在这个过程中，玉器则发生热涨冷缩物理变化，因而产生绺裂。

绺裂呈起层状，是因为玉理内、外的温度不相一致，膨胀系数不能均等，在缓慢变化中所形成的。

绺裂之所以不能均匀分布，是因为玉石的生长纹理。当玉石存在"中空现象"时，中空处所含有的水分因温度而变化，并对玉石产生直接影响。

When the jade ware deeply stored underground, the moisture in soil permeated into jade, because of the change of temperature, had been frozen sometimes or alleviated sometimes. In this course the jade ware occur the physical change that expand when hot and shrink when cold, thus producing tuft crack pattern.

Tuft crack pattern submits layer shape, as the inside and outside temperature of the jade is not uniform, and coefficient of expansion can not be equal, which forms in slow change.

Tuft crack pattern can not distribute evenly for the growth veins of jade. When jade has "hollow phenomenon", the moisture that contains change with temperature and produces direct influence with jade.

图 173 玉龟 （牛河梁五号冢1号墓出土）
尺寸：高 9.4cm(右)9cm （左）
Picture 173 Jade tortoise (unearthed in the No.1 tomb
from the No.5 stone mound of Niuheliang)
Size: 9.4cm high (right) 9cm high (left)

缮裂斑，由于人为不能逼真仿作，它成为我
们鉴定玉器真伪其中一项重要参考依据。

The tuft crack pattern spot, because of which can'
t be artificially imitate lifelikely, it becomes a important
reference basis that we appraise jade ware real or fake.

图 174 玉龟局部放大
Picture 174 Jade tortoise partly enlarged

图 175 方圆形玉璧（牛河梁五号冢 1 号墓出土）

尺寸：直径 12cm（左）12.9cm（右）

Picture 175 square-circle-shaped jade(unearthed in the No.1 tomb from the No.5 stone mound of Niuheliang)

Size: diameter 12cm (left)   diameter 12.9cm (right)

图 176 方圆形玉璧局部放大

Picture 176 square-circle-shaped jade partly enlarged

绺裂斑，由于人为不能逼真仿作，它成为我们鉴定玉器真伪其中一项重要参考依据。

Tuft crack pattern spot, because of artificial can not lifelike imitate make, it become us appraisal jade ware really fake in which a important reference basis.

图 177 玉羊首

尺寸: 高 10.2cm

玉质: 青玉质

牛河梁第二地点一号冢 21 号墓出土。

Picture 177 Jade sheep head

Size: 10.2cm high

Jade texture: blue–green jade

Unearthed in The No.21 tomb from the No.
1 stone mound at the No.2 location of
Niuheliang

图 178 玉象首

尺寸: 高 2.8cm

玉质: 青黄玉

Picture 178 Jade elephant head

Size: 2.8cm high

Jade texture: blue–yellow jade

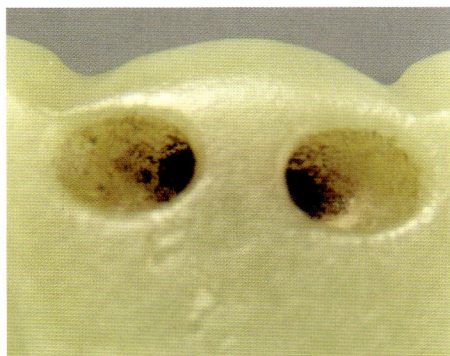

图 179 玉象首背部系佩孔放大

Picture 179 back hanging hole of jade elephant head enlarged

这两件呈黄色的玉器，并非真正黄玉所制。其原本颜色应为淡青色。由于土壤中存在可以改变玉石颜色的元素，长时间浸蚀，从而使其产生色与质变。

These two jade wares that present yellow are not genuine made by topaz. Its former color should be light cyan. As there is the element that can change the jade color in soil, and it is corroded for a long time to make it change in colour and texture of jade.

图 180 马鞍形玉佩
尺寸：高 4.7cm 宽 8.2 cm
玉质：青玉
（听雨堂珍藏）
Picture 180 Horse-saddle-shaped jade pendant
Size: 4.7 cm high   8.2 cm wide
Jade texture: blue–green jade
(Collection of "rain–hear hall")

图 181 马鞍形玉佩器背
Picture 181 The back of horse-saddle-shaped jade pendant

图 182 玉璧
尺寸：高 7.8cm
　　　宽 10.6 cm
玉质：青玉
（听雨堂珍藏）

Picture 182 a kind of Jade(a doughnut-shaped piece of flat jade with the hole⬚ diameter shorter than the width of the rim)
Size: 7.8 cm high   10.6 cm wide
Jade texture: blue–green jade
(Collection of "rain–hear hall")

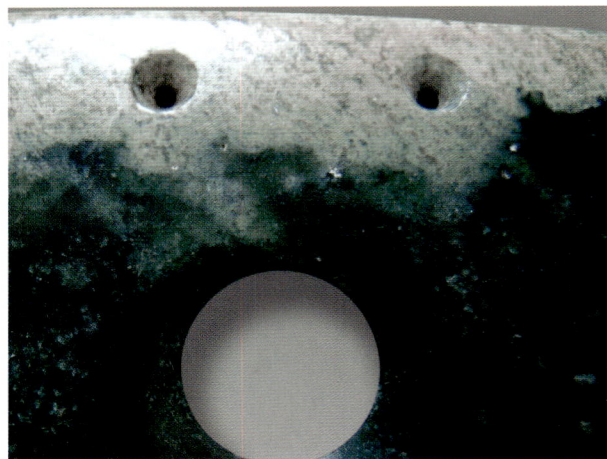

图 183 玉璧局部放大
Picture 183 a kind of jade partly enlarged

无论发生钙化或石化玉器，除具有明显包浆外，其沁色皆存在过渡性。

No matter what occuring, calcification or petrifaction of the jade ware, except having obvious baojiang, whose infiltration colour all exist transition.

图184 玉龟（辽宁省阜新县胡头沟墓地1号墓出土）
尺寸：高3.9cm 宽3.6cm
Picture184 Jade Tortoise(unearthed in the No.1 tomb from Hutou ditch graveyard at Fuxin county of Liaoning province)
Size: 3.9cm high   3.6cm wide

蛇纹石类玉质刻划硬度约在3.5度左右，由于玉石的致密度稍差，所以玉器在遭受浸蚀后、玉质被破坏也较严重。因此我们说，在同一环境下，由于玉质的不同，其沁象也各有所不同。

The carved hardness of snake veins stone jade tex–ture is about in 3.5 degree. As jade density is a little small, so after jade ware suffered erosion, jade texture have been destroied seriously, too. Therefore we say that under the same environment, for different jade texture its infiltration is different from one another.

图185 玉龟局部放大
Picture 185 Jade Tortoise partly enlarged

图 186 鸟兽复合神佩

尺寸：高 5.3cm 宽 7.3 cm

玉质：青玉

（听雨堂珍藏）

Picture 186 Bird and beast compound supernatural pendant

Size: 5.3 cm high 7.3cm wide

Jade texture: blue-green jade

(Collection of "rain-hear hall")

图 187 玉鸟器背

Picture 187 The back of jade bird

此器沁象真实自然。玉器表面大部分完好，而从器背看，内腐严重。各种有害玉器元素正是通过玉石微小瑕疵处侵入玉理，形成由内向外逐渐漫延性浸蚀，甚至直到将玉器内里掏空。凡真古玉器皆比同玉质、同体积新器重量略轻。

The infiltration of this ware is true and natural. The surface of jade ware is most of intact, and we see from the back of ware that it is much corroded inside. The various harmful elements of jade ware invade jade only through jade small flaw, which form gradual ductility corrosion from inside to outside, even until drawing out the ware empty. All real ancient jade ware is a little lighter than identical jade texture and volume.

图 188 玉鸮 (辽宁省阜新县胡头沟墓地 1 号墓出土)

尺寸：高 3.1cm

Picture188 Jade bird (unearthed in the No.1 tomb from Hutou ditch graveyard at Fuxin county of Liaoning province)

Size: 3.1cm high

　　这是一件被石化了的玉鸮。玉器在石化前先完成钙化，钙化了的玉质变的较为松软，这时土浆与土壤中的多种元素随之浸入、凝结，并改变玉石质地。玉石由原来的半透明体，改变玉质不再透明。通过对玉鸮的局部放大可以看到，玉器石化处沁象变化十分复杂，人为永远不能仿作。

　　This is a jade bird that has petrified. Before Jade ware petrifying, it first complete calcification, the texture of cal-cification jade is relatively soft, so at this time many kinds of elements in earth immersed, condense, and changed the tex-ture of jade. The jade is changed from former translucent body to an opaque one. Through enlarging partly of jade bird we can see that the infiltration of jade ware petrifaction place changes very complexly, so it can't be imitated artificially forever.

图 189 玉鸮局部放大

Picture189 Jade bird partly enlarged

图 190 双联玉璧
（牛河梁第二地点出土）
尺寸：高 13cm
玉质：已钙化
Picture 190 Double joined jade
(unearthed in the No.2 location of Niuheliang)
Size:13cm high
Jade texture: already calcification

图 191 玉龟
尺寸：高 5.4cm 宽 4.2cm
玉质：青玉（已钙化）
（听雨堂珍藏）
Picture 191 Jade tortoise
Size:5.4cm high   4.2cm wide
Jade texture: blue-green jade
(already calcification)
(Collection of "rain-hear hall")

图 192 玉鸟
尺寸：15 高 cm
玉质：青玉
（听雨堂珍藏）

Picture 192 Jade bird
Size：15cm high
Jade texture: blue-green jade
(Collection of "rain-hear hall")

　　无论钙化或石化玉器，皆有许多沁后共同特征：包浆明显，温润亮泽，器面可见钙化或石化前因浸染和浸蚀而成的色斑、麻斑等形态方面变化。沁象皆表现真实自然。

　　No matter what jade ware calcification or petrifaction, they have many common features after infiltration: baojiang is obvious, moist and bright, and can see for dip and erosion, the colour and hemp spot etc. changes on form, which is on the ware surface before calcification or petrifaction. The infiltration all shows true and natural.

图 193 玉祖神
尺寸：高 16cm
玉质：青玉
（听雨堂珍藏）

Picture 193　Jade numen

Size: about 16cm high

Jade texture: blue-green jade

(Collection of "rain-hear hall")

图 194 玉神祖局部放大
Picture 194　Jade numen partly enlarged

图 195 玉蛾
尺寸：高 7.1cm 宽 12.9cm
玉质：青玉
（听雨堂珍藏）

Picture 195 Jade moth

Size: 7.1cm high　12.9cm wide

Jade texture: blue-green jade

(Collection of "rain-hear hall")

　　无论钙化或石化多严重的真古玉器，皆有明显包浆。

No matter how serious the calcification or petrifaction real ancient jade ware is, there is obvious baojiang.

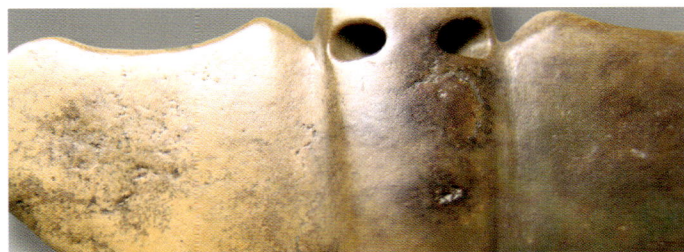

图 196 玉蛾器背放大
Picture 196 The back of jade moth enlarged

图 197 玉璧（牛河梁 16 号墓出土）
尺寸：直径 11.5cm
Picture 197 a kind of Jade(a doughnut-shaped piece of flat jade with the hole's diameter shorter than the width of the rim) (unearthed in the No.16 tomb of Niuheliang)
Size: 11.5cm in diameter

图 198 玉璧局部放大
Picture 198 Jade partly enlarged

钙化，是由于土壤中的多种微量元素，尤其酸、碱、生石灰类物质，在直接与间接与玉器相接触后，玉石中所含有的矿物成分恰与这些元素能够溶合，而不能有效抵御，因而发生化学反应，由此改变玉石原有质地形成钙化。钙化了的玉器表面色斑具明显深浅过渡变化，形成多色性。人为无法仿制。

Calcification shaped with the various trace elements in soil, many kinds of material like soda and raw lime

After contacting with jade ware directly and indirectly, the mineral composition contains with these elements can dissolve to suit in jade coincidentally, which can not resist efficiently, so chemical reaction occurred. Change jade original quality from this to form calcification. Calcification of jade ware on surface color spot obviously depth transitional change form multicolorness. It can not be copied artificially.

图 199 玉蝗　　　Picture 199 Jade locust

尺寸：长 28cm　　Size: 28cm long

玉质：青玉　　　Jade texture: blue-green jade

（听雨堂珍藏）　（Collection of "rain-hear hall"）

图 200 玉蝗局部放大

Picture 200 Jade locust partly enlarged

图 201 玉蝗另面
Picture 201 another side of Jade locust

玉蝗在钙化之前首先受到其它元素浸染，因此玉器表面可见变化复杂的沁色。玉器的受沁过程是无法改变的，这就是自然科学规律。

凡钙化玉器，器表皆存在深浅不一灰白色斑块或条纹。纯白色，或无任何浸染玉器在鉴定时当慎重。

Jade locust first gets dip from other elements before calcification, therefore the surface of jade ware can be seen complex change infiltration colour. the infiltration course of jade ware is can not change, which is the regular of natural science.

All calcification jade ware, ware surface has the difference of depth of the pale spot pieces or stripes.Pure white, or do not have any dipped jade ware should be cautious in appraisal work.

图 202 玉蝗另面局部放大
Picture 202 another side of Jade locust partly enlarged

图 203 玉鸟神佩
尺寸: 高 27cm 宽 12.4cm
玉质: 青玉
（听雨堂珍藏）

Picture 203 Jade bird pendant
Size: 27cm high   12.4cm wide
Jade texture: blue-green jade
(Collection of "rain-hear hall")

　　凡可见沁色玉器，沁色的统一性、完整性、过渡性非常重要。"三性"缺一则不能下最终结论。
　　此器正、背两面，无论钙化程度、绺裂痕、沁色的过渡基本完全一致，因此我们鉴定此器为红山文化真古玉器。

All evidently infiltration colour jade ware, the integrity and the unity of infiltration colour and transition is very important. If one of " The three kinds of properties" is short can not draw the last conclusion.

On the front and back of this ware, no matter what the calcification degree, tuft crack pattern and infiltration colour transition is basically consistent completely, therefore we appraise this ware that it is Hongshan-culture real ancient jade ware.

图 204 玉鸟神佩另面
Picture 204 another side of Jade bird pendant

图 205 玉鸟（辽宁省阜新县胡头沟墓
地 1 号墓出土）

尺寸：高 2.5cm

Picture 205Jade Bird(unearthed in the No.1
tomb from Hutou ditch graveyard at Fuxin
county of Liaoning province)

Size: 2.5cm high

图 206 双兽首三孔器（牛河梁 16 号墓
出土）

尺寸：长 9.2cm

Picture206 Three-holes ware with double
beast heads(unearthed in No.16 tomb of
Niuheliang)

Size: 9.2cm Long

由于玉器长时期处于水的浸泡中，客观封闭了其它元素的浸入。所以在玉器的表面不见其它金属
元素的浸染痕迹。

只要玉器所处的环境具备受沁客观条件，各种元素皆能对其进行有效浸染，这就是沁色。

从这件双兽首三孔器上可以看到，黑色的水银沁已深入玉之肌理，并伴有明显的土沁斑痕。

Since the jade ware is soaked in the water for a long period, which have enclosed other elements to immerse. So
we can't see other metal element contaminating trace on the surface of jade ware.

It can be contaminated efficiently by any kind of elements so long as the environment of located jade ware has
objective condition to receive infiltration, which is infiltration colour.

From this Three-holes ware with double beast heads, we can see that black mercury infiltration has gone deep
into the skin texture of jade, and accompany obvious earth infiltration spot mark .

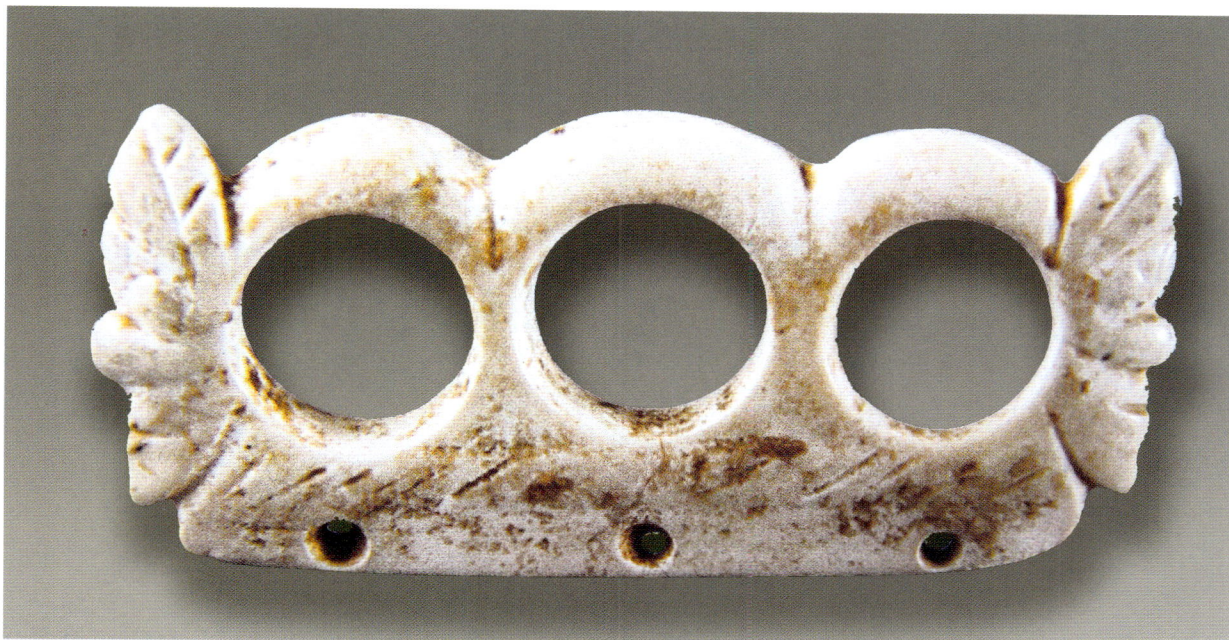

图 207 双人首三孔器(牛河梁第二地点一号冢 12 号墓出土)

尺寸:长 7cm

Picture 207 Three-holes ware with double mankind heads (unearthed in the No.12 tomb from the No.1 stone mound at the No2 location of Niuheliang)

Size: 7cm long

这两件玉器之所以完全同样钙化，存在多种因素。其中最主要还是因为玉质的特殊性。它所含有的矿物元素在特定环境和自然条件下，恰与葬墓中某些元素快速吸纳和溶合，从而产生化学反应形成严重钙化。

从器表我们可以看到，其它元素并没有作用于玉器而形成沁后色斑，说明完成钙化的时间和过程很短。

This two jade wares has the same calcification, there is various factors. The most major reason is the particularity of jade texture. Under specific environment and natural condition, the mineral element it contained exactly absorbed and blended with some elements in grave to produce chemical reaction to form serious calcification.

From the ware surface, we can see that other element do not take affect on jade ware to form colour spot after infiltration, which show that the time and course is very short to complete calcification.

图 208 蚕形玉器（牛河梁二号冢 1 号墓出土）

尺寸：高 12.7cm

Picture 208 silkworm-shaped jade ware(unearthed in the No.1 tomb from the No.2 stone mound of Niuheliang)

Size:12.7cm high

图 210 双联璧形器另面
Picture 210 another side of double joined jade

图 211 双联璧形器局部放大
Picture 211 double joined jade partly enlarged

　　此器长时期处于含水量较大土层中，由于土中含有微量酸碱性物质，对其浸蚀形成钙化。从已钙化的玉器表面可以看到深浅有致的过渡变化。

　　This ware is in the earth layer contained greater water in a long period, as the soil contains trace acid and soda material that corrodes the ware to form calcification. We can see the transitional changes that have right depth from the surface of jade ware that have already been calcification.

图 212 鸭形佩
尺寸：高 13 cm
玉质：青玉
（听雨堂珍藏）

Picture 212 duck-shaped pendant
Size: 13 cm high
Jade texture: blue-green jade
(Collection of "rain-hear hall")

图 213 鸭形佩另面
Picture 213 another side of duck-shaped pendant

图 214 鸭形佩局部放大
Picture 214 duck-shaped pendant partly enlarged

特殊的玉质，形成特别的沁象。

这种呈鸭蛋青色的玉器，由于玉石自身所含有的矿物元素，在微量酸碱浸蚀下多出现点状麻坑或蚕食状麻斑。

Special jade texture forms special infiltration phenomenon.

This kind of jade ware present duck's egg cyan, as the mineral element that jade itself contains, there would appear drop-shaped spot hole or circle-gap-shaped spot under the corrosion of trace acid and soda.

图 215 玉鱼
尺寸：长 34.3cm 宽 10.4cm
玉质：青玉
（听雨堂珍藏）

Picture 215 Jade fish
Size: 34.3 cm long 10.4cm wide
Jade texture: blue-green jade
(Collection of "rain-hear hall")

图 216 玉鱼另面
Picture 216 another
side of Jade fish

图 217 玉鱼局部放大后可见蛀孔与蚁状沁深入肌理。
Picture 217 Jade fish partly enlarged can see moth hole
and ant-shaped infiltration deep into the jade

玉鱼沁象真实自然，具统一性与完整性。尤其孔洞，形似虫蛀，边缘参差不齐，有一定深度，人为不易仿作。

Jade fish infiltration phenomenon is true and natural, have unity and integrity. Especially the hole of it, whose shape is just like moth, edge is not neat, a certain depth, imitate not easily by artificial.

红山文化古玉真品赏析

红山文化古玉真品赏析

　　常言道：识真才能辨伪。不知真古玉器应具备的各方面特征，所有收藏皆因盲目而徒劳。有人收藏古玉数十件，甚至耗尽了大半生积蓄与精力，结果无一件真品。这是为什么？因为他整日里在赝品堆里靠侥幸心理试图捡漏寻宝，也或许为他人所诱导，所以才走进一个完全不能自拔的收藏误区。

　　古玉收藏需要悟性。悟，是分析，认知，求证。悟，要以唯物主义观点进行论证。有人开创了一条古玉收藏新路：图书馆—博物馆—古玩市场，逐步完成从感性到理性的认识过程。这就是科学收藏。

　　有些古玉收藏者非常自信，自信没有什么不好，但偏激和固执的坚持己见，硬把赝品认定为真品就很危险了。自信，要建立在正确的思维方式、严谨的科学态度、理智而客观分析和认识问题的基础之上。否则，盲目自信只能导致最终彻底失败。

　　现今世界，是高科技十分发达的时代。很多人将希望寄托在以先进的高科技设备和技术鉴定文物。作者数年前在上海复旦大学现代物理研究所与专家进行过仪器鉴定方面的交流。事实说明，当前所引进的高精端设备对玉器多项指标测定，不能形成鉴定结果。通过仪器只能分析出玉石的形成年代、矿物成分、物理结构、刻划硬度。而对于玉器的制作工艺，自然受沁变化与人为仿作无法正确区分。无论碳14测定，还是热能检验，只能在特定环境下，和玉器自身必须具备应有因素，才能够达到最准确测试结果。这对于长期散失在民间被收藏的古代玉器来说，已失去这种条件，因此不适合于科学仪器鉴定。

　　由于红山文化覆盖面积广、所处年代、葬墓特征、土壤中微量元素、环境、玉质、造型、制作工艺、受沁变化多有所不同，无疑给科学仪器鉴定数据库的建立，造成了许多无法解决的困难。正是这些困难，让科学仪器鉴定陷入僵局，并且永远无法摆脱。

　　目前，我们对中国古代玉器的鉴定主要还是凭借实践经验。这种经验来自于对科学发掘出土玉器的充分认知，来自于长期工作的积累，来自于对客观事物所进行的科学分析。在科学仪器无助的情况下，做为鉴定师，更要严肃认真对所鉴器物进行有理、有据的科学分析，以得出正确鉴定结论。任何草率、盲目、主观臆断，都将给古玉鉴定工作造成重大失误。

　　"玩玉者，要讲玉德。"这是古训，同时又是道德规范。无论从事收藏、研究、鉴定玉器的人，都要严格遵循这一原则。"不讲玉德者，不能玩玉。"这也是对所有玩玉者的道德约束与限制。著书立说，弘扬和传播中华民族优秀传统文化是好事，但必须要严肃谨慎，善待读者。读过一些研究红山文化玉器方面的书，也看过一些个人网站，在所展示的红山文化玉器中，很少有真器，大多为赝品。这种不良宣传误导了很多人。也许这些传播者对红山文化玉器研究尚不够深透，并非出自主观故意。但又令人产生怀疑，有些传播者，是否为达到某种个人目的"挂羊头，卖狗肉。"如果确如此，这种行为实在令人不齿。因为有很多红山文化玉器爱好者因为对其充分相信和追随而付出了沉重的代价。我想不久的将来，我国会在图书出版、网络宣传、文物鉴定方面进行立法，对进行虚假宣传而误导民众的行为和因此所造成的严重后果，应该承担相应的法律责任。对文物、古玩鉴定工作中的严重失误而造成的损失，同样必须承担法律与经济赔偿责任。以此扼制不良道德倾向，让人类社会走向更和谐。

"红山文化古玉真品赏析"一章所展示的红山玉器，是作者从千余件藏品中精选出来的，并经过反复研究最终确定的真、精品。为此愿意为每一件藏品承担法律责任。希望广大红山文化古玉收藏爱好者在阅读本章时，除加深对前几章的理解和认识，并能从民间藏品鉴识中提高自己鉴赏能力，并希望在阅读过程中吸纳可以得到帮助部分，并提出自己不同意见。

Appreciation of genuine Ancient Jade Articles in Hongshan-culture

The saying says: Knowledge really can distinguish false. If we don't know every aspect of feature that genuine ancient jade articles should have, all the collections are in vain because of blindness. Someone collects ancient jade about tens of articles, which even exhausted over half life savings and energy, but they do not have a genuine article. Why is this? Because they were in piles of fakes relying on lucky mentality to attempt to pick up ignored articles and seek treasures, or maybe inducing by others, so they just walked into a mistake collect district that can not be recovered.

There must be comprehension that collects ancient jade articles needs. Comprehension, is to analyze, is to accept to know, and is to try to prove. Comprehension also must discuss and prove with materialism viewpoint. Somebody has started a new road of ancient jade articles collecting: library – museum – antiques market, which completed the cognition process step by step from the perceptual to rational. This is the scientific collection.

Some ancient jade collectors are very confident. There's nothing wrong with self–confidence, but with radical and stubborn certainty, what we insisted to deem fakes as genuine one is very dangerous. Self–confidence is necessary to establish on the base of correct thinking way and rigorous scientific approach, rational and objective analysis and understanding. Otherwise, blind self–confidence can only lead to the eventual total failure.

Nowadays, world is the times of very developed high–tech. Many people entrust with hope in advanced high–tech equipment and technology to authenticate the cultural relic. A few years ago, the author conducted the exchange with experts on equipment identification in the Institute of Modern Physics, Fudan University of Shanghai. The facts show that we can't get the result of authentication by calibrating a few of fingerposts of jade articles with the high–precision equipment of current introduction. We can only analyze the formation of jade articles through instruments in a few aspects of mineral composition, physical structure, and carved hardness. And for the produce technology of jade articles, we can't distinguish correctly between natural oozing changes and artificial imitating. Whether mea–sured by carbon 14, or thermal testing, only in specific circumstances, jade article itself must have the necessary factors to achieve the most accurate test results. For the ancient jade article collections that have been lost in civil for long time have lost such conditions, therefore it is not suitable for scientific equipment identification.

Being the Hongshan culture, covering a wide area, in era, graves features, soil trace elements, the environment, the quality of the jade, the shape, the production process, and varied of oozing, which undoubtedly make many insuperable difficulties in founding the scientific equipment identification database. These difficulties make the identification with scientific instruments into impasse, and will never be able to be rid.

At present, our authentication for Chinese ancient jade articles still mainly relies on practice experience. This kind of experience comes from the full awareness with the scientific unearthed jade articles, from the long-term work accumulation, and from the scientific analysis of objective things. In the situation of scientific instruments helpless, as an authenticating master, must seriously analyze the authenticated articles more scientifically and rationally, in order to get the correct conclusions. Any rash, blind and subjective assumptions will cause significant errors in authenticating ancient jade articles.

"To appreciate jade articles must obey jade virtue." This is ancient standard, and at the same time are moral norms. No matter who is engaged in collecting, studying and authenticating jade articles, must be strictly adhered to this principle. "Someone who doesn't obey jade virtue can not appreciate jade articles ". This is the morals restrictions and limitations for all the people who appreciate jade articles. It is good ideas to compose books to promote and propagate the excellent traditional culture of Chinese nation, but we must be serious and prudent and treat readers carefully. I have read some research about Hongshan-culture jade articles, and also read some personal website, which was displayed about Hongshan-culture jade articles, few of which is genuine articles, most of which are fakes. This adverse publicity misled many people. Maybe those disseminators for research of Hongshan-culture jade articles are not profound and thorough, and not the result of subjective intent. It is doubtful that some promoters want to achieve some personal ends, "to hang up a sheep's head and sell dog meat is to try to palm off something inferior to what it purports to be." If it is true, such behavior is contemptible. There are many lovers of Hongshan-culture jade articles because of its fully believing and following, then paid a heavy price. I think that in near future, China will legislate in the publishing, network publicity, and the authentication of cultural relic. People would bear the corresponding legal responsibility about the acts of disseminating false information and misleading the public and the serious consequences they caused. For the serious fault of cultural relic and antiques authenticating work and the damages they have caused, people must undertake legal and economic liability. With this to suppress bad morality, then let human society become more harmonious.

"Appreciation of genuine Hongshan-Culture ancient jade articles," in which displayed the Hongshan jade articles is from more than 1,000 most-prized holdings of the author which are the genuine and fine articles that ultimately determined through studying again and again. The author will assume legal responsibility for every collection. We hope when the majority of Hongshan-Culture ancient jade collection enthusiasts are reading this chapter, in addition to deepening the previous chapters of comprehension and understanding, it can improve their appreciation ability from the appreciation of private collections and hope that they can absorb the useful parts during reading and put forward their own views.

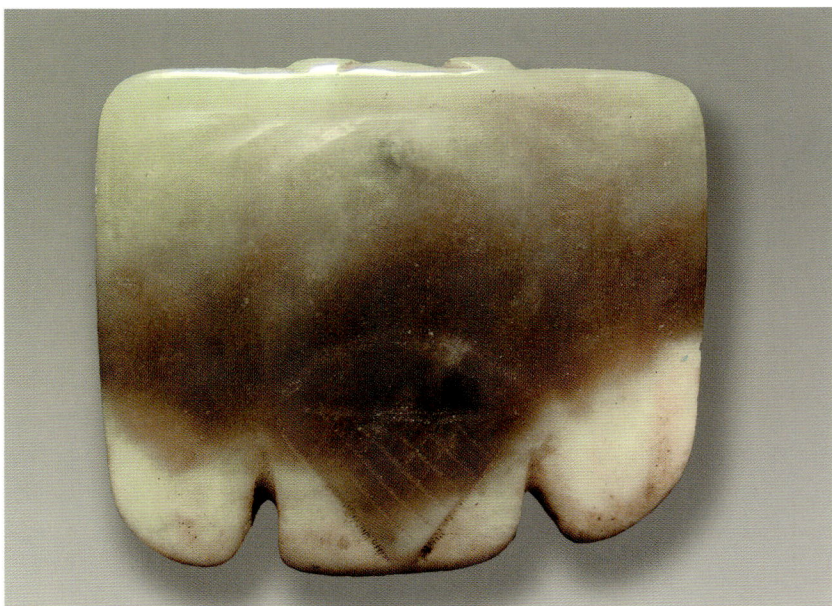

图 218 玉鸟
玉质：青玉
尺寸：高 4.7cm 宽 5.4cm
（听雨堂珍藏）
Picture 218 jade bird
Jade texture: blue-green jade
Size: 4.7cm high   5.4cm wide
(Collection of "rain-hear hall")

图 219 玉鸟之器背
Picture 219 back of jade bird

这件玉鸟极好的表现了玉器受沁后沁色的变化过程与渐变顺序：

1. 由青色玉沁后变为淡青色。（现在所见颜色已非玉石之本色）。

2. 由淡青色逐渐过渡为糖色。

3. 由糖色再白化为乳白色。各种颜色变化之间无明显分界线，而是以缓慢过渡形式相衔接。

The jade bird well shows the process of change and the tradition sequence after the jade get infiltration:

1. The jade changes from blue jade to light blue jade after infiltration. The present color is not the jade's original color.

2. Then the color changed from light blue to sugar color.

3. It became milky white from the sugar color. There are no clear dividing lines between all kinds of colors change, instead of they connected in the form of slow transition.

图 220 龙形玉佩
玉质：青玉
尺寸：高 cm
（听雨堂珍藏）
Picture 220 jade dragon
Jade texture: blue-green jade
Size: 6cm high
(Collection of "rain-hear hall")

图 221（玉佩之另面）
Picture 221 another side of jade dragon

龙形玉佩工艺精湛，包浆明显，沁象真实自然。

玉佩底端呈刀状，受沁严重，出现钙化斑。玉器之最薄处，当是玉器受沁最重处，符合受沁自然科学规律。

玉器受沁先出现糖色，然后逐渐钙化。糖色与钙化间自然过渡，无明显分界线。

人为制做钙化斑多无过渡糖色，所做出的钙化斑呆板，僵化，缺乏灵动感。

我们在鉴定古玉器时，除玉质、器形、工艺外，分析与研究沁象形成的科学性是最为重要的。前者可以选择和模仿，而对后者的判断必须严肃认真。

The process of jade dragon is exquisite, its baojiang is obvious and infiltration phenomenon is real natural.

The bottom of jade dragon presents sword shape, serious infiltration and has calcification spots. The thinnest place of jade is the most serious infiltration place, which conforms the natural scientific rules.

The jade first appeared in sugar color, and then gradually calcified. The transition between sugar color and calcification is no obvious boundary.

The calcification spots by artificial usually have no transitive sugar color, and the spots are stiff, rigid, and inflexible.

When we appraise the jade, the research of infiltration phenomenon is the most important, besides of jade texture, jade shape or the craft, which can be imitated. So we must take seriously to the judgment of jade's infiltration phenomenon.

图 222 玉鸟神佩　Picture 222 bird jade pendant
玉质：青黄玉　Jade texture: blue-yellow jade
尺寸：65 高 cm　Size: about 6.5cm high
（听雨堂珍藏）　(Collection of "rain-hear hall")

图 223 神佩器背
Picture 223　back of god jade

　　此器呈板状，器背打洼，形如鞋拔。我们所见此器颜色为黄色，其实并非黄玉所制，这是沁后颜色，原本应为淡青色玉质。器表糖色沁遍布器身，沁色过渡真实自然，人为所不能仿。沁色的自然变化是衡定是否真伪古玉器的重要条件。在深浅过渡变化中深含着悠久的岁月与历史，是历经数千年在外因作用下一天天缓慢集累的结果。从包浆、沁色、工艺等诸多方面分析，认定此器为红山文化真古玉器。

　　The jade is plate-type, digging hollow on the back, and like a shoehorn. The color we see is yellow, but actually it is not made by topaz, which is the colour of after infiltration. The jade's original color is light blue-green. The sugar color covered the whole jade, and the transition of infiltration color is real and natural which can not be imitated by artificial. The natural transition of infiltration color is the important condition to appraise the jade ware. There contains long times and history in the depth transitional change, which is the result accumulated by the external action day by day for thousands of years. From baojiang, infiltration color and craft, we appraise the jade is a real Hongshan-culture jade ware.

图 224 玦形玉兽　Picture 225 jade coiled animal
玉质：青黄玉　Jade texture: blue-yellow jade
尺寸：高 5.9 cm　Size: 5.9cm high
（听雨堂珍藏）　(Collection of "rain-hear hall")

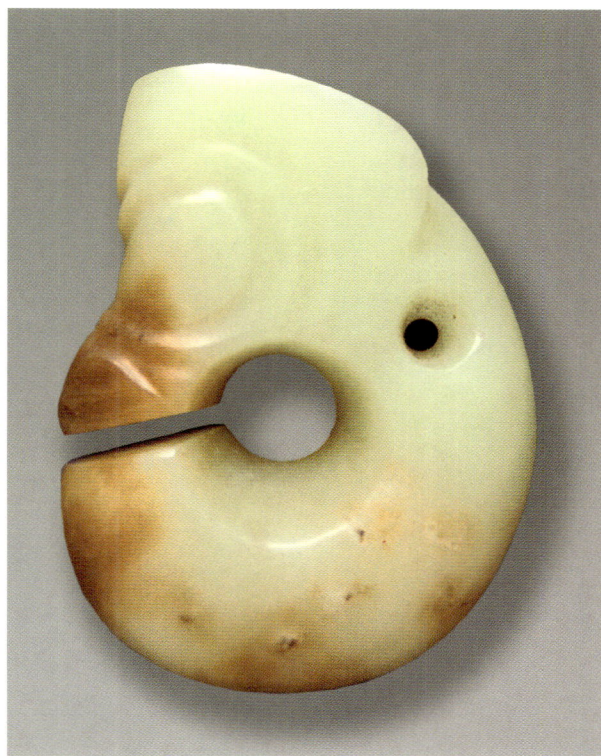

图 226 玦形玉兽另面
Picture226 another side of jade coiled animal

　　许多致密度较高红山文化玉器，因所处环境干爽而沁色不能深入，甚至沁色浮于器表，感觉亮丽如新。但我们不能因此而否定它的真实性。仔细观察，你会发现真品的许多与众不同，从细微处着手，用严谨的科学态度分析玉器所给我们留下的蛛丝马迹，这就是鉴定家应有的责任。

　　Most of Hongshan-culture jade wares with higher density don't have deep infiltration color because of arid climate. The color floats on the surface, looks bright and new. But we cannot deny its authenticity for this. You will discover the real one has a lot of difference, through careful observation, it give us the traces with strict scientific attitude analyzing jade ware that left which is the responsibility an expert should have.

图 227 动物形玉
玉质：青黄玉
尺寸：高 6.8 cm
〔听雨堂珍藏〕

Picture 227 animal-shaped jade
Jade texture: blue-yellow jade
Size: 6.8cm high
(Collection of "rain-hear hall")

图 219 动物形玉另面

Picture219 another side of animal-shaped jade

图 228 天地神佩
玉质：青黄玉
尺寸：长 9cm
（听雨堂珍藏）

Picture 228 compound jade baldric for heaven and earth
Jade texture: blue yellow jade
Size: 9cm long
(Collection of "rain-hear hall")

　　无论玉质多坚密的玉器，当被土壤覆盖后，土壤中的水分都会浸入玉理中。这些借助玉石棉、绺、瑕渗入的水分存留久时便会从玉石内部形成浸痕。透光观察玉理，有一种从中被掏空的感觉，让玉石内所含之棉、绺、璺更为明显。

　　当逆光观察这件玉器时，器面的打洼处明显不够平整，可以看出手工加工痕迹。朴拙的加工工艺、神秘的造型、真实的沁象、厚重的包浆，这一切皆能够认证其年代特征与真实性。

　　When the jade was covered by soil, no matter how hard and dense its texture is, the water in the soil would certainly soak into the jade. The water, getting into the jade with the jade stone cotton, crack or flaw, would leave soaked trace from interior. Observing the jade texture through the light, you will find that the jade looks like empty from inside, which make the cotton, tuft and crack in the jade more obvious.

　　When observing the jade through backlight, we will find that the digging hollow place on the surface is not smooth enough, and there are obvious processing trace by handwork. Simple and unadorned processing craft, mystical modeling, real infiltration phenomenon and thick baojiang, all above which can prove the age characters and authenticity of the jade.

图 229 神佩另面
Picture 229　another side of jade god wear

图 230 对神佩逆光观察
Picture 230　observing jade god wear through backlight

图 231 玉神祖　　Picture231jade numen
玉质：青玉　　Jade texture: blue-green jade
尺寸：高13.4cm　　Size: 13.4cm high
（听雨堂珍藏）　　(Collection of "rain-hear hall")

图 232 玉神祖器背
Picture 232 back of jade numen

　　玉神祖原玉质为青色，因为受沁而变为糖色，然后由糖色再钙化成白色。此器工艺精湛，沁象真实自然，人为永远无法仿制。

　　玉神祖头部放大后，可见白色钙化斑呈雾状由外向内漫延，从而形成明显的沁色过渡。器背放大可见系佩孔上部陈旧绺裂痕，呈现强烈年代感与真实性。玉神祖这两处沁后特征，无论动用任何高科技手段皆无法逼真仿出。

This jade texture is blue-green jade formly, it became sugar color after being infiltration and finally calcified to white. The jade has exquisite craft, real natural infiltration phenomenon, which will never be imitated by artificial.

　　We can see the white calcified spots expanded from outside to inside when the head of jade numen enlarged, so it formed a obvious transition of infiltration color. There are old tuft cracks at the hanging hole when the back of jade numen enlarged, which displayed strong age feeling and authenticity. These two characters of the jade numen can not be imitated no matter what kind of high scientific methods use.

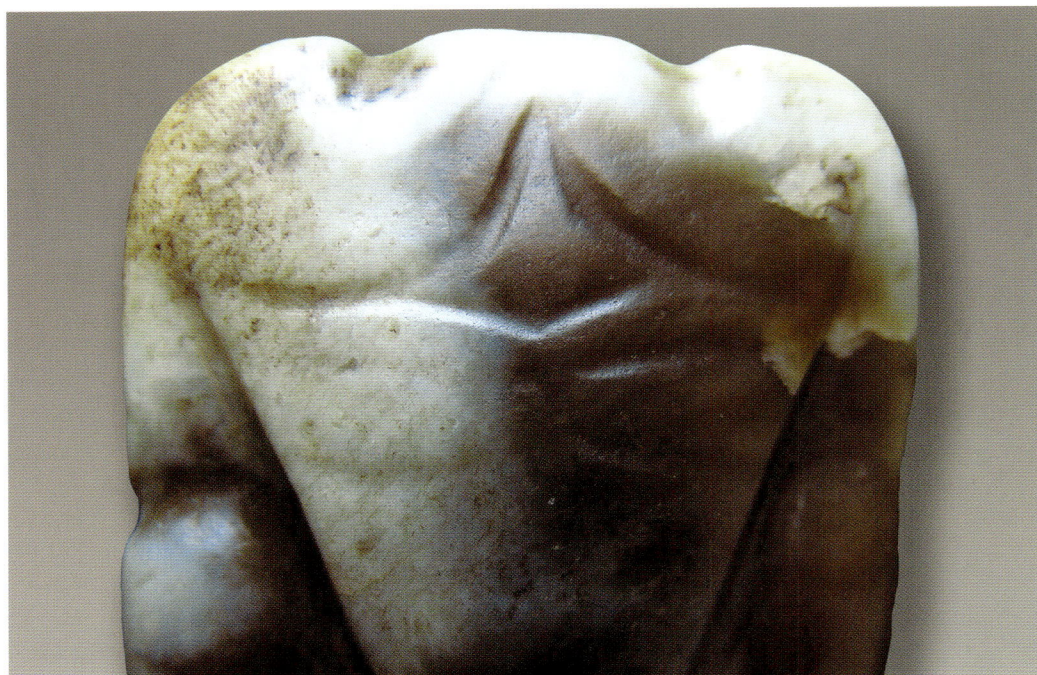

图 233 玉神祖头部放大
Picture 233 the head of jade numen enlarged

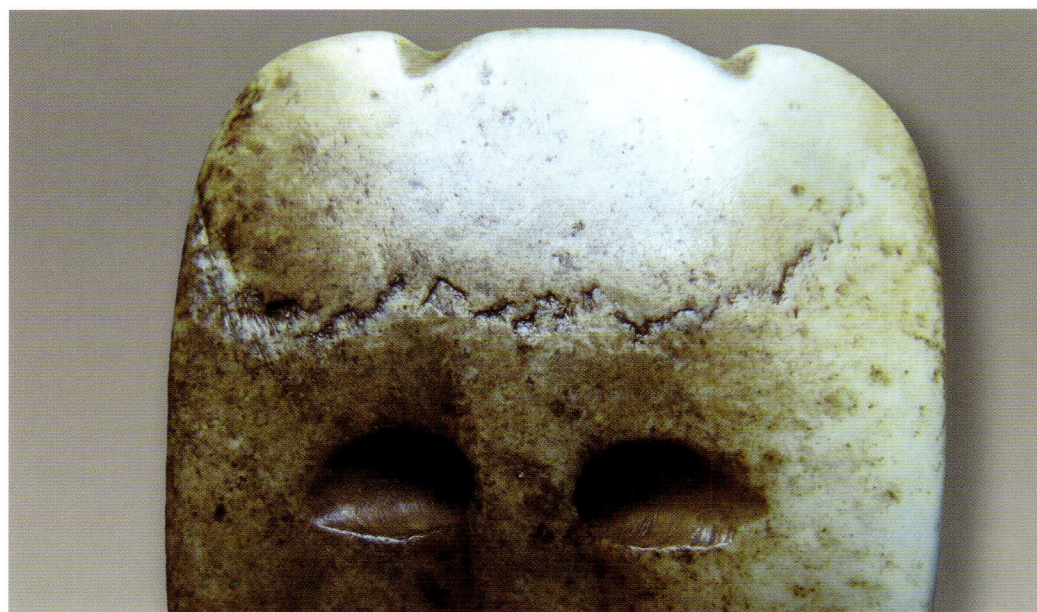

图 234 玉神祖器背放大
Picture 234 the back of jade numen enlarged

图 235 玦形玉兽
玉质：青玉
尺寸：高 9.5 cm
（听雨堂珍藏）
Picture235 jade coiled animal
Jade texture: blue-green jade
Size: 9.5cm high
(Collection of "rain-hear hall")

此器原本颜色为淡青，因受沁而变为黄色。 我们所见红山文化玉器已非本质颜色，而是沁后色。透闪石硬度极高，尽管以刀刻划不能留痕，但玉石中仍然或多或少含有棉、绺、瑕等细小中空。当玉石与土壤接触某种元素随水分进入玉体后，皆能对玉石外部和内部造成伤害。从沁后玉表或逆光透视则能看出，此时玉理已发生了某些变化，犹如水雾状的内蚀白斑几乎充斥了整个玉器。

This jade's original color is light blue-green, and it becomes yellow because of being infiltration .

The color of Hongshan-culture jade ware is not original color, which is after being infiltration color.

The tremolite has extremely high degree of hardness. Though it will not leave marks when it is carved with a knife, but there is more or less some cotton, tuft cracks or flaws etc. tiny hollows in it.

Some of elements may enter the jade with water when the jade contacted to the soil, which will cause the damages to the jade from the interior.Through the surface of jade after infiltration and backlight perspective, we can see the jade texture has already had certain changes, and the entire jade ware is full of white spots that look like mist.

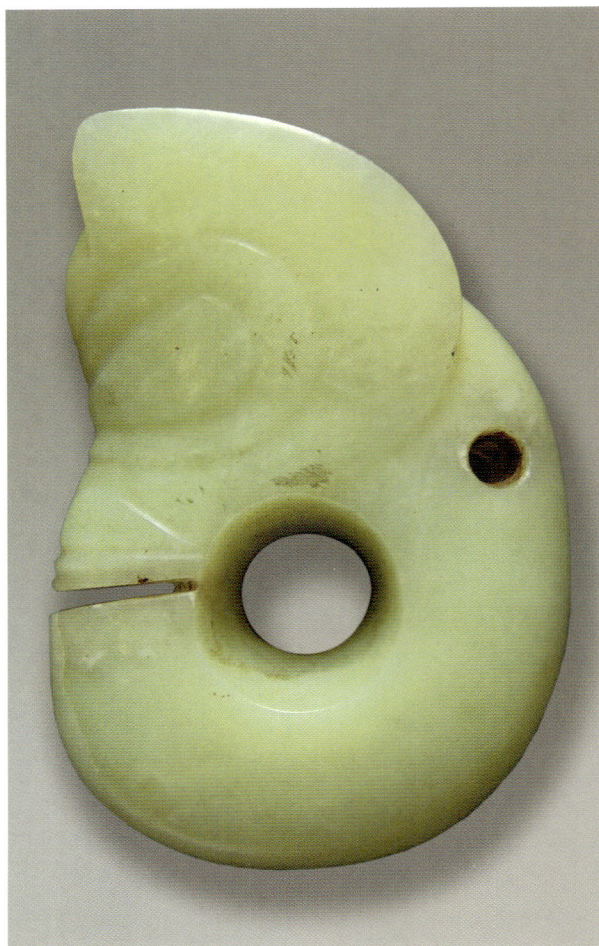

图 236 玦形玉兽
Picture 236 jade coiled animal

图 237 玦形玉兽另面
Picture 237 another side of jade coiled animal

图 238 玉龙
玉质：青玉
尺寸：高 13.7cm 宽 13.5cm
（听雨堂珍藏）

Picture 238 jade dragon
Jade texture: blue-green jade
Size: 13.7cm high   13.5cm wide
(Collection of "rain-hear hall")

在鉴定高古玉器时，除玉质、器形、加工工艺外，沁象将起到百分之七十的决定性作用。因为前三项均可以人为选择和仿制，而真正出土古玉器的受沁变化，却永远无法逼真仿制。

此器局部白化直到系挂孔内，白化过渡自然。边缘处尤为受沁严重，淡黑沁色直深入白化层，绺斑呈起层状。这一切特征皆能客观解释此器之真实性。

器背绺裂痕与器面绺裂相一致，说明玉龙在特定环境中沁象的完整统一和自然变化的科学性。

In the appraisal of high-ancient jade ware, besides the jade texture, the shape and processing craft, the infiltration phenomenon will play a decisive role of 70%. As the first three could be chosen and imitated by artificial, but the real infiltration change in the unearthed ancient jade ware which can not be imitated vividly.

The white partial transition to the link hole is very nature. The edges are serious infiltration particularly. The light black color goes deep into the white layer, so the tuft cracks present layer shape.These characteristics can objectively explain the authenticity of the jade.

The tuft cracks on the jade back and the ones on the surface are identical, which show the integrity and unity of jade dragon and the scientific feature of natural changes.

红山文化古玉鉴定

Hogshan-cultural ancient jade appraisal

图 239 玉龙器背
Picture 239 back of jade dragon

图 240 玉龙局部放大
Picture 240 jade dragon partly enlarged

图 241 玉龙局部放大
Picture 241 jade dragon partly enlarged

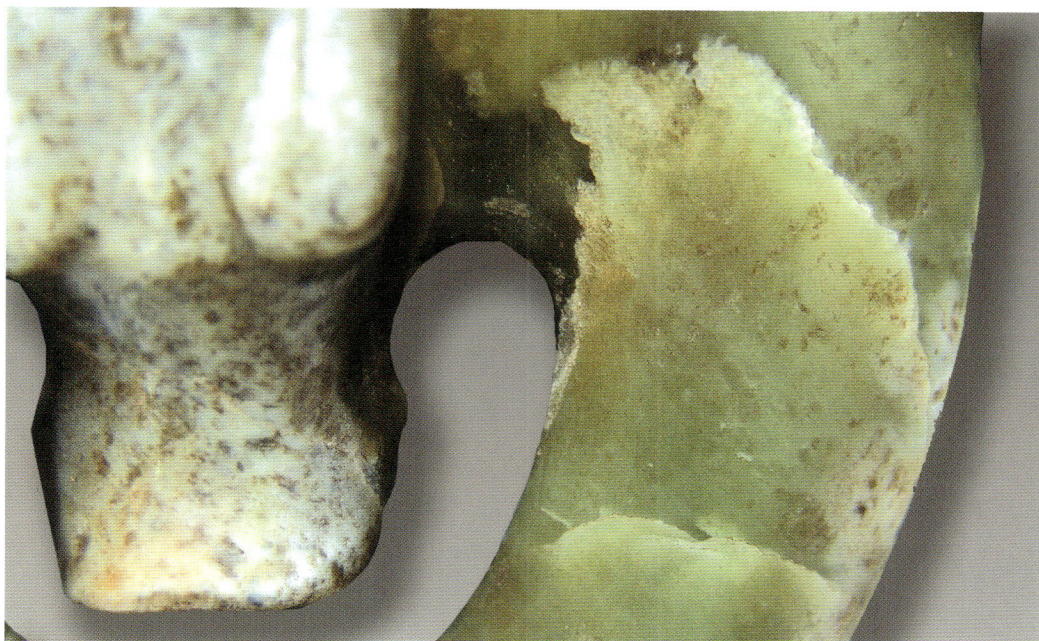

图 242 玉龙绺裂放大
Picture 242 jade dragon's tuft crack pattern enlarged

图 243 玉龙局部放大
Picture 243 jade dragon partly enlarged

对玉龙局部放大后可见微小麻斑覆盖器表。

玉龙下部出戟处较薄，白化尤重，并直到器背。

放大后的绺裂可见边缘处浅淡，并逐渐向玉理深入。这一特征由玉石生长纹所决定的。

玉龙双目下部突起，接触土壤自然面积大些，此处受沁明显较重。这些细微特征昭示着自然科学规律的不可更改性。

After jade dragon partly enlarged, we can see the micro spots covering on the surface.

Jade dragon's downside where the halberd comes out is thin, whiten is serious, and it goes until the back.

From the enlargement of tuft cracks, we can find that the edges are light and thin, gradually go deep into the jade texture. That was decided by the jade's growth veins.

Downside of the jade dragon's eyes protruded and the area contacted to the soil is large, so it was obviously heavier to receive infiltration.These characters show the inalterability of natural scientific laws.

图 244 玉鸟
玉质：青玉
尺寸：高 14.2cm 宽 13cm
（听雨堂珍藏）

Picture 244 jade bird
Jade texture: blue-green bird
Size: 14.2 cm high 13cm wide
(Collection of "rain-hear hall")

玉鸟工艺精湛，包浆明显，沁象真实自然，属大开门之器。

局部放大，可见鸟首处麻斑、层层绺裂、沁色的过渡变化、温润的包浆，可谓真品特征俱全。

器背系挂孔沿润滑，无刺手之感，均符红山文化真古玉器特征。

The jade bird has exquisite craft, Baojiang is obvious, real and natural infiltration phenomenon which belongs to a grand jade ware.

From the enlargement we can see that the spots on the bird's head, tuft cracks layer upon another, the transitional changes of infiltration color and mild baojiang which can be considered the characters of real one are complete.

The back of the hanging hole is smooth and no rough feeling which are all conformed the characters of real Hongshan-culture jade ware.

图 245 玉鸟器背
Picture 245 back of jade bird

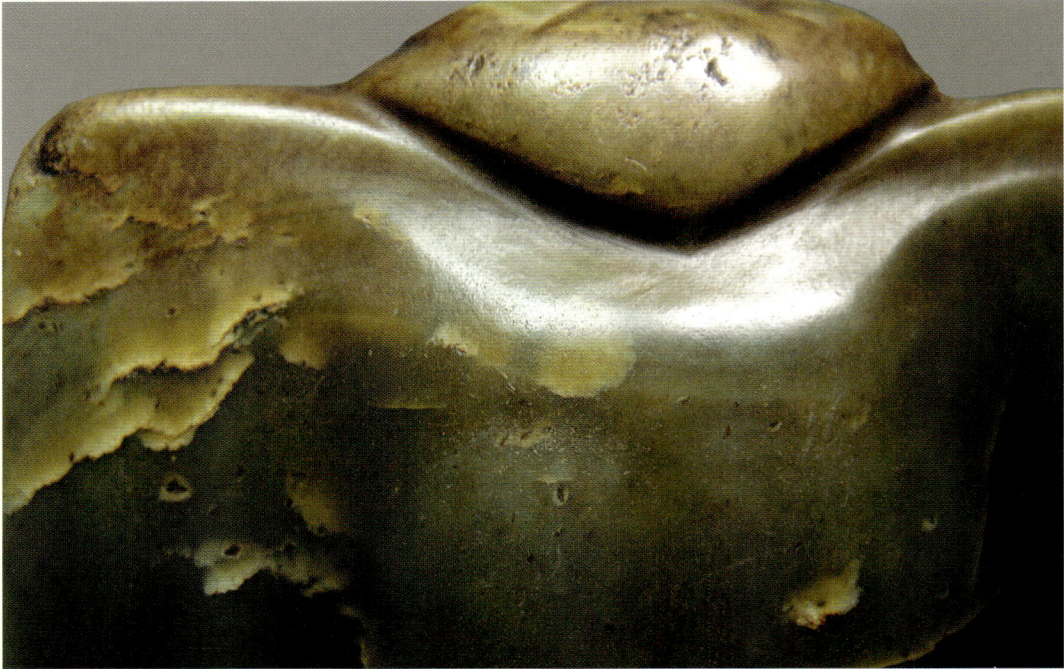

图 246 玉鸟局部放大
Picture 246 partial enlargement of jade bird

图 247 玉鸟器背局部放大
Picture 247 partial enlargement of jade bird's back

图 248 玉鸟神
玉质：青玉
尺寸：高 8.1cm 宽 7.4cm
（听雨堂珍藏）

Picture 248 jade god bird
Jade texture: blue-green jade
Size: 8.1cm high 7.4cm wide
(Collection of "rain-hear hall")

玉鸟神周边受沁明显较重，因为玉器此处与土壤接触面积较大，因而产生必然关系。这种现象就是自然科学规律的不可改变性，所以沁象更真实和生动。

玉鸟神器背可见明显自然形成之绺裂斑痕，进一步说明此器真实性。

通过局部放大可清楚看到青玉质的玉鸟神逐渐钙化过程，这就是沁色的过渡性。

真沁之过渡犹如绘画中的喷绘，人为无法逼真仿制。

The edge of jade god bird has been infiltration seriously because the jade has large areas contacting to the soil, so it produces necessary relation. That is the immutability of natural scientific laws, so its infiltration phenomenon is more real and lively.

We can see the natural tuft cracks on the back of jade god bird, which further prove the authenticity of the jade ware.

We can see the process of a blue-green texture jade bird gradually being calcified. That is the transition of the infiltration color.

The transition in a infiltration is just like spraying paint in painting, which can never be imitated by artificial.

图 249 玉鸟神之器背
Picture 249 back of jade god bird

图 250 玉鸟神尾部放大
Picture 250 enlargement of jade god bird's tail

图 251 天地神佩
玉质：青玉
尺寸：高 9.8cm 宽 21.3cm
（听雨堂珍藏）

Picture 251 compound jade baldric for heaven and earth
Jade texture: blue–green jade
Size: 9.8cm high 21.3cm wide
(Collection of "rain–hear hall")

红山文化古玉，无论片状、板状还是圆雕作品，皆采用"压地隐起法"工艺表现每件器物的形态与神态，给人以简洁而朴拙之感。

"压地隐起法"，即以缓坡打洼剔地，突出线条和表现神态，以增强立体感效果。

此器工艺精湛，线条流畅，包浆厚重，沁象真实自然。器面可见绺裂斑，针刺状孔洞及连片浸蚀斑。

"压地隐起法"工艺看似简单，实际加工并不容易。尤其片状玉器，稍有不慎前功尽弃。

The Hongshan–culture ancient jade, No matter what the piece shape, plank shape or round carved works, all used the craft we called "digging hollows" to show the shape and manner of every jade ware, which give us simple and unadorned feelings.

The "digging hollows" craft actual is digging hollows and pick position with slow slope to protrude lines and behavior to stress effect of three–D sense.

This jade has exquisite craft, smooth lines, thick baojiang, and natural infiltration phenomenon. We can see tufe cracks, acupuncture–shaped holes and slice–shaped infiltration spots on the jade.

The craft seems simple, but not easily to process. You may waste all previous efforts if not carefully enough especially in slice–shaped jade ware.

图 252 天地神佩另面

Picture 252 another side of compound jade baldric for heaven and earth

图 253 天地神佩局部放大

Picture 253 partial enlargement of compound jade baldric for heaven and earth

图 254 天地神佩局部放大

Picture 254 partial enlargement of compound jade baldric for heaven and earth

图 255 天地神佩局部放大

Picture 255 partial enlargement of compound jade baldric for heaven and earth

图 256 天地神佩逆光观察

Picture 256　observing compound jade baldric for heaven and earth against light

器面所出现针刺状蚀孔，与土壤中所含某种有害玉质微量元素有直接关系，并因此浸蚀而成。

绺裂层叠，裂隙处泛白，陈旧性破损，张显了悠久历史沉淀。

逆光下观察器表，不但线条流畅，而且剔地处缺乏平整感，显露出手工打磨痕迹与年代特征。

The acupuncture–shaped holes on the jade surface have direct relations with certain harmful elements in the soil, which formed after being corrasion.

The tuft cracks lay one upon another, the crack place is white, and the damages are old, which demonstrate a long history sediment.

Observing the jade against the light, you will find not only its lines are very smooth, but also picking position lacking neat sense which displays manually polished trace and the times character.

图 257 玉鸟   Picture 257 jade bird

玉质：青玉   Jade texture: blue-green jade

尺寸：长 11.4 cm   Size: 11.4cm long

（听雨堂珍藏）   (Collection of "rain-hear hall")

　　玉鸟器身遍布绺裂与孔洞，半伴有白色钙化斑。

　　人为制造绺裂多先将玉器进行烧烤，然后放入冷水中，这时做出的绺裂实为强制性炸裂，这种炸裂多往纵深走，而并非呈起层状。

　　古玉器自然形成之孔洞边缘参差不齐，并有一定深度。这是因为玉器表面先天存在酸、碱可进入缝隙点。在首先完成钙化后再逐渐形成微小虫蛀孔，蛀孔向外扩展便成孔洞。孔洞不易仿造。人为制作麻斑多以铊头顶压而成，不具自然形成之真实感。

The jade bird is covered with tuft cracks and holes with white calcified spots.

To make the tuft cracks by artifical, first roasting the jade on the fire, and then put it in the cold water. The cracks made in this way is actually forced crack, which always go deep inside, not layer shape.

The edge of holes which formed by nature is not uniform, and has a certain depth. That is because there are the points where acid and alkali can enter. It formed little holes gradually after being calcified, and then expanded outside. The holes can not be imitated easily. The man-made spot holes always made by pressing with a steelyard, not having the real authenticity.

图 258 玉鸟之另面
Picture 258　another side of jade bird

图 259 玉鸟局部放大
Picture 259　partial enlargement of jade bird

图 260 玉鸟局部放大
Picture 260　partial enlargement of jade bird

图 261 玉蝉
玉质：青玉
尺寸：高 8.2cm 宽 8.2cm
（听雨堂珍藏）

Picture 261 jade cicada
Jade texture: blue-green jade
Size: 8.2cm high 8.2cm wide
(Collection of "rain-hear hall")

鉴定古代玉器，绺裂成为其中重要条件与依据。因为自然形成之绺裂人为不能逼真仿制。

对玉蝉局部放大后，可以看到自然形成绺裂缓慢进入肌理。

我们强调沁象的统一性。这件玉器正、反两面无论沁色、绺裂等沁象完全相一致。以河漠玉制作仿古玉也常见较真实自然形成绺裂痕，但多在玉器单面，不具沁象的完整与统一性。

The cracks are the most important conditions and basis when we appraise an old jade ware. That is because the natural cracks can not be imitated.

From the enlargement of jade cicada, we can see that the natural tuft cracks going deep into the jade texture.

We emphasize the unity of the infiltration phenomenon. Both sides of this jade are completely the same no matter what the infiltration color and tuft crack. The imitated old jade by Hemo jade also has real natural cracks, which always in the single side jade, not having the integrity and the unity of the infiltration phenomenon.

图 262 玉蝉另面
Picture 262 another side of jade cicada

图 263 玉蝉局部放大
Picture 263 enlargement of jade cicada

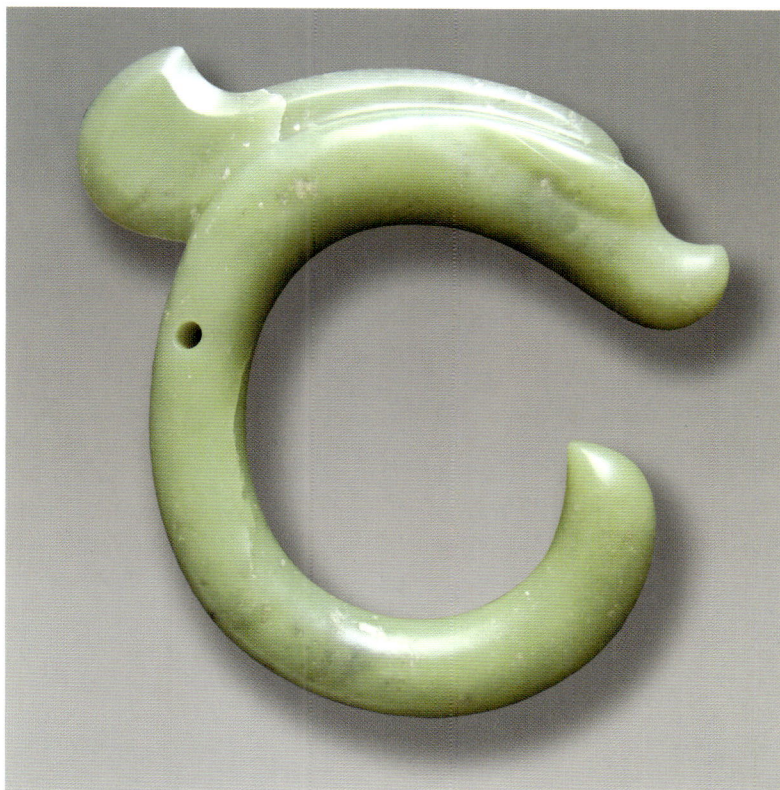

图 264 玉龙
玉质：青黄玉
尺寸：高 15.4cm 径 2.2cm
（听雨堂珍藏）

Picture 264 jade dragon

Jade texture: blue yellow jade

Size: 15.4 cm high diameter 2.2cm

(Collection of "rain-hear hall")

　　玉龙呈青黄色，这是沁后颜色。当一件玉器藏入地下若干年后。由于土壤中所含多种元素的浸染，其质地与颜色都会有所改变。这件以透闪石制作的玉龙，由于质地坚密相对受侵害要小一些，但我们仍然从玉龙的头部、鬣部与龙身处看到明显的绺裂痕，绺裂呈起层状，多不向纵深发展。透闪石类玉器，尽管玉质硬度较高，但因历经数千年，我们仍可以发现玉器表面由于各种有害玉质元素的浸蚀所形成较明显的微小麻斑。

　　The jade dragon infiltration color is blue-yellow. When a jade was under the ground for years, its texture and color would certain changed because of being infiltration by kinds of elements in the soil. The jade dragon made of tremolite is smaller infiltration because of its close quality. But we still see the obvious cracks at the dragon's head and body. The cracks layer one upon another, not going deep into the jade. the temolite jade has high hardness; however, we can also see obvious spots on the surface formed by being infiltration with some harmful elements in thousands of years.

图 265 玉龙之另面
Picture 265 another side of jade dragon

图 266 玉龙局部放大
Picture 266 partial enlargement of jade dragon

185

图 267 龙形佩　Picture 267 jade dragon
玉质：青玉　Jade texture: blue-green jade
尺寸：高 9.3–9.5cm　Size: 9.3–9.5cm high
（听雨堂珍藏）　(Collection of "rain-hear hall")

透闪石类玉器质地非常坚密,受沁后多无较大变化。但从此二器中仍能看到较为明显的沁后变化，这就是只有受沁方能见到的玉石生长纹及器尾处的逐渐过渡色变。

精湛的工艺，温润的包浆，流畅的线条，透闪石类玉器质地非常坚密，自然真实的沁象，受沁后多无较大变化。给玉凤更增加许多美感。

The texture of he tremolite jade ware is very dense and it will not change toomuch after being infiltration. However, from these two jade ware,we can see obvious changes. That is the growth veins only being see onthe jade after being infiltration and thetransition of color change gradually atthe tail of the ware.

Exquisite craft, mild and moist baojiang, smooth lines, and natural and realinfiltration phenomenon, which increaseesthetic sense for jade phoenix.

图 268 玉凤　Picture 268 jade phoenix
玉质：青玉　Jade texture: blue-green jade
尺寸：高 10.1cm　Size: 10.1cm high
（听雨堂珍藏）　(Collection of "rain-hear hall")

图 269 乌形佩
玉质：青玉
尺寸：高 13.5 — 13.8cm
（听雨堂珍藏）

Picture 269bird shape jade pendant
Jade texture: blue-green jade
Size: height 13.5–13.8cm
(Collection of "rain-hear hall")

　　从鸟形佩由青色玉受沁渐变为黄色给了我们许多新的启示。就是说，我们通常所见很多红山文化黄色玉器物，许多都是因为受沁后而改变其原本颜色。因此目前所见颜色并非玉之本色。

　　The color transition of bird shape jade plaque from blue-green to yellow gives us much new enlightenment. That is to say, most yellow Hongshan-culture jade we usually see changed their original color after being infiltration. Therefore, the present color is always not the jade's original color.

图 270 玉鸟
玉质：青玉
尺寸：高 5.3cm 宽 7cm
（听雨堂珍藏）

Picture 270 jade bird
Jade texture: blue-green jade
Size: 5.3cm high 7cm wide
(Collection of "rain-hear hall")

玉鸟包浆明显，温润亮泽，沁象真实自然。

对玉鸟局部放大后，逆光观察，你会发现尽管这种透闪石类玉石质地坚密，但由于岁月漫长，仍在玉器表而浸蚀出密集微小麻坑。

器背处由于接触酸碱性物质，可见多处白色沁斑，沁斑分布错落有致，色变过渡自然。

The jade bird has obvious baojiang, moist bright, real natural infiltration phenomenon.

Observing the partial enlargement of jade bird against the light, you will find that although the tremolite has close quality, there still would be many little pits on the jade surface.

The back of jade contacts to acid and alkali elements, so there are white infiltration spots at some places. can see a lot of place white infiltration spot, and the transition of the infiltration color is very natural.

图 271 玉鸟之背面
Picture 271　back of jade bird

图 272 玉鸟局部放大
Picture 272　partial enlargement of jade bird

图 273 玉神祖
玉质：青玉
尺寸：高 12.4cm
（听雨堂珍藏）

Picture 273 jade numen
Jade texture: blue-green jade
Size: 12.4cm high
(Collection of "rain-hear hall")

图 274 器背面
Picture 274 back of jade

透闪石类玉质比较坚密，但仍可见沁后明显特征：包浆十分明显，有被蒸煮熟透了的感觉。头部因温度变化而出现绺裂。逆光观察器背，可见沁后所形成的点状麻斑。

对神祖头部放大，可见鼻两侧与嘴部打洼处明显镙纹状刮削痕，符合当时制玉特征，因此鉴定为红山文化古玉真品。

The texture of tremolite is much dense, but we can also see the obvious feature after infiltration: baojiang is obvious like being steamed entirely. The tuft cracks appeared on the head because of the temperature change. Observing the ware back against the light, we can see the drop spots generated after being infiltration.

From the enlargement of jade numen head, we can see that two sides of nose and the digging hollows place of the mouth have obvious whorl trace, which conform to the processing character at that time. So we appraise the jade is a real Hongshan-culture ancient jade.

图 275 玉神祖头部放大
Picture 275　enlargement of jade numen head

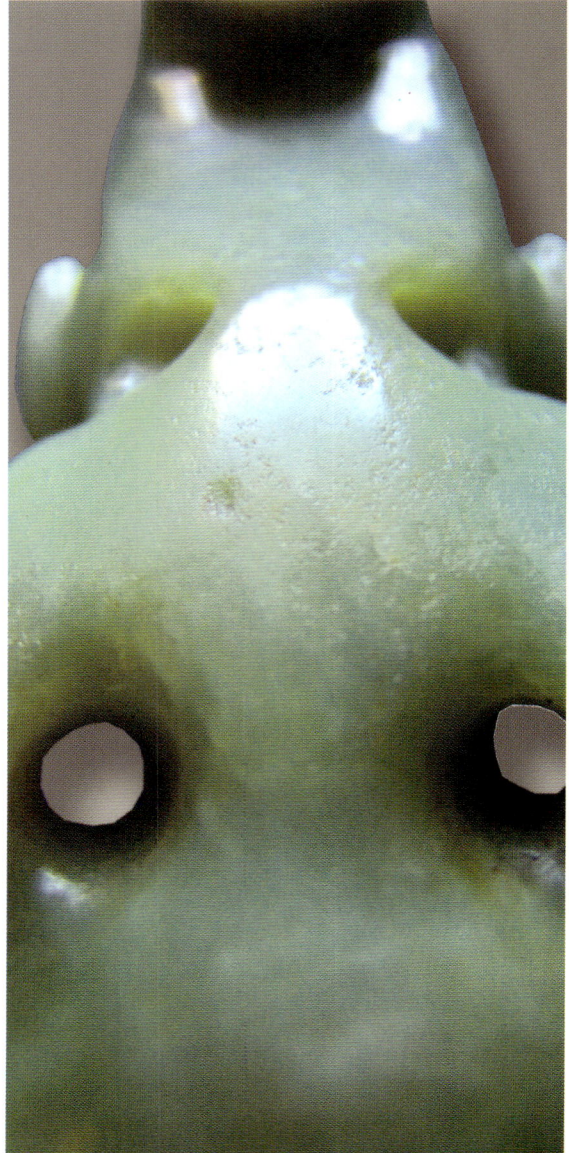

图 276 器背局部放大
Picture 276　enlargement of jade back

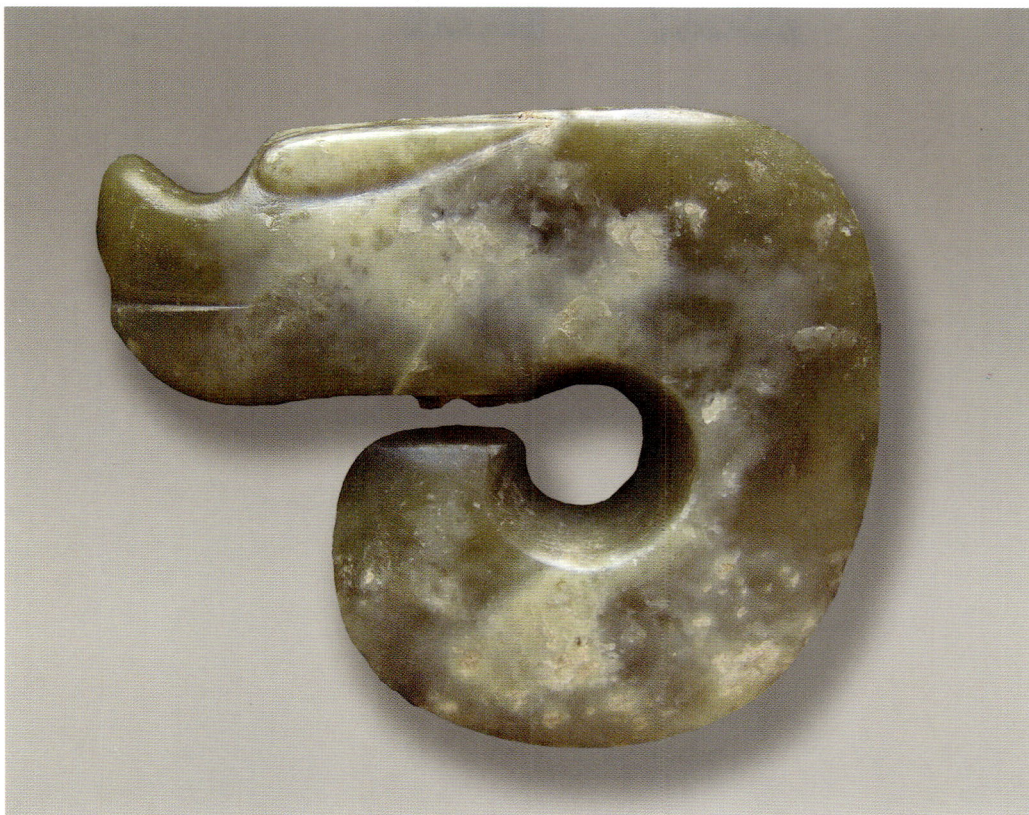

图 277 龙形玉　　　　Picture 277 jade dragon

玉质：青玉　　　　　Jade texture: blue-green jade

尺寸：高 7.8cm　　　Size: 7.8cm high

（听雨堂珍藏）　　　(Collection of "rain-hear hall")

　　经过漫长的岁月，玉器在受沁后皆已改变原本颜色。俗话道："无孔不入"，凡玉器中的沁色皆有进入点，并由一点逐渐向外扩散，则形成沁色的过渡性。由此器可以看到白化斑的深浅有着明显的色差变化，这就是玉器受沁点与晕散扩展所形成的主要特征。

　　The jade has already changed its original color after being infiltration through long years. It is said that to get in by every opening. All infiltration color of jade ware has a point to get in, and it gradually expands outside from one point to form the transition of color. We can see there is obvious color change at the depth of white spots, and this is the major feature of the infiltration point and halos expanding of jade ware.

图 278 龙形玉另面

Picture 278 another side of jade dragon

图 279 虎形佩　　　　Picture 279 jade tiger

玉质：青玉　　　　　Jade texture: blue-green jade

尺寸：高 11.9cm　　Size: 11.9cm high

（听雨堂珍藏）　　　（Collection of "rain-hear hall"）

这种质地较坚密的玉器受沁后玉质不易受到严重破坏，但岁月仍能在它的表面浸蚀出颜色和斑痕。这些细微的沁象变化还是为我们鉴定玉器的真伪提供了有效证据。

The jade with dense texture is not easily destroyed seriously after being infiltration. However, there would be eroded into some color and spots on the surface through long years. The infiltration phenomenon provided us valid evidences to appraise the authenticity of jade ware.

图 280 块形玉兽　　　　Picture 280　jade coiled animal
玉质：青玉　　　　　　Jade texture: blue-green jade
尺寸：高 21.4cm　　　　Size: 21.4cm high
（听雨堂珍藏）　　　　（Collection of "rain-hear hall"）

　　玉器在土壤中含有一定水分，由于温度的变化而出现绺裂。绺裂处脱落则积存玉石内分泌矿物质与水渍，因此形成结痂，我谓之"蚀斑"。蚀斑较沁色颜色浓重，陈旧感强烈，人为制作不易。

　　古人云：入土千年古玉则腐为泥土。此器残破处已见内里确实腐如泥砂状。外表润泽而内腐严重者，自然为真古无疑。并由此可以认为，凡同体积、质地玉器，受沁与未受沁其重量是不一样的，受沁真古玉器重量要明显低于仿古玉器。

The jade has some water in the soil, and the tuft cracks will come out when the temperature changes. The tuft cracks comed off to accumulate some internal secretion and water stain of jade to form the scab, which we call "eroded spots". The eroded spot is deeper than infiltration color, having strong old feeling and not easily made by artificial.

The old people said that the jade would be rotten to soil after being in the earth for thousands of years. We can see something like muddy inside the jade where it damaged. The surface is moist but eroded inside, so it must be a real old jade. We can think that the jade after being infiltration is heavier than the ones not being infiltration, though they may have the same volume and texture.

图 281 块形玉兽之另面
Picture 281 another side of jade coiled animal

图 282 玦形玉兽蚀斑放大

Picture 282　enlargement of jade coiled animal`s spots

图 283 玦形玉兽局部放大可见内腐严重

Picture 283 eroded seriously seeing from the enlargement of jade coiled animal

图 284 玉龙

玉质：青玉

尺寸：高 25.1cm

（听雨堂珍藏）

Picture 284 jade dragon

Jade texture: blue-green jade

Size: 25.1 cm high

(Collection of "rain-hear hall")

　　青玉质玉龙受沁后发生万千沁色变化，在这些变化中蕴含着多种颜色的和谐衔接与过渡，这种自然形成的沁象，人为永远无法仿制。

　　The blue-green jade dragon has kinds of colors changes after being infiltration, which contain the connection and transition of all colors. The infiltration phenomenon formed naturely can not be imitated by artificial.

图 285 玉龙之另面

Picture 285 another side of jade dragon

图 286 玉龙之局部放大

Picture 286 partial enlargement of jade dragon

图 287 地母神佩　Picture 287　earth goddess jade

玉质：青玉　Jade texture: blue-green jade

尺寸：高 15.2cm　Size: 15.2cm high　8.8cm wide

宽 8.8cm　(Collection of "rain-hear hall")

（听雨堂珍藏）

图 288 地母神佩器背图

Picture 288 back of earth goddess jade

图 289 地母神佩局部放大

Picture 289 partial enlargement of earth goddess jade

　　此器温润亮泽的包浆、自然形成的绺斑、错综复杂的沁色变化、器背的浸蚀麻斑与完全符合时代特征的加工工艺，综合诸多方面特征认定此器为红山文化真古玉器。

　　This jade has mild and moist baojiang, natural formed tuft cracks, intricate changes of infiltration color, eroding spots on the jade back and the craft which completely conformed to the times characteristics. For all above reasons we can appraise this jade is a real Hongshan-culture ancient jade ware.

图 290 玉神面
玉质：青玉
尺寸：高 25.5cm 宽 22cm
（听雨堂珍藏）

Picture 290 jade god face
Jade texture: blue-green jade
Size: 25.5cm high 22cm wide
(Collection of "listening to rain" hall)

　　玉神面外凸内凹呈瓢形玉器。玉器受沁后内外沁象统一而完整，沁色丰富多彩，包浆温润亮泽，沁象真实自然。

　　对玉神面器背局部放大可见自然形成绺斑与石化斑。二者共存器背，有充分理由证明并非原生沁河漠玉所制和人为仿作。

　　石化处有黑斑入肌理，并可见沁色明显进入点，为有源之沁，后天所形成。因此鉴定此器为红山文化古玉真品。

The jade god face protrudes outside but concaved inside like a gourd-shapede jade ware. The infiltration phenomenon is unified and integral, the color is rich, baojiang is mild and moist, and the infiltration phenomenon is real and natural.

From the enlargement of jade god face's back, we can see tuft cracks and petrifaction spots, two of which exist on the ware back together. We have sufficient reasons to prove that the jade is not made by Hemo jade that is original infiltration and not imitated one by artificial..

The petrifaction place has black spots infiltration into the jade texture, and there are obvious points where infiltration color got in, which called "infiltration with a source" which formed by acquired. So we can appraise it is a real Hongshan-culture ancient jade ware.

图 291 玉神面器背
Picture 291   back of jade god face

图 292 玉神面局部放大
Picture 292   partial enlargement of jade god face

图 293 勺形玉祖
玉质：青玉图
尺寸：长 18.2 cm
（听雨堂珍藏）

Picture 293 spoon-shaped jade Zu
Jade texture: blue-green jade
Size: 18.2cm long
(Collection of "rain-hear hall")

　　玉器受沁必须具备一定客观因素，这就是玉石先天形成时存在的棉、绺、璺等。

　　正是这些先决条件，提供了沁色浸入的可进入点。凡无进入点之沁色，皆称无头沁。凡无头沁，大多属玉石先天形成时火山灰等物质内含玉理之包裹体。

　　勺形玉祖沁色进入点明确，沁象真实自然。

There must be some certain objective factors when the Jade ware receives infiltration. They are cotton, tuft or cracks which already existed when the jade innately formed.

Because of these prerequisites, it offer a point where infiltration color could soak in. The infiltration color without the point is called "no-head infiltration". Most of "no-head infiltration", belong to jade mostly congenital form the materials such as volcano ash the parcel that contains jade texture body.

Spoon-shape Jade Zu has a clear infiltration color point, and the infiltration phenomenon is real and natural.

图 294 玉祖局部放大

Picture294 enlargement of Jade Zu

图 295 玉祖局部放大

Picture295 enlargement of Jade Zu

296 玉祖器背

Picture296 back of Jade Zu

图 297 璜形神鸟佩
玉质：青玉
尺寸：高 3.7cm 宽 7.7cm
（听雨堂珍藏）

Picture 297　Huang-shaped jade bird
Jade texture: blue–green jade
Size: 3.7cm long　7.7cm wide
(Collection of "rain–hear hall")

玉器受沁玉质已发生明显变化。

逆光观察器面工艺特征与受沁变化，可见琢磨痕与受沁后所出现微小麻斑。

此器包浆明显，温润亮泽，左边缘处白化斑真实自然。

The infiltration of jade has already had obvious changes.

Observing the craft characters and infiltration changes on the jade surface against the light, we can find that the grinding marks and micro spots after infiltration.

The baojiang of this ware is obvious, mild and moist, and its white spots at left edge are real and natural.

图 298 逆光观察器面受沁变化
Picture 298   observing the jade surface against the light

图 299 璜形佩之器背
Picture 299   back of the Huang-shaped jade bird

图 300 龙形玉
玉质：墨玉
尺寸：高 10.7cm 宽 9.5cm
（听雨堂珍藏）

Picture 300 jade dragon
Jade texture: black jade
Size: 10.7cm high 9.5cm wide
(Collection of "rain-hear hall")

这是一件由墨玉制成的器物，黑色的器表虽然不易看见明显沁色，但我们仍然可以看到较明显的、符合科学规律的沁象特征。玉器自然受沁一般多为从边缘到中间，从薄处到厚处，这是自然科学规律。

这件龙形玉呈刀状的脊背与尾处受沁最重，已经趋于钙化并逐渐向内延伸，在延伸过程中形成沁色的过渡性。并且从器表看到玉器制作年代特征痕迹和厚重的包浆，因此我们鉴定此器为红山文化古玉真品。

Ihis is a jade made of black jade.We can not easily see the infiltration phenomenon on the back surface, but we still can see obvious infiltration characters conformed to the scientific rules. The jade is always being infiltration from edge to center, from the thin to the thick, which is the natural scientific rules.

The back and tail of the jade dragon presenting knife shape were infiltration seriously. They have gradually calcified inside and formed the transition of infiltration color. From the surface of the ware, the age characters and thick baojiang, we can appraise the jade is a real Hongshan-culture ancient jade ware.

图 301 龙形玉之另面
Picture 301 the other side of jade dragon

图 302 玉鸟
玉质：青玉
尺寸：高 6.8cm 宽 13cm
（听雨堂珍藏）

Picture 302 jade bird
Jade texture: blue-green jade
Size: 6.8cm high 13cm wide
(Collection of "rain-hear hall")

图 303 玉鸟器身局部放大
Picture 303 partial enlargement of jade bird

玉鸟受沁后色彩斑斓，沁象真实自然。沁后特征除绺裂斑、钙化斑外，尤其沁色变化十分丰富，无论沁色的过渡性与真实感可谓不容质疑。玉鸟局部所出现的绺裂层次分明，毫无做作之感，这是因为玉器在土壤中含有一定水分，在冷热变化中，器内、表温度不能均衡，由于膨胀系数的不同，因而产生玉器的表面炸裂。玉器的沁色正是通过这些裂隙而进入玉理。

The jade bird is colorful after infiltration and the infiltration phenomenon is real and natural. The infiltration characters are tuft cracks, calcified spots, and the infiltration color change is especially rich. There is no doubt about the transition of infiltration color and authenticity. The tuft cracks of jade bird's layer is one upon another, not having affected feeling. The jade has some water in the soil, and when the temperature changes, the degree inside and outside of the ware is not balance, as the coefficient of expansion is different, so it cracks on the surface. The infiltration color went into the jade texture through the cracks.

图 304 玉鸟之器背
Picture 304 back of jade bird

　　玉鸟器背与正面沁象基本一致，证明玉器是在完成后所受沁，并非以河漠玉所制作。因而以此确定了其真实性。

　　系挂孔内与玉鸟表面沁象一致，说明沁象之完整性。

　　玉鸟右翅膀处出现较大面积钙化斑。因此处较薄，在局部与酸、碱或生石灰相接触过程中，由于玉质和其它特殊因素决定了此处出现自然钙化。钙化需要一定过程方才能够逐步形成：先有玉石中空缝隙为元素浸入做首决条件，元素浸入后开始漫延、扩大，然后其它元素随之侵入并破坏玉质，甚至改变原有沁色。这样就在沁色与钙化间形成明显过渡，白色钙化斑并非纯白，其中蕴含着已改变了原本颜色的沁斑。这种沁斑千变万化，人为所不能仿制。

The infiltration phenomenon on the back of the jade bird is almost the same as the front one, which proved the jade was infiltration after complete. It is not made by Mohe jade, so we can ensure its authenticity.

The infiltration phenomenon in the hanging hole is the same as what on the jade surface, which can prove the jade's integrity.

There is large area of calcified spots on the bird's right wing. Because this place is a little thin, when the jade partially contacted with acid, alkali or lime, it appeared natural calcified spots at the place. The calcification need a long process: there must be some cracks on the jade as the entrance, then the elements get in and expand, finally more elements seep in and destroy the jade texture, even change the jade's original color. So it forms a obvious transition between the infiltration color and the calculation. The white spots are not absolute white, and it also contains the spots which changed its original color. These infiltration spots are ever changing, which can not be imitated by artificial.

图 305 玉鸟器背钻孔处放大

Picture 305 enlargement of jade bird's back hole

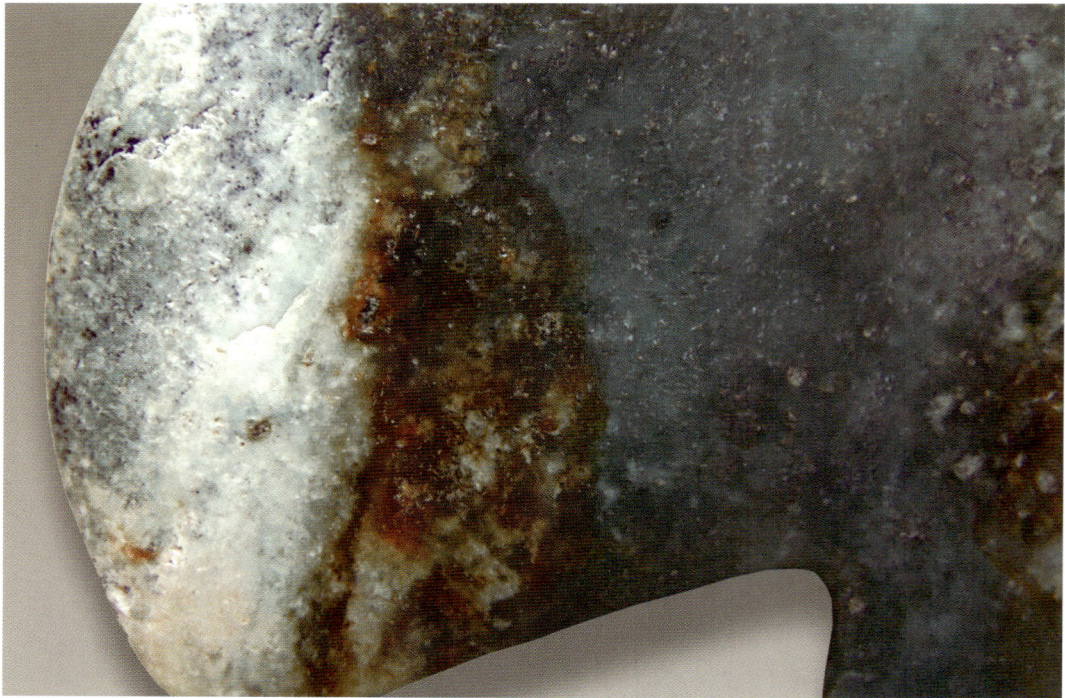

图 306 玉鸟翅膀处放大

Picture 306 enlargement of jade bird's wings

图 307 玉鸟
玉质：青玉
尺寸：高 9.6cm 宽 9.2cm
（听雨堂珍藏）

Picture307 jade bird
Jade texture: blue-green jade
Size: 9.6cm high　9.2cm wide
(Collection of "rain-hear hall")

此器以青玉制作，在入土后先受到土壤中水银所沁，出现条状黑色沁纹。

黑色沁纹具方向性与流动感，这与玉石生长纹理有关。

玉鸟双翅由边缘向内逐渐石化，石化处可见赭石色条纹，这是被石化了的水银沁纹。

由边缘向中间、由薄处到厚处、先受沁后钙化的自然受沁规律，向我们提供了可靠的科学鉴定依据。

从局部放大图我们可以看到沁色直到系挂孔内，这就是沁色的完整性。

This ware was made of blue-green jade, it was infiltration by mercury in the soil and showed strip-shaped black infiltration veins.

The black infiltration veins have a clear direction and a sense of movement, which has relationship with the jade growth veins.

图 308 玉鸟器背
Picture 308 back of jade bird

图 309 玉鸟器局部放大

Picture 309 partial enlargement of jade bird

图 310 具方向性的水银沁纹

Picture 310 mercury veins having the direction

Double wings of the bird petrified from edge to inside. The petrified place has reddish-brown veins which is the mercury veins being petrifaction.

The natural rule, being infiltration first and then calcified, from the edge to the center, from the thick to the thin, which provided us reliable scientific basis.

From the partial enlargement we can see the infiltration color goes until the hanging hole, that is the integrity of the infiltration color.

图 311 玉鸟
玉质：青玉
尺寸：高 10.5cm 宽 10.4cm
（听雨堂珍藏）

Picture 311 jade bird
Jade texture: blue-green jade
Size: 10.5cm high 10.4cm wide
(Collection of "rain-hear hall")

玉鸟受沁后呈浅黄色，器身大部布满赭石色沁斑并深入玉理。此种沁象极为少见。从沁象看，人为永远不能仿制，因此我们鉴定为红山文化古玉真品。

从玉鸟背面观察，沁色的完整性，统一性与过渡性特征极为明显。自然形成之绺裂与微小残破痕充分展现了在漫长岁月下所饱受的经历与苍桑。

The jade bird became light yellow after being infiltration and most of the jade is covered with reddish brown infiltration spots going deep into the jade texture.This kind of infiltration phenomenon is rarely seen. From the infiltration phenomenon, that is can not be imitated by artificial, so we appraise this jade is a real Hongshan-culture ancient jade ware.

Observing from back of jade bird, we can see the integrity, the unity and the transition of infiltration color are very obvious. The natural tuft cracks and the little damaged traces fully showed the experiences during the long years.

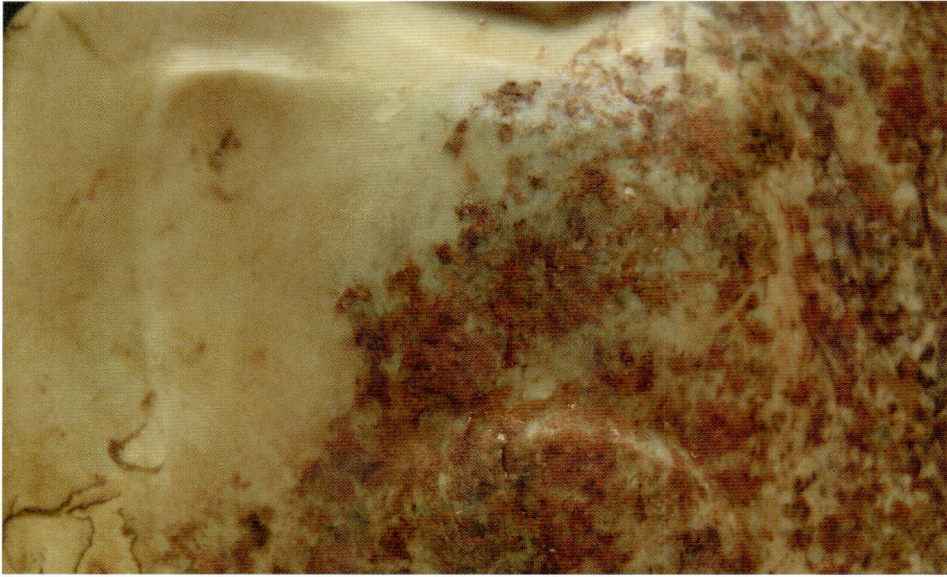

图 312 玉鸟受沁处局部放大
Picture 312 partial enlargement of jade bird□ infiltration place

图 313 玉鸟之背面
Picture 313 back of jade bird

red 图 314 兽面佩

图 314 兽面佩
玉质：青黄玉
尺寸：高5.9cm 宽6.3cm
（听雨堂珍藏）

Picture314 jade beast face pendant
Jade texture: blue yellow jade
Size: 5.9cm high   6.3 cm wide
(Collection of "rain-hear hall")

　　兽面佩之器表与器背，由于受土壤中各种元素所浸蚀形成密集微小麻斑。这些麻斑是历经了无数个日日年年所形成的。岁月不但可以改变玉器表面形象，而且能够改变玉之质地与颜色。

　　温润亮泽的包浆与绺裂，钻孔处所留下的镙旋痕，这一切充分展现了这件玉器无可挑剔的真实性。

　　逆光下我们可看到器背受沁后遍布密细的麻斑。人为制造麻斑多为酸蚀，经过酸蚀后的玉器不但可嗅到刺鼻化学药品味，而且避免不了泛出大量白灰，这些白灰经盘化或涂油可暂时退去，但放置久了仍会再三泛出，数年不退。

　　Both surface and back of the jade beast face pendant were covered with spots, which formed after being infiltration by kinds of elements in the soil. The spots finally generated after thousands of years. The years could not only change the jade's surface, but also change the texture and the color of jade ware.

　　The moist bright baojiang, tuft cracks and the helix trace drilling left hole, all which have displayed the actuality of this jade ware fully.

　　We can see numerous spots at the back by observing the jade against light. Man-made spots were always eroded in the acid. The jade being eroded in the acid not only smell like chemical medicines, but also it can not avoid coming out much white ash. The ash can be moved back by paint oil temporarily, but they will come back again after a long time laying, which can not be moved back for years.

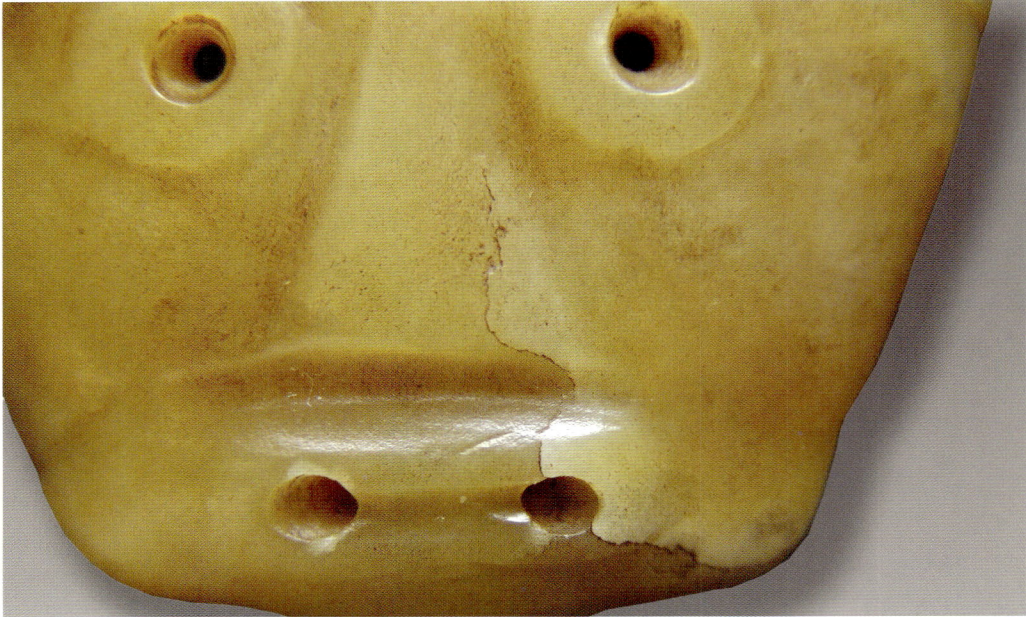

图 315 兽面佩局部放大
Picture 315　partial enlargement of jade beast face pendant

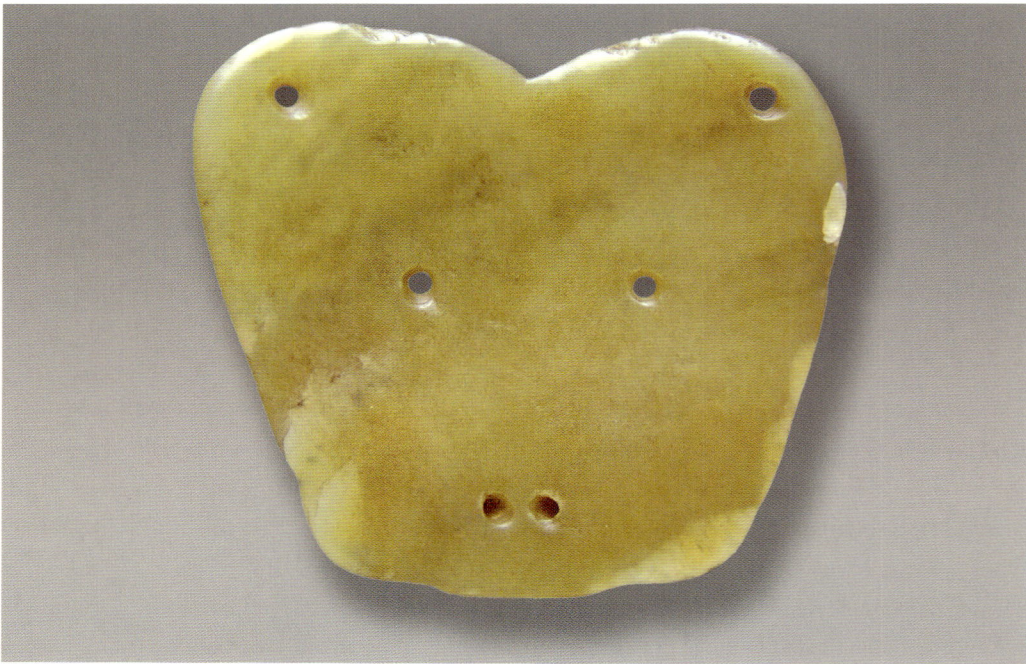

图 316 兽面佩之器背逆光观察
Picture 316 observing back of jade beast face pendant against light

此器正面全部石化，石化后的玉器表面褐色沁斑密集深入玉理，具丰富层次感。器背青色玉地除微细麻斑外，正面石化斑已漫延过来，与玉地和谐相连接。女神头部刮磨痕真实的反映出当时的制作工艺。

此器无论包浆、沁色、工艺充分展示了年代特征与绝对真实性。

The front side of this jade is completely petrified, and the brown spots on the surface went deep into the jade texture, having a rich sense of layering. Besides of the spots at the back, the petrified spots at the front has already stretched and connected with the jade. The caving traces at the head of jade goddess reflect the processing craft at that time.

The ware regardless of baojiang, infiltration color and the craft fully displayed the age characters and the absolute authenticity.

图 317 祖先女神　Picture 317 jade goddess

玉质：青玉　　　　Jade texture: blue-green jade

尺寸：高9.7cm　　Size: 9.7cm high

（听雨堂珍藏）　　(Collection of "rain-hear hall")

图 318 祖先女神器背

Picture 318 back of goddess jade

图 319 祖先女神头部放大

Picture 319 partial enlargement of goddess jade's head

213

图 320 块形玉兽
玉质：青玉
尺寸：高 14cm 宽 10.5cm
（听雨堂收藏）

Picture 320 jade coiled animal
Jade texture: blue-green jade
Size: 14cm high   10.5cm wide
(Collection of "rain-hear hall")

此器一面受沁较轻，而另面石化严重。这是因为尽管在相同条件下，但玉石生长纹理所形成瑕疵所分布于器身位置不同所致。石化严重一面可以明显看到曲线形玉石生长纹，受沁正是从这里开始的并向周边扩展的。

从局部放大可以看到，玉石由青色先行白化而后再石化，其间要经历漫长的过程方能逐渐完成。白化与石化间形成很自然的过渡。

One side of The jade was light infiltration, but on the other side it was serious petrifaction. The spots formed by jade's growth veins which distributed at different places, though they were in the same conditions. The serious petrifaction side appears obvious curve-shaped growing veins, where the infiltration started and then expanded around.

From the partial enlargement we can see that, the jade first became white from blue, and then being petrifaction. The period is quite long, and there would form a natural transition between the petrifaction and the white.

图 321 块形玉兽之另面
Picture 321 another side of jade coiled animal

图 322 玦形玉兽局部放大
Picture 322 partial enlargement of jade coiled animal

图 323 玦形玉兽局部放大
Picture 323 partial enlargement of jade coiled animal

图 324 玦形玉兽局部放大
Picture 324 partial enlargement of jade coiled animal

图 323 可见明显的绺裂线纹与浸蚀后所形成微小麻斑。

图 324 中间呈岛形青色玉地，因为质地较为坚密，因此尚未被浸蚀。但日久终会被蚕食。

图 325 较明显的玉石曲线生长纹，是玉器大面积石化的主要原因。

Picture 323 there are obvious tuft cracks and spots after being eroded.

Picture 324 The middle is island-shaped blue-green jade. It has not been eroded because of its dense texture. But it will be eroded in a long time.

Picture 325 there are obvious growing veins, which is the main reason of large area petrifaction of jade ware.

图 325 玦形玉兽局部放大
Picture 325 partial enlargement of jade coiled animal

图 326 玉鸟神
玉质：青玉
尺寸：高 14.5cm 宽 24.5cm
（听雨堂珍藏）

Picture 326 jade bird god
Jade texture: blue-green jade
Size: 14.5cm high   24.5cm wide
(Collection of "rain-hear hall")

玉鸟神受沁后全部石化。石化过程：玉器首先受到土壤中各种元素浸染形成不同色斑。然后在外因条件下逐渐钙化，此时玉质已变的较为松软。随之泥浆及其它物质浸入玉之肌理，并与玉相溶合、凝结而改变了玉石质地与颜色。石化了的玉器所发生的质变，完全改变了玉石特有的微透明特性。

The whole jade bird god was petrifaction after being infiltration. The process of petrifaction is that the jade first was dipped by kinds of elements in the soil and formed different spots. Then it gradually calcified in external conditions, and at that time the jade texture was becoming very soft. Then the mud and some other elements went into the jade and changed the jade's texture and color. The texture changes of the petrifaction jade completely changed the jade's little transparent character.

图 327 玉鸟神器背
Picture 327 The back of jade bird god

图 328 玉鸟神局部放大
Picture 328 partial enlargement of jade bird god

图 329 玉鸟神器背局部放大
Picture 329 partial enlargement of jade bird god's back

　　我们在鉴定红山文化古玉时,一定要注意器面细微变化。这些形如针刺状的麻斑，人为无法逼真仿制。

　　放大后的玉器表面，绺斑与微小孔洞是历经数千年逐渐浸蚀而成，其中饱含着岁月的苍桑。这就是古玉器的年代感。

　　鸟尾处受沁后绺裂脱落形成蚀斑。石斑处凹进，呈参差不齐状。

　　右边系挂孔上方可见明显刮磨痕。这是红山文化玉器加工典型特征。

We need to pay attention to slight changes on jade's surface when we appraise the jade ware. The spots like acupuncture-shaped can not be imitated by artificial.

On the enlargement of jade surface, the tuft cracks and little holes formed after being eroded thousands of years, which were filled with the vicissitudes of years.It was the age sense of ancient jade ware.

The tail of jade bird was infiltration first and then it formed cracks there. The place with spots is concaved, not uniform.

The hanging hole on the right has obvious caving traces. That is the Hongshan-culture jade's typical characters

图 330 兽面神器
玉质：青玉
尺寸：高 17.1cm 宽 7.5cm
（听雨堂珍藏）

Picture 330 jade beast face
Jade: blue–green jade
Size: 17.1cm high 7.5cm wide
(Collection of "rain–hear hall")

此器受沁后大部分石化。

无论石化程度如何严重，真古玉器皆有包浆。

包浆是衡定玉器真伪的重要条件。凡无包浆之玉器皆不能认定为真古玉器。

此器上端石化尤为严重，但仍看到厚重的包浆。

Most of this ware was petrifaction after being infiltration.

No matter how serious the petrifaction degree is, the real jade always has baojiang.

The baojiang is the important condition to judge the authenticity of a jade ware. The jade ware without baojiang we can not appraise it is a real ancient jade ware.

The upside of the jade ware was serious petrifaction, but we still can see its thick baojiang.

图 331 兽面神器器背
Picture 331 back of jade beast face

图 332 兽面神器局部放大

Picture 332　partial enlargement of jade beast face

图 333 兽面神器局部放大

Picture 333　partial enlargement of beast face jade

图 334 兽面神器局部放大
Picture 334　partial enlargement of beast face jade

图 335 兽面神器局部放大
Picture 335　partial enlargement of beast face jade

曾访问江南一位仿古玉高手，问及仿古玉何为最难，他答曰：包浆和沁色。

人为制作包浆仍以抛光为主，所发出的光泽呈"贼光"，有刺眼感。

还有人将制作完的玉器进行浸腊处理，然后再除去器表腊层制作假包浆。以此制作出的包浆手感滞涩，一旦退腊，原形毕露。

真实包浆看上去温润而亮泽，这是因为玉器表面微小麻斑能够吸收光线的原因。

通过局部放大图我们完全能够感受到沁色的多变性与神秘感。它就象一幅泼彩山水画，色相变幻气象万千。大自然的刀斧神功非人为所能做到。这就是真古玉器的真实感。

When was asked what's the most difficult in the imitation, a expert in south of Yangtze River answered: baojiang and the infiltration color.

Artificial produce baojiang is still polished mainly, the lustre presents " thief light", which is always offending to the eye.

Some people put the jade in the wax, and then removed the wax on the surface to make out fake baojiang. The baojiang made in this way feels unsmooth. It will reveal that the wax once removed.

The real baojiang looks mild and bright. That is because the spots on the jade surface can absorb the rays.

From the partial enlargement we can feel the variability and mystery of infiltration color. It likes a color splashed landscape painting. The color changes irregularly and it is majestic in all its variety. The superlative craftsmanship is not a person can imitate. That is the authenticity of the real ancient jade.

图 336 玉鸟神器
玉质：青玉
尺寸：高 10.4cm 宽 12.8cm
（ 听雨堂珍藏 ）
Picture 336 jade bird god
Jade texture: blue-green jade
Size: 10.4cm high 12.8cm wide
(Collection of "listening to rain" hall)

图 337 玉鸟神器局部放大
Picture 337 partial enlargement of jade bird god

图 338 玉鸟神器器背
Picture 338 partial enlargement of jade bird gods back

此器正面大部分石化，器背仍可见青色玉地与沁痕和蚀斑。沁象之所以真实与自然，因为其中内含着万千种沁色的无穷变化。这种变化，任何高科技手段都永远无法完成，这就是真古玉器的绝对真实性。

Most of jade front side was petrifaction, but we can see the blue-green jade texture on the back, the infiltration trace and the spots. The infiltration phenomenon is real and natural, that is because it includes kinds of infiltration color changes, which will never be imitated by any scientific methods. That is the authenticity of real ancient jade ware.

图 339 玉神祖
玉质：青玉
尺寸：高 12.3cm 宽 6.5cm
（听雨堂珍藏）

Picture 339 jade numen
Jade texture: blue-green jade
Size: 12.3cm high   6.5cm wide
(Collection of "rain-hear hall")

图 340 玉神祖另面
picture 340 another side of jade numen

　　玉神祖呈板状，周边浸蚀较重，已经白化，并逐渐向器中扩展。沁色过渡真实自然，包浆明显。根据自然受沁特征：由边缘向中间，由薄处向厚处之客观规律，鉴定此器为红山文化真古玉器。

The jade numen is plate-shaped, and its edge has been eroded seriously to whiten and gradually expanded to the center. The transition of infiltration color is real and natural, the baojiang is obvious. According to the natural rule, the objective laws that the jade was infiltration from the edge to the center, from the thick to the thin, we can appraise this jade is real Hongshan-culture ancient jade ware.

图 341 玉龙
玉质：青玉
尺寸：高 26cm
（听雨堂珍藏）

Picture 341 jade dragon
Jade texture: blue-green jade
Size: 26cm high
(Collection of "rain-hear hall")

　　玉龙为青玉质，受沁后则发生色变。因土壤湿度较大，其中所含微量酸碱或砌筑墓穴石灰岩质石材风化因而成沁。器表整体满布灰白斑，灰白斑过渡有致。自然绺裂真实，包浆明显，这些特征人为难以制作。因此鉴定此器为红山文化真古玉器。

　　The jade dragon is made of blue-green jade, but it changed its color after being infiltration.Because humidity of the soil is much big and the soil. Among it, the acid, alkali or limestone built grave because of weathering became into infiltration. The surface of the jade is covered with gray-white spots. The transition of these spots is natural, the cracks are real and the baojiang is obvious. All above characters is difficult to be imitated by artificial. So we appraise the jade is a real Hongshan-culture ancient jade ware.

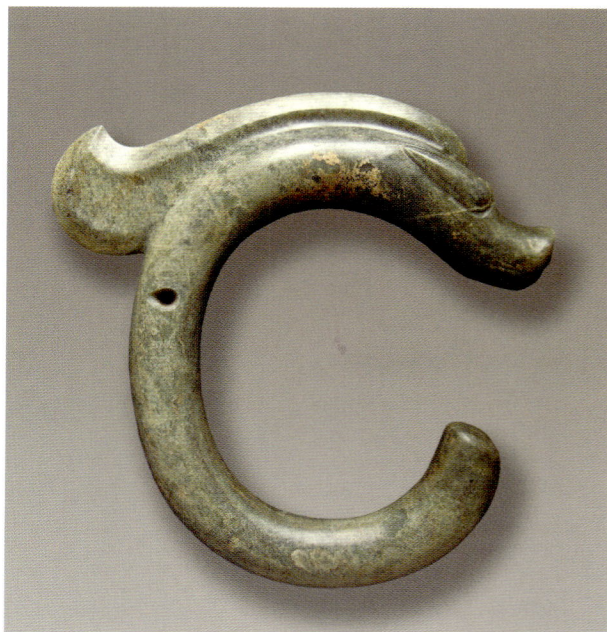

图 342 玉龙另面
Picture 342   another side of jade dragon

图 343 玉龙局部放大
Picture 343　partial enlargement of jade dragon

图 344 玉龙局部放大
Picture 344　partial enlargement of jade dragon

图 345 玉神祖
玉质：青玉
尺寸：高 8.9cm
（听雨堂珍藏）
Picture 345 jade numen
Jade texture: blue-green jade
Size: 8.9cm high
(Collection of "rain-hear hall")

这种玉质呈绿颜色的玉器极易钙化和石化。这与它们所含矿物成分恰与土壤中某种元素能够快速溶合发生化合反应有直接关系。

This kind of blue-green jade is extremely easy calcification and petrifaction. That has direct relationship with the mineral it contains could dissolve with some kind of element in the soil and take chemical reaction.

图 346 玉神祖器背
Picture 346 The back of jade numen

图 347 玉神面
玉质：青玉
尺寸：高 19.5cm 宽 14.2cm
（听雨堂珍藏）

Picture 347 jade god face
Jade texture: blue-green jade
Size: 19.5cm high 14.2cm wide
(Collection of "rain-hear hall")

已发生质变的玉神面边缘处尤重，并逐渐向内扩展，从而明显看出沁色的过渡性。

The edge of jade god face has had serious texture changes, which gradually expanded inside, so we can obviously see the transition of infiltration color.

图 348 玉神面器背
Picture 348 the back of jade god face

图 349 角形器
玉质：青玉
尺寸：长 19cm
（听雨堂珍藏）

Picture 349 horn-shaped jade
Jade texture: blue-green jade
Size: 19cm long
(Collection of "rain-hear hall")

玉器的受沁是逐步完成的。玉石在数十万年形成过程中自然存在绺、棉、瑕、璺，我谓之玉石的"中空现象"。土壤中的各种元素正是通过这些瑕疵而进入玉理，从而形成对玉质的浸染与破坏。我们对玉器的局部进行放大可看到，沁色的变化是缓慢完成的，并由于浸蚀逐渐形成微小的麻斑与孔洞。受沁严重处，玉质变的更为松软，甚至钙化后的玉器表面更利于颜色的快速进入，从而形成过渡性沁色。

The jade got infiltration step by step. The tuft, cotton, flaw and the crack in the jade for thousands of years we call it "hollow phenomenon". All kinds of elements in the soil went into the jade texture through them and destroyed the jade. The change of infiltration color is very slow, and the point we can see from the enlargement of the jade. In the serious infiltration place, the jade texture is more loose, even beneficial for the color to get in quickly, and finally formed transitional infiltration color.

图 350 角形器局部放大
Picture 350 enlargement of horn-shaped jade

图 351 玉龟

玉质：青玉

尺寸：高 16.5cm

（听雨堂珍藏）

Picture 351 jade turtle

Jade texture: blue-green jade

Size: 16.5cm high

(Collection of "rain-hear hall")

229

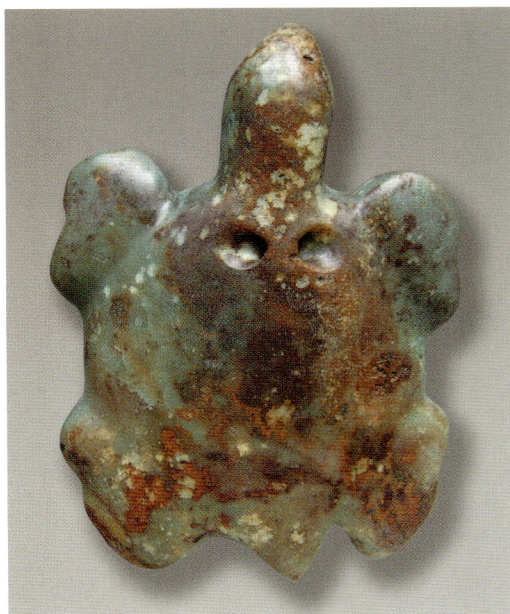

图 352 玉龟背部

Picture 352 back of jade turtle

玉龟受沁后沁色变化十分丰富。尤其铁红色，错落有致分布于器身多部位，看起来真实而自然，具有典型的统一性、完整性与过渡性。从系挂孔处可见沁色直入玉石肌骨，又从局部放大可见沁色的变化过程与浸蚀严重处所形成的孔洞。这些特征是人为永远无法做到的，因此我们鉴定此器为红山文化古玉真品。

The color change of jade turtle is rich after being infiltration. The iron-red color distributes different places of the jade, look real and natural and has typical integrity, unify and transition. The infiltration color directly went into hanging hole, and from the enlargement we can see the infiltration color transition and holes at the seriously infiltration place. The characters can never be imitated by artificial, so we appraise the jade is a real Hongshan-culture ancient jade ware.

图 353 系挂孔处局部放大
Picture 353 enlargement of hanging hole

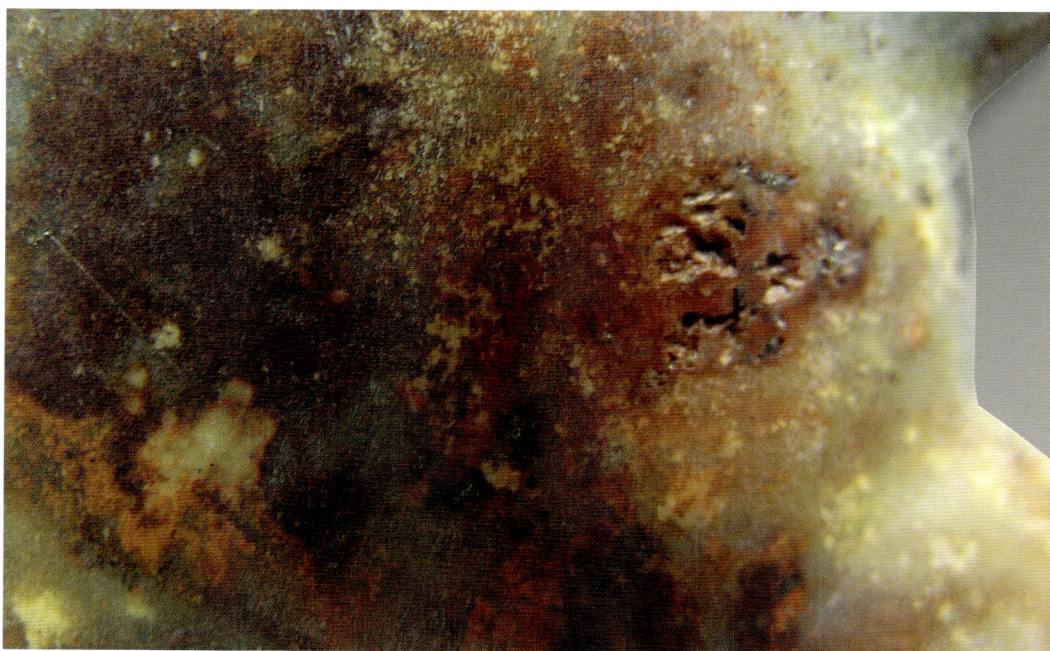

图 354 器背局部放大后所见蚀孔
Picture 354 enlargement of jade turtle□ back hole

图 355 玉祖

玉质：青玉

尺寸：长 24.5cm

（听雨堂珍藏）

Picture 355 Jade Zu

Jade texture: blue-green jade

Size: 24.5cm long

(Collection of "rain-hear hall")

　　玉祖多处受沁形成石化斑，这是由于玉石局部存在中空现象所致。玉石最弱点，正是玉器受沁最重处。

　　石化斑的形成，必须首先完成钙化，然后土浆随之渗入玉理而凝结并相互交织，从而让玉性变成石性，随之失去透明度。

　　石化斑同样存在过渡性，这是自然完成沁象之特征。

Some parts of ancestral jade have petrified spots, which formed because there was space inside. The thinnest point the jade having is just the most serious infiltration place.

The petrifaction spots formed after the calcification. The soil went deep into the jade texture and then interweaved with the jade. Finally the jade texture became stone texture, lost its transparency.

The petrifaction spots also have a transition, which is the character of being infiltration naturally.

图 356 玉祖局部放大

Picture 356　partial enlargement of Jade Zu

图 357 玉祖局部放大

Picture 357 partial enlargement of Jade Zu

图 358 玉神面
玉质：青玉
尺寸：高 7.3cm 宽 8.4cm
（听雨堂收藏）

Picture 358 jade god face
Jade texture: blue-green jade
Size: 7.3cm high 8.4cm wide
(Collection of "rain-hear hall")

　　从玉神面正、背两面沁色来看，色入肌理、五彩纷呈，人为不能做成。颇具统一性、完整性、过渡性之受沁特征，属大开门之器，因此我们鉴定为红山古玉真品。

　　玉神面器背系佩孔采用锥形钻低速对钻，呈马蹄形。

　　钻具表面较粗糙，添加粗颗粒解玉砂磨削而成。孔壁处可见螺旋纹，这是红山文化古玉钻孔最常见加工工艺。

Seeing infiltration color from both sides of jade god face, the color goes deep into the jade texture and the color is rich, which can not be imitated by artificial. The jade has the characters of integrity and unification, so it's a grand jade ware. We appraise this is a real Hongshan-culture ancient jade ware.

The hanging hole at the back of jade god face was drilled to U-shape at low speed.

The surface of drilling tool is rough and the coarse pellets were added into the drilling tool to make U-shape. We can see the whorl at the hole. That is the normal processing craft to drill holes on the Hongshan-culture jade ware.

图 359 玉神面局部特写

Picture 359 special enlargement of jade god face

图 360 玉神面器背钻孔放大

Picture 360 enlargement of hole on jade god face　back

图 361 玉神面器背

Picture 361 back of god face jade

Real Ancient Jade Appraisal

图 362 玉龙

玉质：青玉

尺寸：高 41cm

（听雨堂珍藏）

Picture362 jade dragon

Jade texture: blue-green jade

Size: 41cm high

(Collection of "rain-hear hall")

　　玉龙受土壤中多种元素所浸蚀，器身发生明显色变与质地变化。

　　沁色深入玉石肌理，而且过渡自然，整体保持完整、统一与和谐，非人为所能仿做。龙体下部可见依玉石生长纹沁成钙化斑，沁象真实自然，无人能够局部仿制出来。钙化斑偏上处又可见逐渐白化痕迹，从各种迹象分析，发生钙化处皆为玉石生长层中空石璺。

The jade dragon was eroded by many elements in the soil and its body has had obvious colorful and texture changes.

The color went deep into the jade texture, and the transition is natural. The whole remains integrity, unification and harmony, which can not be imitated. On the downside of jade dragon we can see calcified spots along with the growth veins, and the infiltration phenomenon is real and natural. We can also see the white traces at the upside of calcified spots, occur calcification, it is jade growing layer hollow stone and crack.

红山文化古玉鉴定

Hogshan-cultural ancient jade appraisal

图 363 玉龙之另面

Picture 363   another side of jade dragon

图 364 玉龙钙化处局部放大

Picture 364   partial enlargement of calcification

图 365 双联璧
玉质：青玉
尺寸：高 6.5cm
（听雨堂珍藏）

Picture 365 double joined jade
Jade texture: blue-green jade
Size: 6.5cm high
(Collection of "rain-hear hall")

玉器长时期浸泡于水中所形成之沁象为水沁。因水中含有微量酸、碱或其它元素，所以受沁的玉器多在器面结一层白膜，严重者逐渐钙化并出现孔洞。

从双联璧另面我们可以看到，其边缘处明显受沁严重，并形成由外到内的沁色过渡变化，这些特征完全符合自然受沁科学规律。

When the jade has been soaked in water for a long time, it will form a different infiltration phenomenon, which it is called "water infiltration". Because the water includes micro acid, alkali or other elements, the jade always has a piece of white membrane on the surface and if more serious, it may gradually calcify and appear holes.

From the other side of the double joined jade, we can see that its edge was obvious infiltration seriously, and the infiltration color has a transition change from outside to inside. These characteristics completely conform to the nature scientific rules.

图 366 双联璧另面
Picture366 another side of double joined jade

图 367 玦形玉兽

玉质：青玉

尺寸：高 14cm

（听雨堂珍藏）

Picture 367 jade coiled animal

Jade texture: blue-green jade

Size: 14cm high

(Collection of "rain-hear hall")

　　此器受水沁后，仍保持温润厚重包浆。大面积的水浸白垢几乎覆盖全器，这些白垢已深入玉之肌理形成沁后白化斑。这与人为酸蚀制作皮壳不同，凡经过酸蚀玉器经盘化可退掉，然后复出。而水浸白化斑永不能因盘化而除掉。

　　水沁白斑深浅层次变化十分丰富，人为酸蚀则呆板。

This jade still remains the mild thick baojiang after being infiltration in the water. The large area of white limescale almost covers the entire jade ware, which already went deep into the jade texture and formed the white spots. That is different from the man-made scale. The jade which soaked in acid will fade after being boiled in water, and then return. However, the water soaked white spots will never fade.

The depth level changes of water soaked white spots are very rich, but the man-made ones eroded by acid are quite stiff.

图 368 玦形玉兽另面
Picture 368 another side of jade coiled animal

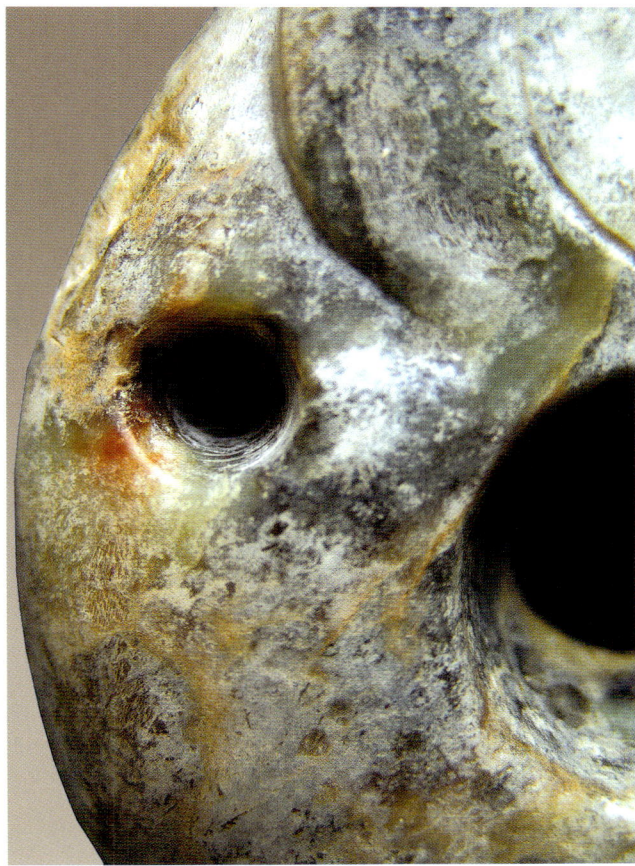

图 369 玦形玉兽局部放大
Picture 369 partial enlargement of jade coiled animal

图 370 玉鸟
玉质：青玉
尺寸：高 12.1cm 宽 10.8cm
（听雨堂珍藏）

Picture370 jade bird
Jade texture: blue-green jade
Size: 12.1cm high 10.8cm wide
(Collection of "rain-hear hall")

图 371 玉鸟器背
Picture 371 back of jade bird

玉鸟长期受水浸泡，玉质已发生严重质变。由于水中含有一定酸碱成分，给玉器表面罩上一层深厚浆膜，状如渍垢。

玉器的表面抛光尽管能够一定程度抵御有害元素的浸蚀，但受沁严重时完全可以掏空玉理，甚至整体石化。

The nature of jade bird has already had serious texture change because of being soaked in the water for a long time. The water contains acid and alkali and they form a thick membrane on the surface of the jade ware, like the limescale.

The surface polishing of the jade can resist the erosion by the harmful elements in certain degree. But when the jade is infiltration seriously, the jade texture may be pulled out to empty completely, even is petrifaction entirely.

图 372 玦形玉兽

玉质：青玉

尺寸：高 16cm 宽 10.8cm

（听雨堂珍藏）

Picture 372 jade coiled animal

Jade texture: blue-green jade

Size: 16cm high　10.8cm wide

(Collection of "rain-hear hall")

图 373 玦形玉兽另面

Picture 373　another side of jade coiled animal

此器两面沁象一致。青色玉质由于受土壤中所含生石灰、微量酸、碱所浸蚀，玉器表面出现变化较为复杂的钙化斑。这些斑痕完全依玉石生长纹理而形成深浅不同变化，这种变化真实而自然。白中透青，青中有白，青、白中可透析出多种色标。这些错综复杂魔术般的颜色变化与符合年代特征的加工工艺及厚重的包浆直接展现了这件器物的苍桑年轮。这些沁后特征人为所不能仿，这就是真实感。

The infiltration phenomenons on both sides are the same. It came out complicated calcification spots on the surface because the soil contains acid, alkali and lime. The trace is different along with the jade growth veins, the change is real and natural. Blue out of white, white out of blue, there can be seen some different colors out of blue and white. The magic color change, the processing craft, and the thick baojiang directly displayed the age feeling of jade. The infiltration characters can not be imitated by artificial, and that is the authenticity.

图 374 天地神佩
玉质：青玉
尺寸：高 7.2cm 宽 16.2cm
（听雨堂珍藏）

Picture 374 compound jade baldric for heavn and earth
Jade texture: blue-green jade
Size: 7.2 cm high 16.2 cm wide
(Collection of "rain-hear hall")

此器为青玉所制，受生石灰所沁出现大面积白化斑。器两面沁象一致，具统一性、完整性、沁色的过渡性等鉴定古玉之要点。

一件玉器在相同环境与条件下受沁有轻重，源自玉石生成之质地。玉石含棉、绺处是各种元素进入点，并逐渐扩散，漫延，因而出现明显的沁色过渡，这是人为所不能完成的。

仔细观察玉器表面所形成的白化斑，我们可以从中看到沁色的细微过渡变化，正是这些统一为白色的深浅无穷变化，饱含着岁月的延伸。可以简单的认为，凡人为无法完成之沁象，则为真沁。

The jade was made of blue-green jade; it came out large area of white spots after being infiltration by lime. On both sides of jade, the infiltration phenomenon is the same, integrity, and unity, which is the key point to appraise the jade.

Infiltration phenomenon is not the same even on a jade in the same environment and condition, lighter or deeper. The jade contained cotton and crack as the entrance point, which expanded outside and formed the transition of infiltration color, which can not be imitated by artificial.

Observing the white spots on the jade's surface, we can see the transition of infiltration color. It is the endless depth changes of white show extend of age. We can simply think that the real infiltration is the infiltration can not be imitated by artificial .

图 375 神佩之另面
Picture 375　another side of compound jade baldric for heavn and earth

图 376 神佩局部放大
Picture 376 partial enlargement of compound jade baldric for heavn and earth

此器已全部钙化，局部并被赭石色元素所浸染，但仍能看到淡青色玉地。

在钙化成鸡骨白色的器表，我们从中所看到的并不是完全的纯白色，而是错综复杂的多种颜色相交织。这是因为玉器在钙化之前，首先被其它多种金属元素与非金属元素所浸染，然后才形成钙化。此器沁色过渡有致，包浆明显，给人以强烈自然真实感。

The jade has been calcification completely. It was partly soaked by brown element, but we still can see the light blue jade.

What we see at the white surface which caused by calcification is not the absolute white, it is a mix color of kinds of colors instead. Before the jade was calcification, the jade was soaked by many kinds of mental elements and nonmetallic elements, and then it was calcified. The jade has disordered transition, obvious baojiang, and show the people strong natural authenticity.

图 378 块形玉兽之另面

Picture 378 another side of jade coiled animal

红山文化玉器存世数量

Quantity of Hongshan-Culture Jade Wares

红山文化玉器存世数量

　　红山文化玉器到底存世有多少？这是多种学科专家都在分析研究的问题。有考古学家认为，红山文化玉器大约存世 300 件左右。这 300 件分别为：文物部门考古发掘及所征集的约 100 件，散失在民间的约 100 件，历经数千年被收藏的约 100 件。尽管考古学家这一结论不知以什么科学依据所推定，但"300"件的理论，至今仍然影响和干扰着国家文物管理及相关领域一些人的思想，并因此致使我国在红山文化研究方面进度缓慢，甚至停滞不前，处于一种非常尴尬的境地。这一思想观念不改变，中国红山文化的研究工作势必因此而受阻，将来历史给我们的评价只能是极大的遗憾与悲哀。

　　试用一道最简单的算术题计算：红山文化距今 5000 — 6000 年，这一时期前后历经 1000 年。如果完全按手工磨制，一年制作一件玉器计算，当有 1000 件玉器问世。试问，在偌大个地域，众多的部落必须到只有一人可以制作玉神器？尽管疑问种种，但答案却是肯定的，红山文化玉器的存世数量决不是 300 件。这不是考古学家思想保守的问题，而是一些人完全缺失正常的思维方式和科学的判断理念。

　　要正确的计算出红山文化玉器的真正存世数量，必须以历史唯物主义的观点，认真分析这一历史时期先民们的宗教意识、生产力的发展、分布的区域及民族特点，并在考古发现中寻找科学依据。

　　我们已经知道，在距今 7000 — 8000 年查海文化新石器时代的早期，我们的祖先就已经出现爱玉、崇玉、葬玉的习惯。到红山文化时期，人们已不再将玉器作为饰物所佩带，而是随着原始宗教意识的产生和发展，已将玉器进一步升华为神器。崇神与敬神，已成为精神领域至高无上的意愿，从而产生神器使用极大的广泛性。不但上层权贵，就是平民百姓同样企盼得到神灵的保护。从辽西牛河梁红山墓发掘情况可以印证这一点，除中心大墓中所葬玉器较多外，其他葬墓中都或多或少葬有玉器，只是数量不同而已。因此我们说，红山文化时期人们对玉神器的普遍需要，完全决定着当时玉器的生产和以后的存世数量。

　　我们已经从红山文化玉器的制作工艺客观分析出，这一时期应该已经掌握了冶炼技术，并有红铜或青铜类工具问世，并制作了以木为框架结构的专门用于玉器加工的设备和工具，已形成手工业作坊生产模式。制玉设备的问世，不但大大的提高了生产力，而且造就了一支专门制作玉器的专业技术队伍。由于摆脱了完全靠手工制作玉器的落后局面，所制作的玉器无论是质量还是数量都得到很大提升。这些大量玉神器不但按照个人需要用于佩带，而且还将一些大型神器提供给寺庙、祭坛或者家庭用于供奉和祭祀活动。从已发现的牛河梁宗庙和大型祭坛遗址可以充分说明，这一时期以部落或部族为单位的宗教活动应该相当频繁。并形成一定规模。玉器已成为祭祀活动中必不可少、具有重要意义、代表某种理念的神灵为人们所崇拜。

　　考古学家将红山文化分为前红山、后红山，红山前和红山后。而我们所见类同于红山文化器形和工艺特征玉器皆统称为红山文化玉器。从已发现的红山文化玉器地域来看，除辽宁西部，内蒙古的东部及临近河北一带皆有红山文化玉器出土以外，近年来，在吉林和黑龙江省部分地区也有红山文化玉器面世。从地理特征看，红山文化存在地皆为水源充足，树茂草丰之处，并始终未离开大辽河流域，因而红山文化被称为草原文化和游牧民族文化。如此广大地域分布的红山文化形成了北方地区特有的文化类型。从大量来源于民间的红山文化玉器信息说明，辽西牛河梁只是这一地区的政治、经济、文化中心，而不能错误认为这就是红山文化的全部。一些末被考古部门发现和发掘的红山文化遗址应该仍有大量存在。

从已知所发现红山文化玉器地域来看，横贯辽宁、吉林、黑龙江、内蒙、河北。而我们将红山文化中心锁定在牛河梁地区，显然就此而论定红山文化玉器存世数量是远远不够的。从目前考古发掘和民间发现的红山文化玉器的数量来看，早已远远超出300件，甚至3000件。因此说，300件的理论，难免让人感觉荒谬至极。

红山文化葬墓大都选择在山坡处，这里形成面积不等的平台，人们称此为"台地"。葬墓距地面较浅，墓穴窄小，周边多以石块或石板砌成，上面以石板或石条封顶，然后夯土，并在土层上面堆积石块，因此我们称此为"积石　"。

由于积石　位于山坡处，墓穴较浅，所以常在暴雨、山洪后暴露于地面。在农业学大寨年代，因修筑梯田和农民垦荒不时捡拾到红山文化玉器。又因为积石琢具有特明显的记号，这给不法分子盗墓创造了有利的条件。因此我们说，由于一些特殊原因，散失民间的红山文化玉器已远远超过考古发现玉器数量。

辽宁考古研究所对辽西牛河梁地区的考古发掘不过几十人，数年来文博部门，从民间所征集到的红山文化玉器也不过几十件。要知道，在如此广阔的红山文化分布区域，在每天都接触土地的无数农民人群中和历经数千年朝代更迭的收藏，您不可能准确计算出红山文化玉器的真正存世数量。由于国家体制和相关文物政策问题，这些散失的文物必然流向市场，流向收藏家或者流向境外。

由于部分专家对红山文化玉器存世数量的误导和不加扼制的造假成风，从而造成文物管理、历史研究、市场流通和收藏领域人们的思想混乱。也正因为人们盲目的相信了某些专家们的权威性，给我们对红山文化玉器的征集、收藏、研究、鉴定工作造成了许多障碍。准确把握红山文化玉器的真正存世数量，对于我们的收藏与研究都具有十分重要的意义。

在过去那些年，笔者经常与辽宁考古研究所名誉所长、我国著名红山文化研究专家孙守道先生交往，并进行有关红山文化古玉器方面的交流与探讨，其中相互时常有激烈辩论，尤其就文物部门民间征集可以认定为真，而对民间收藏品多持怀疑态度这一问题提出许多不同看法。辩论中也曾试图否定并非正式发掘孙先生亲自认定的"中华第一龙"之真实性，以此想改变孙守道先生之观点和认识。

红山文化真古玉器到底存世多少？除国内、外博物馆现有藏品外，对散失在民间的红山文化玉器需要进行全面的普查。对尚未发现、发掘红山文化葬墓遗存玉器数量的科学估算，这是一项十分艰巨的调研工程，除国家行为外，其他任何个人将无能为力。

Quantity of Hongshan–Culture Jade wares

How many Hongshan–Cultural jade wares exist in China? Experts in many fields try to analyze and study this issue. Some experts declared that the existing quantity of Hongshan–cultural jade is no more than 300 pieces, in which about 100 pieces were dug up and collected by archaeological departments, about 100 pieces were lost in folk, and about 100 pieces were owned by collectors. Though we don't know the scientific basis of this conclusion, it still affects and disturbs the administration of the cultural relics and minds of some people in the related fields. For this reason, the research on Hongshan culture is slowly progressing, even in stagnant situation, which is embarrassing. It would be a tremendous sadness that foreign research level would exceed that at home if this situation continued.

Hongshan–culture is far from 5,000 to 6,000 years ago, covering about 1,000 years. Let us calculate quantity of the jade wares with a very simple way: supposing that the jade is completely hand made and produced one piece annually, there would be 1,000 pieces totally. But, in the vast area which Hongshan culture covered, was there only one man having skills of gemstone production in each generation? Though many questions still remained, I'm sure that the quantity of Hongshan–culture jade is absolutely not 300 pieces. The above conclusion was drawn not because the archaeologists are conservative but with subnormal sense and unscientific concept.

To calculate the exact quantity of Hongshan–culture jade objects, we must analyze the religion and productivity of ancestor in this period, as well as environments of the region and archaeological findings with historical materialistic eyes.

We know as early as 7,000 to 8,000 years ago in Xinyue Culture period, Hemudu Culture period, Yangshao Culture period, the ancestors had loved jade, adored jade and used jade in grave furnishings. Till Hongshan Culture period, with the development of religion, jade was used not only for the wearing, but also used as cult instrument. Both high–ranking members and commons esteemed and worshiped god extremely. This widespread god–worship requires a wealth of jade productions, which can be proved by the findings from tombs at Niuheliang site in the west of Liaoning province. Gems could be found in every tomb. In the central grave jade wares were even more. Therefore, we can say jade production then and the quantity of existing jade nowadays depend on the social needs about jade at that time.

Through analyzing the craftsmanship of jade carving, we can say that not only bronze and red brass metallurgy was mastered by our forebears, but also mood–framed equipments and special tools were created. They also built jade producing workshops. Those applications not only improved productivity greatly but also made a special jade–making team. Therefore, the quantity and quality of jade production were enhanced remarkably. Those large numbers of gems were not only for personal wearing, but also for family, temple or sacrificial altar oblation or sacrifice activities. The religious temples in Niuheliang and larger scale sacrificial altars tell us that tribe religious activities were frequent and large scaled at that time. Jade objects had been adored as cult instruments in sacrifice activities at that time.

Archaeologist divided Hongshan Culture into four periods: pre–Hongshan Culture, post–Hongshan Culture, early stage of Hongshan Culture and late stage of Hongshan Culture. All gemstones charactering similar Hongshan Culture style and processing are collectively called Hongshan Culture jade here. Except the west of Liaoning province, east of Inner Mongolia and the region near Hebei province, Hongshan Culture jade objects were also found in Jilin and Helongjiang province. Geographically, Hongshan Culture scattered on places rich in water, grass and trees. We still haven't found Hongshan–Culture jade out of the region of Liao River. So Hongshan Culture belongs to plain cultures or nomadic cultures. Hongshan Culture, which covers so large area in north area, formed its own unique northern culture style. The large gems collected from civilians suggest that Niuheliang of Liaoxi was the political, economical and cultural center of this region, but not center of Hongshan Culture. A lot of Hongshan Cultural relics should still remain under the earth.

Therefore, we are not sure how many pieces of Hongshan Culture jade exist in this world. Now there are much more than 300 pieces even reach to 3,000 pieces Hongshan Culture jade unearthed. So the conclusion that there is only 300 pieces Hongshan-Culture jade is obviously absurd.

Most of Hongshan-Culture tombs were built on hillsides. Form of the graves is like a platform over earth ground inches. Thus we call the tombs Plat Graveyards. The graves are normally shallow and narrow; each inside wall is stone-built. Tombs were also fenced by stones around and covered by stone bars or stone laths, on which soil tightly covered, and then some stones piled again over the soil. We named such kind of grave as Stone Mound.

The shallow Stone Mounds were easily exposed in the air by storms or flood, so farmers picked up some Hongshan Culture jade wares from time to time in mountains in 1960s. Remarkable sign of the Mounds also attracted ghouls. Therefore we say total of the gems should far more than archaeologists' findings.

There are no more than dozens of workers assigned by Archaeological Research Institute who are working at Niuheliang of Liaoxi. Their Hongshan-Culture jade collection is not more than dozens too. It's impossible to calculate the exact existing because jade objects picked up by local farms are beyond the number. Thanks to national systems and policies on cultural relics, those gems must flow into market, to collectors or out of our country inevitably.

Both the experts' wrong presumption on Hongshan-Culture jade quantity and the flood fake jade contribute to the mess of heritage management, history study, market circulation and collection field. Blind trust of some authorities baffled piece together and collection, study and research and appraisal of Hongshan Culture jade. Thus exact quantity of Hongshan Culture jade existing is significant for both collection and research.

In the past years, I exchanged and discussed frequently with Shou-Dao Sun, famous expert on Hongshan Culture as well as Honorary Director of Liaoning Archaeological Research Institute, and learned a lot from him. Many intense debates also occurred between us, especially I brought up many different opinions that the wares in non-governmental circles collected by cultural or historical relics department can be regarded as real one, but they took doubtful attitudes for the collections of non-governmental circles. I once tried to negate the reality of "Chinese foremost jade dragon" presumed by Mr. Sun that not excavated officially, and for this to change the opinion and cognition of Mr. Sun.

How many Hongshan-Culture ancient jades are there? Except domestic, outside museum existing holdings, we also must make a correct estimation of the quantity of real Hongshan-Culture jade in society. We should scientifically estimate the graves of Hongshan Culture that we still haven't discovered and excavated, which is an extremely difficulty research works, except the behavior of nations, and any others are not able to do this.

图 379 牛河梁第二地点一号冢 21 号墓

Picture 379 The No.21tomb from the No.1 stone mound at the No.2 location of Niuheliang

红山文化古玉器究竟存世有多少？有考古专家说，只有300件。这一错误论断数年来一直影响和干扰着我国文化艺术领域文博界上层人士、专业科研人员、国内外收藏家和鉴赏家们的正常思维，甚至很多人不加分析，信以为真。致使国家在红山文化研究方面进程缓慢。

1972年，辽宁省文物考古研究所在开展文物大普查时，仅在辽宁西部八县即发现红山文化遗址上百处，内蒙古敖汉旗发现400余处。牛河梁所发现的20余处红山文化遗址，只不过是这一地域性中心，而并非整个北方地区红山文化的中心。从红山文化的早期到晚期，从黑龙江、吉林到辽西、内蒙、河北局部地区，象牛河梁这样的中心可能还有很多，无人给以确切统计。内蒙古东部地区至少八个旗皆发现红山文化玉器，究竟还有多少处红山文化遗址未被发现？遗存多少玉器？中国的考古学家们二十余年来并没有给出科学合理的答案。

牛河梁第二地点一号冢21号墓中发掘出20件红山文化玉器。象这样的大墓相信决非一例。因此在历经数千年时间里散失在民间的红山文化玉器，应该决不是考古学家所估量的数字。

How many Hongshan cultural ancient jade ware does there exist on earth? Archaeology expert says, has only 300 wares. This wrong inference always affects and disturbs the normal thought of professional researcher, domestic and international collector in the cultural artistic field museum upper circles, and connoisseurs of our country of cultural relic for several years, even others do not analyze to believe it is real, which cause the study process of whole country depelop slowly in Hongshan cultural research aspect.

In 1972 the Liaoning province archaeology research place of cultural relic develop the big general investigation of cultural relic, In Liaoning west Ba country there was discovered over hundred Hongshan-culture sites, and in Mongolia Ao Han Qi over four hundred places. The over twenty Hongshan-culture sites discovered in Niuheliang just is the region center, and not the center of all the north area of Hongshan-culture center. From the early period of Hongshan culture to late, and from Heilongjiang, Jilin to Liao Xi , Mongolia and Hebei local areas, the center like Niuheliang is still probably a lot and no one can give definite statistics. Mongolia eastern area still have eight flags at least to discover the Hongshan cultural jade ware. How many Hongshan-culture sites has there not discovered on earth? How many jade wares had there left? Chinese archaeologists do not give the answer with reasonable science for more than 20 years.

There has unearthed twenty jade wares of Hongshan cultural in the No.21 tomb from the No.1 stone mound at the No.2 location. We believe that such big tomb is just not one. Therefore in thousands of years the Hongshan-culture jade ware was lost in non-governmental circles should not the amount of archaeologist estimating.

图 380 玉人 （牛河梁 16 号墓出土）

尺寸：高 18.6cm

Picture 380 The jade human figure (unearthed in the
No. 16 tomb of Ninheliang)

Size: 18.6cm high

红山文化玉器到底有多少种造型？对这个问题我们需要进行科学的分析和有待于今后进一步发现，目前不敢妄自断定。

数年前，考古专家曾声称：红山文化玉器不可能有玉人存在。直到几年前考古发掘出土了玉人，这些权威人士才默不作声。

我们鉴定红山文化玉器，要就物论物，而不以己所未见为理由给以否定。做一个历史唯物主义者，要客观地分析问题和认识问题。你所未见到的，不能证明此物客观不存在。

How many kind modelings do Hongshan-culture jade ware have? For this problem, we need to carry out scientific analysis and remain to discover in the future that now can not be concluded easily.

Several years ago, archaeology expert professed: Hongshan-culture jade ware is impossible to have the jade human figure. Until a few years ago there unearthed the jade human figure in archaeological studies, these authorities are just silent to not make sound.

We appraise Hongshan-culture jade ware to discuss thing for thing, and not with the reason we not see to negate. Being a historical materialism to know problem and analysis problem objectively. What you do not see, can not prove that this thing is objective to not exist.

红山文化玉器收藏与辨伪

Collection and Identification of Hongshan-Culture Jade Articles

红山文化玉器收藏与辨伪

近年来，国内各地仿制红山文化玉器大肆泛滥，甚至在偏远的县城和山区都能够发现红山文化伪古玉的渗入。从本人所鉴定的古代玉器来源可以看出，"红山文化玉器"几乎已经遍及全国每个角落。

由于红山文化玉器特有的艺术魅力和悠久的历史，尤其被人们所喜爱和收藏。许多刚刚涉足红山文化玉器收藏的朋友，因缺少对红山文化玉器足够的了解，淘宝心情强烈，自认为有一些鉴识经验，因此产生极大的盲动性，试图在成堆的红山文化仿制玉器中侥幸挑选出真品，显然这是不现实的。还有部分人，为避免上当受骗，求助"专家"帮助掌眼，但有些"专家"由于自身经验不足，或徒有虚名，给收藏者带来不小的经济损失。有极个别人，只对红山文化耳闻或略有所知，当在古玩市场发现大量仿制红山古玉后，自以为自己第一个发现了新大陆，不问青红皂白大肆收购。目前社会上还存在一些自称为红山文化玉器鉴赏家、收藏家、行家，以著书立说为手段，或利用自己与古玉鉴定不相关的头衔、知名度，以正人君子面目出现，极力向那些刚刚步入红山文化玉器收藏者兜售自己从古玩市场搜罗来的仿制品，从中牟利。其实，这是一种严重的诈骗行为。所见最多的是一些不法商人，编造各种离奇故事以证明为出土真古玉器，蒙骗了很多收藏者。

奉劝喜爱红山文化玉器收藏的朋友，如果你不想走更多的收藏弯路，更少的交纳学费，就必须亲自对红山文化进行认真的研究，尤其在玉器真伪鉴识方面更要下大力气。同时，也不要轻信一些自称为专家或行家人的错误引导或不负责任的鉴定。要知道，我国在法律方面还有许多盲区。我们有的专家可以信口开河，随心所欲，正确与否，他们并不负法律责任。

目前，古玩市场作伪红山文化玉器之所以大肆泛滥，是因为我们在这一领域并没有进行打假，而且出售者也不可能给收藏者注明"仿制品"的标识。所以我们的收藏家就必须考虑保护自身利益，练就正确识别真伪的火眼金睛，学会在古玩市场这一苍茫大海中鉴真辨伪。要做到这一点并不难，只要我们对真品和赝品进行认真比较分析，从细微处入手，则不难看出真、伪两者之间所存在的根本的差别。搞收藏、交学费在所难免，但有很多人交了非常昂贵的学费却仍然徘徊在误区中，这就很不正常。我所知道个别人，辛苦收藏了几十件甚至近百件红山文化玉器，说起来却从来没有目睹或真正接触过红山文化玉器真品。没有亲身感受，谈何收藏？辨伪必须通真，这是必由之路，没有其他任何捷径，对收藏、鉴赏家都是如此。

多年前，本人到过自称为"相当于最高法院"，具"最终判决权"的国家级鉴定机构，请他们鉴定古玉器，在场多位"专家"竟然连玉和石都分不清，还欲盖弥彰说："现在是高科技时代，利用高科技手段，任何古玉都可以高仿出来。"此话乍听起来似乎有些道理，但仔细分析，则不然。从我们所掌握的情况来看，目前我国尚没有任何科研机构或较大型企业，动用高科技设备和专业技术人员，专门从事古代玉器的仿制。而事实是，他们所说的"高仿"古玉器，仍然不过是采用土办法造出来的，其中并不存在高科技成份。所谓"高科技"，只是人们的主观想象和为知识贫乏所找的一种借口。

红山文化玉器种类很多，但却始终保持它自身明显特征。仿制者尽管依照造型、玉材、工艺、沁象努力做到更逼真，尽量不被人识破，但仍然避免不了还会露出许多蛛丝马迹。这些破绽对于初学者来说看起来可能比较困难，而对于富有经验的人来说，则很容易看穿。经验来自于实践，来自于长时期不间断对真品和赝品进行反复认真分析的科学总结。

可以明确一点，无论作伪者采用何种方法与手段，所仿制的红山文化玉器永远都无法达到可以乱真的程度。因为，真正的红山文化玉器历经数千年，由于历史沉淀所形成的多方面特征，永远不可能被仿制的天衣无缝。目前所见仿制红山文化玉器只不过使用现代化工原料进行浸蚀与染色，根本不存在高科技成份。而且由于作伪者急功近利，不能完全掌握红山文化古玉之真蒂，只能靠一知半解仿其形，却不能仿其神韵，仿其沁象。

一、仿制红山文化玉器的用材特征

从考古发现红山文化玉器的玉种、玉质、及玉器受沁后颜色变化来看，所用玉材仍然有一定的规律性和局限性。而我们所见仿制品，不但玉材种类繁杂，而且很多玉质完全与真正红山文化玉器的玉种严重不符。仿制者所用玉材，与所在地区有直接关系。如辽南地区邻近岫岩，所以仿制者多用岫岩玉。辽西和内蒙部分地区盛产玛瑙，所以常见很多玛瑙仿制器。南方有些地区产一种多棉绺黄色玉，所以这些地方就有许多黄色仿红山文化玉器大量出现于市场。前些年，还有人从缅甸引进一种玉质较软，温润细腻、色泽艳丽的淡黄色玉用以仿制红山文化玉器。在红山文化出土玉器中尽管没有发现纯白色质地玉器，但还是有些人用白玉仿制。近来又有许多合成绿松石红山文化仿制器光顾古玩市场。

玛瑙、黄玉、绿松石，这些材质玉器因为在红山文化出土玉器中并不多见，所以人们对其沁象知之甚少。因而许多收藏家不加分析，错把赝品当真品，一概收藏之。

目前我们所见仿红山文化玉器，多采用岫岩产原生沁玉石和真古残破玉斧等器进行加工和改制。原生沁玉石因距地表较浅，已存在沁象变化，又因其质地松软，容易在原有基础上做色，因此极具欺骗性。以残器改制，多为小件器物。为达到逼真效果多保留部分原生沁，所制作出的玉器因先天受沁，有熟化感，不易被察觉。有相当一部分人听信"专家"所说，确定红山文化玉器所用玉材皆为岫岩玉，认为凡岫岩玉制作红山文化玉器皆为真品，甚至以此作为认定真伪重要标准。有很多人按图索骥，凡与出版物图录相接近者，皆深信其真实性。其实并不然，从笔者看过的多部介绍红山文化玉器书籍图录中，发现其中大多数都是赝品，这无疑给收藏者以误导。最近又看到一部带有图片的红山文化古玉研究书，从头到尾，全书竟然无一件真品。作者真伪不辨，谈何收藏研究，所谓"传世"，完全在蒙骗人。

多年与红山文化玉器收藏家交流发现这样一个问题，很多人只重视玉器外表的完美，从而忽略玉器的真实性。玉质坚密，造型奇特，表面亮丽之玉器，成为众多收藏家争相收藏的目标。正是由于这种刻意追求，致使许多人误入歧途，因为达到十分完美的玉器毕竟极少。我们收藏红山文化玉器，首要考虑的是真实性，因为真实才是价值。反之，无论多么精美的仿制品，它也只是一件现代工艺品，远远失去我们收藏的真正意义。

二、仿制红山文化玉器的造型特征

近些年来，很多大件红山文化仿制玉器涌入市场，其造型古怪、神秘、夸张。并将玛雅文化、奥尔梅克文化玉石器造型揉和进红山文化。一些美术设计人员专门从事仿红山文化玉器的设计，更有别出心裁者在玉器上面镌刻象形文字，由于缺乏对中国历史文化的研究，这些伪红山文化玉器被一些收藏者视为珍宝。

最近几年，仿制红山文化玉器已形成专门企业生产。据了解，一些个体工厂成吨大批量从岫岩购进利于仿制古玉器的河漠玉，形成从设计、开片、磨制、抛光、做沁等一整套生产程序。这些企业很多在当地注册了的玉器厂。因为工商执法对此不打假，所以他们公开仿制不同历史时期的古玉器，尤其仿红山文化玉器已成为这些企业的主导产品。企业规模较大者拥有三四十名员工，由此可见每年伪古玉器的生产量。

由于一些较大型玉器制造厂的出现，红山文化玉器的仿制也由最初小型器向大型器发展。一些人与鸟、动物与人复合型圆雕玉器重达数十斤甚至上百斤。有人寄照片给我，说他所收藏玉龙重达百斤，可谓空前绝后。如此大型的红山文化玉器居然也会有人相信为绝对真品。可见人们的收藏观念意识还需要进一步端正。

目前，我们所见到的红山文化玉器仿制品的造型，绝大部分仍然以我们最常见的鸟、鹰、鸮、龙、玦形玉兽和片状的天地神器为主，有些也依图谱仿制其他一些器形。除此之外，仿制者凭空想象，杜撰了一些不伦不类、光怪陆离的奇特造型玉器，这些玉器多为圆雕可以站立或坐立的较大型玉器。奇特而神秘的造型，常常吸引那些对红山文化略有所知，在新奇中忽视真实性的人们。这种偏爱与收藏者所从事的职业有很大关系。当然也不排除极少数人，贪大求利，梦想着在一夜之间成为暴发户。凡抱有这种幻想的人，不管你有多大的冒险精神，也都还是一种侥幸。把经济利益放在首位，你永远都不会成为名符其实的收藏家和鉴赏家。

三、仿制红山文化玉器的工艺特征

红山文化玉器有它自身诸多工艺特征。由于历史的原因，现代人仍然无法依原来工艺将红山古玉仿制的更逼真。因为现代机械设备和工具的先进性已远远超越红山文化时期。能够快速旋转的机械动力，先进的切割与磨削工具已完全进入机械化和更科学化。因此与古老的木制框架为主体结构的加工机械，以手工磨制的工具，以脚踏或手摇为动力的加工手段相比，两者之间存在很多根本的不同。因此也就出现加工工艺特征的许多不同。红山文化玉器仿制者们虽然在加工时采用了一些老工艺，尽量做到与红山真品相一致。但由于片面追求利润和提高产品数量，不会完全做到全部采用原始工艺，因为这样会大大降低生产力，加大产品成本。正因为如此，产品质量自然不能得到保证，由此它为我们鉴定红山文化玉器真伪留下很多有效的鉴定证据。

红山文化玉器的"压地隐起法"工艺是由多道工序完成的。所以看起来过渡平缓，衔接处有渐隐渐显感觉。而新仿红山文化玉器，粗制滥造，力求一次性完成全部工艺。又在仿制前观察真品仅凭感觉，而在加工时这种感觉往往出现较大视觉差，大部分沟槽较深，而且出明显棱线，缺乏和谐平稳过渡，沟槽两侧与底部横断面多形成三角形。而真品多为圆弧形，横断面呈瓦状，也就是我们通常所说的瓦沟纹。以"压地隐起法"制作工艺塑造的动物、人物、几何体、圆雕或片状物体完整形象，是红山文化玉器的重要工艺特征。正是具备了这些特征，所以红山文化玉器看起来才更质朴而生动。

红山文化玉器绝大部分皆有孔，这些孔多用于系挂或系佩。经对这些孔分析研究认为：钻孔工具当为圆柱体木棒下端固定硬度较高矿物体锥形工具。木棒上固定和缠绕皮条然后连接拉动杆，类似旧时民间用于锔锅盆钻孔工具。反复拉动连接杆，使其旋转，以此完成玉器的对钻孔。当然与锔锅盆工具不同的是，红山文化玉器的钻孔不是靠钻头旋转切削，而是锥形钻头带动解玉砂进行磨削成孔。手工钻孔，由于缺乏稳定性，所以孔的圆度一般不够规则，而且孔沿处圆滑，无刺手感。现代仿制红山文化玉器钻孔，多采用转数较高的机器完成。因稳定性较好，和使用金属钻孔工具，所钻出的孔非常圆，孔沿处锐利刺手。为弥补这一不足，作伪者再用较大号钻具在孔沿处进行"划窝"，看似锥形钻加工。但"划窝"后的孔沿，明显可见"台痕"现象。所以我们在对红山文化玉器进行分辨真伪时，必须了解和掌握古代钻孔与现代机械钻孔两者之间所存在的根本差异。

古时多采用麻丝、兽皮或木棒蘸较细解玉砂对玉器抛光，光泽温润柔和。现时采用转数极高的电动机械，专门的抛光工具和微粒金刚砂进行抛光。抛光后的玉器光泽有明显刺眼感，通常人们称为"贼光"。新仿玉器多不做入土处理，所以这种光泽短时间不易退去，比较容易辨认。

四、仿制红山文化玉器沁象特征

我们所说的沁象，包括沁色、包浆、绺裂、孔洞、蚀斑、白化等不同形象的玉器浸后特征。这些特征直观反映在红山文化玉器表面上，我们依此为科学依据辨别每件玉器的真伪。

1、沁色：

在红山文化玉器中常见多种沁色，如土沁呈土黄色，水银沁呈黑色，铁锈沁呈暗红色等。目前我们所见作伪沁最多的则是铁锈沁、黑色沁和钙化。

凡作伪沁玉器，多选用质地松软或绺、璺、棉、较多玉石制作，这样有利于沁色的进入，便于浸染。凡玉质坚密无棉绺者不易做沁，所以作伪者极少采用此类玉做沁色，因硬度较高玉石做出的沁色多浮于器表，很难达到一定深度。

玉石在有缝隙情况下颜色方能够进入。为使沁色能够深入玉理，作伪者常常需要破坏玉器的表面，在完成初抛光工序后的玉器表面人为制作出许多麻斑、裂隙，以便让颜色从这些麻斑或裂隙中浸入玉理。制作麻斑多用利器敲击和铊头顶压而成，这种沁色只做在玉器某一部分。玉器整体做沁有的采取喷砂法，以强力气泵吹砂击打玉器表面，使玉器表面形成点状绺裂痕，从而让颜色渗入玉理。也有人作伪冰裂纹。首先将玉器进行冷冻，然后突然浸入热水中，使之形成炸裂，然后人工染色。目前市场上见到最多的红山文化伪古玉，多采用强酸、碱、化工原料高温浸泡，将玉器表面浸蚀成麻状斑，然后再做色。以此方法制作出的沁色，表面常常泛出白灰，长久不易退去。当以手盘化久时或涂油白灰能够暂时退去，放置久了，或用温水浸泡后还会继续泛出白灰。这并不是传统鉴玉法所说的"出灰"现象，而是经强酸、碱浸泡后的玉质所起化学反应。被称为"黑皮玉"者，就是用高锰酸钾、氢氟酸、快速金黑染色而成。人工作伪沁色的方法很多，却未见以传统做伪沁方法制作者。显然古时所谓的"血沁"已被人们质疑。目前我们所见到不同颜色的"化学沁"，不但颜色严重失真，而且嗅起来或多或少都有刺鼻的气味，这种气味数年不退。而真正红山文化出土玉器，因与含尸水土壤长时期接触，所以嗅起来多有腥臭气味。

真沁与伪沁，有时做一小实验便可见分晓。我们都知道，猫、狗之嗅觉比人更灵敏。当我们将一件含有化学物的玉器放到它鼻前时，它嗅之即转身离开，绝不回头，因为它不堪化学气味的强烈刺激。而当我们将一件真正出土器放在它面前时，它却嗅之又嗅，因为土古腥臭，甚至它还会以舌舔之。实验很简单，你不妨可以一试。当然，其他有效鉴定古玉器的办法还有很多，有些尚在实验阶段，将来一并奉献给广大古玉器收藏爱好者。

2、包浆：

前面已经讲过，包浆的形成是由于温度的变化，玉器因"出汗"而产生内分泌现象，长时期周而复始凝结于玉器表面的一层保护膜。凡出土红山文化古玉器，不管出土于任何年代，不管受沁到何种程度，稍加擦拭包浆即显露出来。凡无包浆的红山文化玉器皆不能认定为真品。

真古玉包浆具有强烈的年代感、沧桑感、真实感。不要错误理解，凡玉器外表光亮者皆为包浆。伪古光亮为抛光后亮度，它与包浆并不完全一样。伪古看起来光亮刺眼，真古看起来温和润泽。这是因为真古玉器在入土后表面受到浸蚀已退去原有"火气"。而新制作玉器之所以"火气"逼人，是因为不但未曾入土，而且没有经历过长时期的温度变化或者把玩。

目前所见仿制古玉包浆多用浸蜡方法，将制作好的玉器浸泡在热蜡中，待凉却后再将蜡除去，以降低和消除玉器表面光亮度。但浸过蜡的玉器表面手感滞涩，缺少润滑感，经过一段时间盘化，或以温水烫之，光亮依然恢复如初，露出本来面目。还有以酸、碱性化学品对新制玉器表面进行退光处理者，退光后的玉器尽管看起来有些与真包浆相接近，但往往在玉器孔洞和背角处留下不易除去的白灰，嗅之有刺鼻的化学品气味。有些被长时期把玩过的新制玉器，由于油、汗的浸入，经过冷热不同温度的变化，可以出现较簿包浆。本人曾做过实验，将含有一定水分的新制玉器放在电褥子下，经过一个冬天不间断的冷热变化后，玉器表面则出现包浆。但这种人为制造出来的包浆非常簿，经不起长时间盘化，就会逐渐退去。从仿制红山文化古玉情况来看，单纯为玉器制造包浆者较少，而大部分与作伪沁同步进行，并且不是十分重视包浆与其真实性。正因为包浆形成需要足够的时间和特殊的条件，对于急功近利的作伪者来说，望尘莫及。

凡无包浆玉器，皆为赝品。凡真品古玉器皆有较厚包浆，看起来有一种熟透了的感觉。所以包浆的存在与否，包浆的真实性已成为我们鉴定真伪古玉器的重要依据。

3、绺裂：

古玉器的绺裂，是在特殊环境下，由于温度不间断缓慢变化，从而使玉器产生由表及里的炸裂。这种炸裂是在漫长岁月中逐渐形成的，因此玉器自然形成的绺裂无深度，呈起层状，严重者，层层剥离，直使玉器表面损坏。

人为制造绺裂，多模仿玉器自然绺裂形成条件，将玉器放置于冰箱或雪地冷冻，然后再放入热水中使其产生炸裂。以此法仿制的绺裂多往纵深发展，形成明显炸裂纹。主要因温度的变化过于突然，膨胀力没有缓冲余地。所以因此产生的绺裂无起层感，而过于深透直接。凡过于深透炸裂皆为伪绺裂。

目前我们常常看到的一些仿制红山文化玉器，也见有在正常状态下所形成的绺裂，这些绺裂多分布于玉器一面，这是因为采用原生沁河漠玉所制作玉器。有绺裂一面，正是裸露地表或距地表较近处自然所形成之绺裂。因此我们在鉴定红山文化玉器时，还要注意绺裂的完整与统一，不要片面理解凡符合绺裂特征者皆为真品。

因为真实的绺裂不易仿制或者无法仿制，因此成为我们辨别玉器真伪的重要依据。

4、孔洞：

孔洞因其形似虫蛀，所以又被称为虫蛀孔。目前尚未见特意仿制孔洞者，偶尔在一些玉器表面发现伪孔洞，多为做钙化斑时，淋酸时间过长所形成的。这些孔洞多无深度，孔洞边缘处圆滑，有些则形成小面积的残破。真正自然形成孔洞，其边缘处参差不齐，具有一定深度，状如针刺，人为无法仿制。

5、蚀斑：

因蚀斑影响玉器外观形象，因而特意仿制蚀斑者很少。偶见类似蚀斑，这是在仿制红山文化玉器时故意做残，在为其做沁色时，残破处颜色明显吃进较深，形成假蚀斑，这与真正蚀斑相差很远。也有些伪古玉，保留和利用原生沁或残件原有蚀斑充古，这些蚀斑多在玉器一面，为利用这些蚀斑常影响玉器的完整性。鉴识中当谨慎区别。

6、白化：

白化又被称为钙化，是玉器受生石灰浸蚀而形成。白化了的玉器，因玉质遭受严重破坏，变得疏松、脆弱。白化呈两种情况，一种为玉器的局部白化，另一种为整体白化。玉器的整体白化较易仿制，而局部白化不易仿制。因为局部白化，应可见玉器表面所反映出的明显白化过程，就是我们所说沁象的过渡性。它是沁象缓慢完成过程的真实展示，沁象鲜活、灵动而不呆板。

目前所掌握玉器白化作伪有这样几种方法：一种是，将制作完成的玉器包裹生石灰，在压力锅或高压釜内通过高温烧烤，使其迅速白化，这需要严格控制温度和时间。温度和时间过高过长，玉器表面则出现烧裂，通常我们称之为"火劫纹"。整体作白化多为中小型较厚和圆雕玉器，而不适用于板状或片状玉器。另一种是将大块玉原石切割成板块状，或将较小块玉石放入高压釜内高温烧烤，使其白化层逐渐深入玉理，然后再根据玉器制作需要，将这些玉石进行切割，多制作薄板状和片状类玉器。经过烧烤已白化了的玉石切割后因为白化深浅程度不同，看起来似有明显的白化过渡变化，对不明真象的人来说，多以为自然白化所成，所以常常被此所蒙蔽。以此法所制作白化玉器，白化处多连成大片，而且白化斑块多在玉器边缘，器中心处白化较轻微。认真观察，缺少细微过渡变化。除以上两种方法外，还有将制作好的玉器埋置于生石灰土坑中，让其慢慢发生玉质变化。以这种办法作伪需要较长时间，而短时间效果不大，白化程度较浅薄，所以目前已不多用。

7、石化：

由于土壤中多种元素对其长时期浸蚀而发生的玉石质变称为石化。质变后的玉石松软，土浆随之浸入，使之呈半透明的玉石不再透明，状如石头。这种石化玉器其色极不易仿制。目前也未见仿制者。

从市场情况来看，做伪者的手段和方法越来越高，我们必须随时观察掌握，稍有不慎，不但给我们的收藏和鉴定工作造成失误，而且将蒙受很大的经济损失。

Collection and identification of Hongshan–Culture Jade articles

Hongshan–Culture Jade Collection Actuality

In recent years, fake Hongshan–Culture jade inundated market home and abroad. We even found that Hongshan culture had penetrated into outlying counties of the country. My personal appraisal experiences prove that fake Hongshan–Culture jade wares have spread all over the country.

People love and collect Hongshan–Culture jade due to its charming art and long history value. Some newcomer in Hongshan–Culture jade collection field considered themselves experienced but actually lacked enough knowledge on it, and they tried to pick real Hongshan–Culture jades from large numbers of imitate ones. Some other men under the guidance of the so called experts tried to avoid blindness, but still had been deceived many times and suffered economic losses. For those experts are authorities on studying and researching, but actually inexperienced on appraisal. The third kind of people is sciolistic on Hongshan culture. He thought that he was the first one who had found a new land, regarded the mimic articles as the real at market and purchased without restraint. Nowadays some self–assumed Hongshan–Culture jade experts, collectors and connoisseurs imposed their title, which did not concern with Hongshan–Culture jade appraisal, to make profit by selling fake Hongshan–culture jade. Frankly speaking, it's a grift behavior.

I would like to suggest the people who are interested in Hongshan–Culture jade collection that he should study Hongshan culture, especially appraisal carefully by himself to avoid wasting more money and energy. At the same time, he should not be easily mislead and believe irresponsible appraisal of those experts. We should know that the legal system is not perfect at present, thus some experts speak randomly but needn't be responsible for his legal duty.

Nowadays, jade market lacks enough supervision and punishment on selling fake Hongshan–Culture jade. So we should improve our own appraisal skills, learn how to pick out real precious antique in curio market to protect our rights and benefits. In fact, learning appraisal is not very difficult. If we compare the real and the fake carefully, we would improve the appraisal skills quickly. Wasting money on jade collecting is normal for new collectors, but it's abnormal if you still wander along the wrong road after paying a lot of tuition fee. There are a few persons who collected dozens even hundreds of fake Hongshan–Culture jade objects, but never seen any real one. So collection requires knowledge and impression of real Hongshan–Culture jade.

Many years ago, I visited the experts of national appraisal institute, which is the highest court that has ultimate jurisdiction of jade identification in appraisal field, but they even couldn't recognize jade from stones, and spouted that any kind of imitated jade could be produced by high technology in nowadays. What they said sounded very reasonable, but actually not. As we know, there is still no any scientific and research institute or large–scale enterprise specializing in the imitation of ancient jade with high–tech equipments and special technical teams. In fact, fake jade production made by indigenous methods but not high technology. Fake jade made by high–tech just comes from imagination and poor knowledge.

Various Hongshan–Culture jade articles have their own distinct characters. Though imitators try to perfect the fake on every aspect such as texture, style, arts and crafts, infiltration, but many nuances could still not be imitated. Those nuances are difficult to see for the most newcomers, but easily for experienced men. It requires solid basic skills and long-time study.

It is sure that Hongshan-Culture jade can't be imitated as real as the unearthed jade forever, no matter what kinds of methods are used, because real Hongshan-Culture jade contains culture and history deposit of thousand years. Because imitators don't know much about Hongshan culture while seeking quick success and instant benefit, so they just can imitate the shape but not the verve.

I Textures of Fake Hongshan-Culture Jade

Hongshan-Culture jade has its own basic regularity and localization. But textures of fake jade are not only various but also inconsistent with the real Hongshan-Culture jade. Most imitators use raw materials from the local place directly. For example, imitators in Liaonan often use Xiuyan jade since Liaonan is near Xiuyan. While Liaoxi and Inner Mongolia teems with agate, so a lot of fake agate Hongsha-Culture jade appears on market. Some south areas produce yellow jade containing cotton shaped hollows, so there are a lot of Hongshan-Culture yellow jade imitations in those regions. Several years ago, a kind of soft, mild and gentle, exquisite brilliant light yellow jade was imported from Burma for fake jace made. Though no white jade has been found in Hongshan-Culture jade wares, white imitations still appeared on market. Recently a lot of turquoise fake Hongshan-Culture jade also emerged.

People know little information about encrustation situations of agate, turquoise and yellow jade because those jade were seldom seen in unearthed Hongshan-Culture jade. It's also because those kind of jade are too hard to be infiltrated easily; many collectors gathered the fake jade articles as the real ones.

There are also a lot of collectors who are be misled by experts that raw material of Hongshan-Culture jade is made of Xiuyan, so they regard all jade wares real made by Xiuyan. This is one of important rules in Hongshan-Culture appraisal. Some collectors collect Hongshan-Culture jade according to pictures of books or videos. But they don't know most jade in pictures or videos are artificial. This serious problem should appeal our attentions. Recently I saw a book in which there is no piece of real Hongshan-Culture jade object at all.

After exchanging ideas with many Hongshan-Culture jade collectors, I found that many people attach importance on shape of the jade but not the reality and just wrongly pursue hard, high density, brilliant superficially and odd shaped jade. We collect Hongshan-Culture jade because of its long history and culture, as well as its trueness. Otherwise, it has no sense if it's only a modern handicraft no matter how exquisite of this imitation is. Therefore, even if some jade articles have some broken, but we should collect them so long as it is real. For the reality itself is the value.

II Shapes of Fake Hongshan-Culture Jade

In recent years, a lot of fake Hongshan-Culture jade articles charactering as mysterious and exaggerated shape were combined with Mayan culture, Olmec culture and stone style. Even some art designers were employed on shape design. To try to be different, some jade was even carved hieroglyph to cheat those who lack acknowledge of history. Those fake jade wares were even treasured by some collectors.

Recently the special enterprise to produce Hongshan culture jade formed. Reportedly some private companies purchase batches of raw material from Xiuyan, and form lines of designing, cutting, skiving, grinding polishing and infiltrating. Those companies are not illegal but officially registered. They produce jade imitations of various historical periods, and Hongshan-Culture jade becomes a staple production. Large scaled companies own thirty to forty employees, so we can imagine that the quantity of their production is huge.

Thanks to the emergence of large jade companies, Hongshan-culture jade imitations are made bigger and bigger. Weight of human shaped or bird shaped or animal and human compound gems is dozens even hundreds Jin (1 jin = 500 g). Someone told me that his jade dragon reaches one hundred jin. It's unbelievable that so big jade can be recognized as real. So the erroneous concept of collection should be changed.

Nowadays fake jade occurs in a wide range of styles, such as bird, hawk, owl, dragon, and Jue or other shaped according to the pictures in books. Besides, some big, nondescript, strange looking, human shaped or animal shaped or two figures compound jade which can stand or sit was made by imitators who don't know much of Hongshan-Culture jade. Those jade often attract people who work on painting, sculpture, photography, art design, and they have a little knowledge of Hongshan-Culture jade but are just interested in shape and style of jade regardless of its reality. And of course there are also a few people who collect jade only for profit, dreaming to become a millionaire after a night. Putting money as the first target, one would never become a real collator and connoisseur.

III Processing of Fake Hongshan-Culture Jade

Hongshan-Culture jade has its own unique techniques that modern men still can't imitated because modern mechanical equipments and tools are far more advanced than Hongshan culture period, the rapid spinning machinery impetus and advanced cutting and grinding are more mechanized and scientific. There are many distinguished differences between mechanized incising, grinding and cutting tools with wood-frame tools which are used by hand or foot. That results in different processing technic features. Although Hongshan-Culture jade imitators use some old craft in the processing, try to be consistent with the genuine, they aim to pursue profit and product quantity, so the imitators wouldn't fully use the original craft, which would significantly reduce productivity and increased product costs. That is the reason of the natural decline in the quality of products, which also gives us many jade effective identification evidences to judge the jade authenticity.

Shallow Relief on Hongshan-culture jade was completed by many working procedure. Therefore, mild and gentle features appear in the transition and linking up places. But the modern jade is shoddy, and the process was completed with one-time effort. Producer only depended on their feelings and experiences to observe the real jade, then fake jade made according to their impressions. But great visual dispersion often arise in the working procedure, so trenches carved deeper lack of harmony and smooth in transition place. There are clear lines and sub-faces on the imitator. Two sides of the trench often formed as triangle shape with the bottom transect. But real goods are mostly arc-shaped, and transect is like a tile, which we usually call it sulcate dents. It is an important characteristic that Hongshan-culture jade was performed with human, animals or other objects overall image. With these characteristics, Hongshan-culture jade looks more simply and vividly.

Most of Hongshan-culture Jade wares have a hole for wearing. Upon analysis and studies, we think that a round wooden stick are likely to be used as the main part of the tool when drilling a hole, on bottom of the stick fixed very hard taper mineral body, leather strip was twisted on wooden stick and connected with joy stick, which similar to the old times drilling tools to civil pots or tin pots, to complete two-sides drilling. But the difference between the two is that the tools on Hongshan-Culture jade do not depend on the aiguille but the naxium driven by aiguille to circumvolve and cut. Manual drilling lacks relative stability, but the hole was smooth and with no thorns.

Modern high-electrical machinery was used in nowadays, because of stability in burnishing, smoothness in drilling holes but with thorns in the brim. Gloss of Jade after that polishing treatment is glare, which was generally called Floating Light. Most of fake Hongshan-Culture jade wares are never under the earth, so the floating light doesn't disappear easily, which can be easily recognized.

Ⅳ Infiltration of Fake Hongshan-Culture Jade

Infiltration herein includes color, Baojiang, tuft crack pattern, hole, and eroded spot, calcification, etc. These features were directly reflected on the surface of Hongshan-Culture jade, which we could identify authenticity of each piece of jade accordingly. For antique collectors, infiltration existence was one of measures to the authenticity of ancient jade. Precisely because of this, infiltration is extraordinarily important to us.

1、 Infiltration color

Various color changes were found in permeated ancient jade. When jade permeated by soil, the color is like ocher. When permeated by azoth, the color would become black, while iron infiltration represents dark red color. Nowadays most we see is Iron infiltration, azoth infiltration and calcify.

Low-density jade has tuft pattern cracks and hollows, favorable for dip-dye. On the contrary, high-density jade is adverse to make pseudo-color, so imitators wouldn't use hard jade to make fake color infiltration since the color would float on the surface but can't penetrate into the inside of jade. Imitators often produce many speckles on jade exterior after the polishing to let color penetrate into jade. Speckles were made by sharp tools stroke or ingot head press. This method is for part of jade infiltration. The entire jade infiltration was made by pump blowing sands on the jade surface to form point damage. While large jade was soaked into acidic liquid, alkali or other chemical materials to make speckles, and then dyeing is performed. But white ash would appear on the jade surface after that treatment. White ash could be gotten rid off by Pan or oiling, but the white ash would appear again after a long time or when the jade is put in water. Moreover, the dyed color doesn't look lively and smell of the jade is pungent. But the smell of genuine Hongshan-Culture jade is fish-stench since it contacted with dead body for a long time.

We can identify jade by a small experiment. Put a piece of jade in front of a dog, and the dog would?lick the genuine one because of the fish-stench smell, leaving the artificial one due to its pungent smell.

2、Bao Jiang

it had been mentioned above that Bao Jiang formed owing to the temperature change, the jade "perspiration" phenomenon produced a protective film after a long time on the jade surface. Every unearthed Hongshan-culture jade, no matter when it was unearthed and what kind of degree of infiltration was used, Bao Jiang would be reflected on the surface obviously as rubbing the jade with slight force. Any jade that doesn't have the film can not to be recognized for the real one.

Bao Jiang of real aged jade is not easily simulated, because Bao Jiang can only formed after a very long time. Not all light of jade is Bao Jiang. Actually light is produced by polishing, and this kind of light is different from Bao Jiang. The former looks like luminous and dazzling, while the latter looks like gentle and moist. This is because erosion retreats the original radiance of jade after buried in the earth for long, but light of new manufactures is harsh. The light could not retreat completely in a short time even if the jade is buried under the earth for several years.

At present wax was used for Bao Jiang imitation. The jade was put in the hot wax, and then the wax was removed after cooling down. Finally, the jade surface radiance would be reduced after this treatment. But such jade surface feels rough and lacks the smooth feeling. Panning jade after certain time, the dazzling light would restore. If the jade is reproduced by acid or alkalinity chemical, Bao Jiang will look like the real one, but could still not achieve real degree, and often leave lime in holes and carry-over that couldn't be easily gotten rid of. If some new jade is held appreciatively for a long time, thin Bao Jiang will appear because of the oil penetration, perspiration immersion and temperature change. Some people put newly made moisture jade under the electricity mattress, and Bao Jiang would also appear on the jade surface through a winter of uninterrupted cold-hot change. But this kind artificial Bao Jiang cannot withstand the long-time panning, and can retreat gradually. Imitators seldom make Bao Jiang alone, but do with false infiltration. Imitators are not attaching importance on the authenticity of Bao Jiang. Actually real Bao Jiang is hard to be imitated, because its formation needs enough time and special conditions. Therefore Bao Jiang existence is important basis for jade appraisal.

3、Cracks

Temperature change caused cracks in long time. The cracks are?laminated, even peel off the jade.

How to imitate cracks? The only way is modeling the natural crack circumstance; put the jade into icebox or in snow, then transfer it to hot water. But cracks made in this way are deep and narrow because the temperature change is too sudden.

There are also natural cracks in fake Hongshan-culture jade articles; such jade was reproduced from aged Hemo jade.

4、Hole

Hole is also called because it seems to be eaten by moth. We haven't found designedly-made hole until now. The imitated holes are normally the sideline product when the calcified speckles are produced. Those holes are shallow and smooth. Natural holes can't be imitated easily too, so it's an important basis to appraisal.

5、Speckles

Speckles can affect jade image, so speckle imitation is less. Once in a while, false speckles were found and they were intentionally incomplete. When infiltration color was performing, color of the broken site is deeper obviously, forming false speckles. These false speckles differ very far from the real ones. There is also fake ancient jade that retains and uses raw infiltration or incomplete original speckles to be real. These speckles are mainly in one side, and the integrity of jade article is frequently affected in order to use these speckles. We should be cautious to distinguish.

6、Whiten

Whitening, which is also called calcification, is made by calces infiltration. Texture of whitened jade damaged seriously, so it became loose and fragile. Whitening presents two conditions: one is local whitening, and the other is overall whitening. Overall whitening of jade article is easy to copy, while local whitening is no easy to copy. Since local whitening, whose process should be obviously reflected on the surface of jade article, is what we claimed the transition property of infiltration herein. It is the slow and complete course of infiltration truely demonstrating, and infiltration presentation is fresh, flexible and active and not rigid.

Now fake whitening of jade article have some kinds of methods as follows. The first: the complete jade article is wrapped up with raw lime in pressure cooker or the cauldron of high pressure, and through high temperature the jade is burned to make it quick whitening. This needs strict control of temperature and time. When temperature and time are growing too high, the jade will be split and the surface of jade article appears to burn cracking. Usually, we called this "fire burning veins" Whole whitening is often used in medium or small thick and round vulture-shaped jade article, but not suitable for board-shaped or flat-shaped jade article. The second: cut original jade stones of large size into board-like pieces, or put jade stones of smaller size into the cauldron of high pressure and high temperature, burn to roast, make its whitening deeper gradually. Then these jades were cut according to the specific jade article. This time more thin board and flat shaped jade articles were made. Through burning and roasting, whitened jade was cut, and has obvious whitening transition changes because of different whitening depth. For the person who does not understand true condition, he will consider it natural, so as to be deceived. With this method, batches of whitening places are usually joined together and on the edge of jade article. It is lighter in ware center. Observing carefully, we can found such whitening lacks subtle transitional changes. Besides the two methods mentioned above, another method is to bury the jade article in raw lime, let it change slowly. This method requires longer time, so it is used less frequently.

7、Landification

In soil, jade is perennially eroded by various elements in the earth, so the property of the jade is changed. The jade after qualitative change is soft, and liquid earth soaks to enter. Therefore, the jade is not semitransparent any more just like stones. This kind of landification jade color is not easy to copy. Now, no copier is found. According to market condition, the method and means of being fake are more and more high wise, we must observe at any time to grasp. Any time if we are careless, we will not only make a fault collection, but suffer great pecuniary loss.

图 381 仿红山文化玉人
Picture 381 imitating Hongshan Culture Jade Person

图 382 仿红山文化玉人
Picture 382 imitating Hongshan-Culture Jade Person

图 383 仿红山文化玉蚕
Picture 383 imitating Hongshan-Culture Jade Silkworm

此三件玉器以岫岩玉制作，皆经过酸处理做沁。

图 381 玉人与图 382 玉蚕在做白化斑的同时，又在高温下以高锰酸钾浸泡，已改变玉原生颜色。

图 383 玉人在制作完成后将其呈俯卧状浸泡于强酸中，使玉人白化，以制作钙化斑。

This three jade wares made of Xiu rock jade, processing by acid to make infiltration.

The jade person of Picture 381 and Jade Silkworm of picture 382 have changed jade raw color while making white calcification spots, it also soaked under high temperature with potassium permanganate ,

After completing Jade Person of Picture 383, they soaked it in strong acid on stoop liying down to make Jade Person white alcification in order to make calcification spot.

图 384 仿红山文化玉神祖
Picture 384 imitating Hongshan Culture   Jade Numen

图 385 玉神祖器背
Picture 385 imitating Hongshan Culture   the back of Jade Numen ware

图 384 玉神祖与图 386 虎形器皆采用先将玉器毛坯进行高温烧烤，然后再进行细部加工。这样制作完成后的玉器不但可显露玉地，又能形成沁色的过渡感。以此方式制作出的玉器皆无包浆。

图 387 锥形白玉鸮，玉质松软。我们所看到的褐色沁为人工所作。红山文化考古发掘中尚未见白色玉质器物。

Jade Numen of Picture 384 and tiger-shaped ware of Picture 386 adopted the method that roasted jade ware with high temperature then processed the details. So the jade ware after producing can not only show jade land, but also formed the transitional sense of infiltration colour. With the way to make jade ware all has no baojiang .

The cone-shaped white jade bird of Picture 387 is soft. The brown infiltration colour that we see made by artificial. We have not seen white jade texture wares in Hongshan-culture archaeology excavate.

267

图 386 仿红山文化虎形器图
Picture 386 imitating Hongshan Culture   tiger-shaped ware

387 仿红山文化锥形白玉
Picture 387 imitating Hongshan Culture cone-shaped white jade bird

图 388 仿红山文化玉鸟
Picture 388 imitating Hongshan Culture Jade Bird

图 389 玉鸟器背
Picture 389 the back of Jade Bird ware

　　这两件玉器皆为原生沁河漠玉仿红山文化玉器。河漠玉多临河道或距地表较浅玉石，历经数千年甚至数万年而自然受沁。以河漠玉仿制古玉已有很长历史。剥离玉皮或利用玉石表层加工之玉器，尽管沁象具真实感，但仍与真古玉器整体受沁有着明显不同。

The two jade wares are all infiltration that Hemo jade imitated Hongshan culture jade ware. Hemo jade is more close to river course or the jade shallow from the surface of land. All through thousands of years even ten thousands of years receive natural infiltration. With Hemo jade imitating ancient jade had a very long history. After peeling off the jade leather or processing with jade surface, though infiltration had the sense of reality, but still have obvious difference with the real ancient jade ware that received infiltration in a whole.

图 390 仿红山文化玦形玉兽
Picture 390 imitating Hongshan-Culture Jade Coiled Animal

图 391 玦形玉兽另面
Picture 391 another side of Jade Coiled Animal

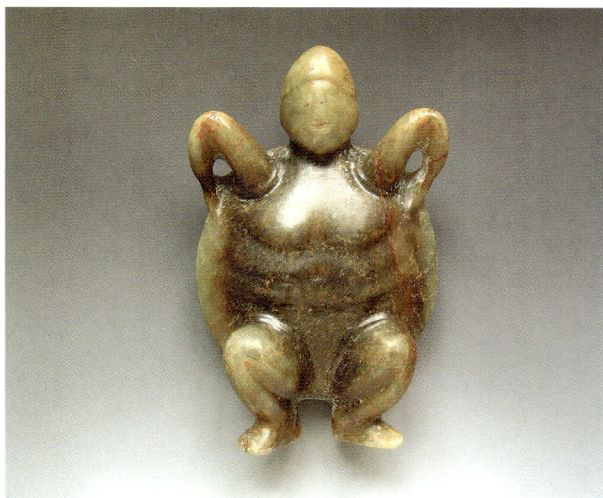

图 392 仿红山文化人物形龟神
Picture 392 imitating Hongshan Culture　Figure-shaped tortoise god

图 393 仿红山文化玦形玉龟
Picture 393 imitating Hongshan Culture　Jade Coiled Tortoise

　　上图二器皆采用高温烧烤，强行做色于玉理方法制作。

　　做沁色由玉器表面裂隙浸入玉理多呈僵死条纹状，缺少过渡感。

　　艳丽的红色严重失真，既不似铁锈沁，又非土沁。如此夸张伪沁较易辨认。

　　下图仿红山文化玉神祖作了淋酸处理。白化斑分布均匀，明显违犯科学规律，因而失去了它的真实性。

The two wares of left picture all roasted with high temperature，and forced to make colour into jade texture.

Make infiltration color to soak by the surface crack of jade ware into jade texture, much is to submit stripe form, which is dead and lack to transitional sense.

The bright red is serious distortion，which seems not rust infiltration and not earth infiltration. So exaggerate fake infiltration is easy comparatively to identify.

The imitating Hongshan-Culture Jade Numen of Picture387 have made by pouring sour. The distribution of white calcification spot is even, which violates scientific regularity obviously, thus have lost it's actuality.

图 394 仿红山文化玉神祖
Picture 394 imitating Hongshan Culture　Jade Numen

图 395 仿红山文化虎形器
Picture 395 imitating Hongshan Culture Tiger-shaped ware

图 396 仿红山文化兽面人
Picture 396 imitating Hongshan Culture   jade person of beast face

397 仿红山文化天地神佩
Picture 397 imitating Hongshan Culture   Compound Jade Baldric for Heaven and Earth

图 398 仿红山文化玉龟
Picture 398 imitating Hongshan Culture   Jade Tortoise

这些都是经过高温酸浸泡作旧的仿红山文化玉器。看上去色脏、无包浆、死气沉沉。

These are imitating Hongshan Culture jade ware that soaked by the acid of high temperature to make old. Looks that the colour is dirty, without baojiang and lifeless.

图 399 仿红山文化玉鹰
Picture 399 imitating Hongshan Culture
Jade Hawk

图 400 玉鹰另面
Picture 400 another side of Jade Hawk

这些都是以新岫玉制作，局部经过酸腐蚀做出伪沁的仿红山文化玉器。经过人为高温烧烤所形成绺裂，多往玉理深处走，而非呈起层状。看上去，新而脏。

These are produced in soapstone, whose part is made by sour corrosion to make into fake infiltration of imitating Hongshan-Culture jade ware. Through artificial high temperature roasting to form tuft crack pattern, most of which is deep into jade texture and not subimit layer form.So looks new and dirty.

图 401 仿红山文化玉兽
Picture 401 imitating Hongshan Culture　Jade animal

图 402 仿红山文化玉鸟
Picture 402 imitating Hongshan Culture　Jade Bird

图 403 玉鸟器背
Picture 403 the back of Jade bird ware

图 404 仿红山文化蝉形玉
Picture 404 imitating Hongshan Culture Cicada-Shaped Jade

图 405 仿红山文化刀形人
Picture 405 imitating Hongshan Culture　Knife-Shaped jade Person

　　这些均为"旧玉新作"，以残破石斧改制的仿红山文化玉器。它们巧妙的利用了原受沁钙化斑。

All these are "old make to new" jade, with broken stone axe altering into imitating Hongshan-culture jade ware. They ingeniously used the calcification spot of raw infiltration.

图 406 仿红山文化玉神祖
Picture406 imitating Hongshan Culture　Jade Numen

这些以原生沁河漠玉仿制的红山文化玉器皆生涩无包浆。

These imitating Hongshan-Culture jade ware with Hemo jade of raw infiltration is all not smooth and have no baojiang

图 407 仿红山文化玉蝉
Picture 407 imitating Hongshan Culture　Jade Cicada

图 408 玉蝉器背
Picture 408 the back of Jade Cicada ware

图 409 仿红山文化玉头骨佩
Picture409 imitating Hongshan Culture　bone pendant of Jade head

图 410 仿红山文化玉龙
Picture 410 imitating Hongshan Culture　Jade Dragon

图 411 玉龙另面
Picture 411 another side of Jade Dragon

这是一件用河漠玉仿作的红山文化玉龙。从原生沁玉石剥离下来的玉料，在加工后仍然能明显看出器两侧受沁变化的诸多不同。

This is a imitating Hongshan–Culture jade dragon made by Hemo jade. The jade material peeling off from raw infiltration jade, we can still find out obvious infiltration changes of two sides of wares after processing.

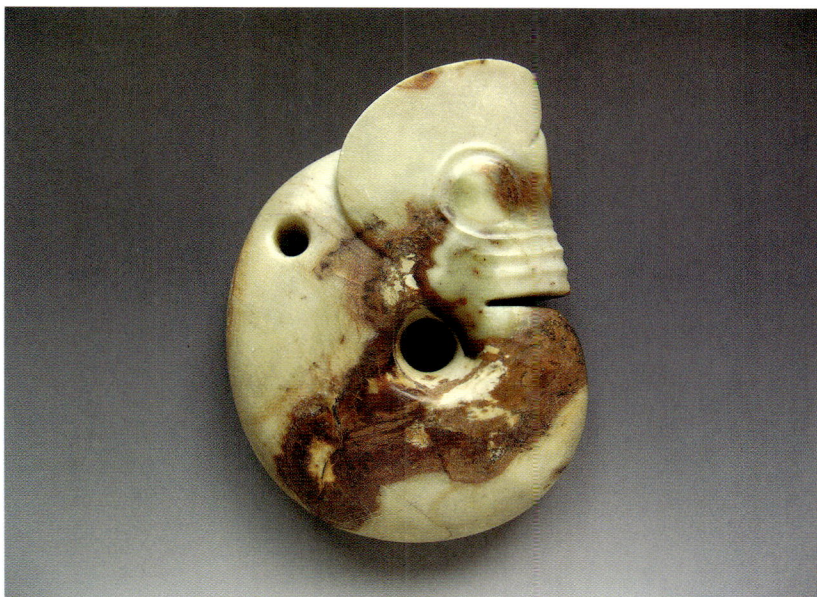

图 412 仿红山文化玦形玉兽
Picture 412 imitating Hongshan Culture　Jade Coiled Animal

图 413 仿红山文化玉蚕
Picture 413 imitating Hongshan Culture　Jade Silkworm

　　这是经过人工作色仿红山文化玉器。在染色前先对玉器进行加温，玉石可改变原本颜色，同时利用加热后较细裂纹，趁热将颜色注入玉理。

　　人工所做沁色呆板，无明显过渡性。

　　从玦形玉兽、玉蚕两件玉器看，器表均干涩无包浆。不具自然受沁年代特征。

This is the imitating Hongshan Culture jade ware through painting colour by artificial. Before dyeing, first to warm up the jade ware, which can change formerly color, and at the same time using fine crack veins after heating, so put the color into the jade texture while heat.

The artificial infiltration color is stiff, and has not obvious transition

Seeing from Jade Coiled Animal and Jade Silkworm the two jade wares, the ware surface is all dry and not smooth without baojiang, which do not have nature infiltration time feature.

图 414 仿红山文化玉凤
Picture 414 imitating Hongshan Culture　Jade Phoenix

图 415 玉凤另面
Picture 415 another side of Jade Phoenix

图 416 仿红山文化玦形玉兽
Picture 416 imitating Hongshan Culture　Jade Coiled Animal

图 417 玦形玉兽另面
Picture 417 another side of Jade Coiled Animal

上图沁色艳丽多彩，乍看沁象颇具真实感。仔细分析你会发现，这是一件以原生沁玉石制作的红山玉器仿制品。从钙化程度分析，玉原石当为椭圆形小块玉。此器无包浆、干涩和缺乏年代感。

下图为原生沁河漠玉仿红山文化玉器。原石应为河卵石状玉石，先天受沁。此器尽管沁象自然，但无明显包浆，对此认真分析：器两侧沁色不一致，一侧可见蚁状黑斑，而另侧却无，而且沁后差别较大。试想，玉器受沁依玉石纹理而形成，所形成的沁色应统一而完整。显然此器违背了自然科学规律。

The infiltration colour of this ware in picture 414 is bright and polychrome, and quite have reality sense at the first sight. You can find through careful analysis that this is an imitating Hongshan culture ware made by raw infiltration jade. Analysing its calcification degree, the original stone is ellipse-shaped little piece jade. This ware does not have baojiang, dry, not smooth and lacks time sense.

This ware of picture 416 is an imitating Hongshan-culture jade ware made by raw infiltration of Mohe jade. Original stone should be river cobble form jade received infiltration congenitally. Though the infiltration of this ware is nature, but it is obvious to do not have baojiang, Analysing carefully for this, the infiltration color of two sides of the ware is not uniform, one side is ant-shaped black spots and another side has not, so the difference is greater after infiltration. Think that the jade ware receives infiltration to depend on jade veins to form, which should be uniform and intact. Obviously, this ware has violated the law of natural science.

图 418 仿红山文化玉兽面
Picture 418 imitating Hongshan Culture　Jade beast face

图 419 玉兽面器背
Picture 419 The back of Jade beast
face

　　这是一件以圆形原生沁玉石制作的玉器。玉器正面几乎全部石化，器背露青色玉地，沁色多变。这块玉石可能历经数万年，甚至更长时间，因此沁入层深厚。当将玉石切割开来后，器背仍能显露真实沁象，但器正面与器背沁象却截然不同。从玉器加工工艺来看，完全背离红山文化时期古玉琢磨特征。因此鉴定为仿红山文化之器。

　　This is a jade ware made of circular jade of raw infiltration. Almost all the front side of this ware is petrifaction. The back of this ware expose to the blue-green jade texture, whose infiltration color changes a lot. Maybe this jade is through several ten thousands of years or even longer, therefore the infiltration layers is deep. When cutting off the jade, the bake of the ware can still show real infiltration phenomenon, but the infiltration phenomenon of front and back is entirely different. Seeing from the process of the jade ware, it is completely deviated from the carving and polishing features of Hongshan Culture period. So it was appraised as imitating Hongshan-culture ware.

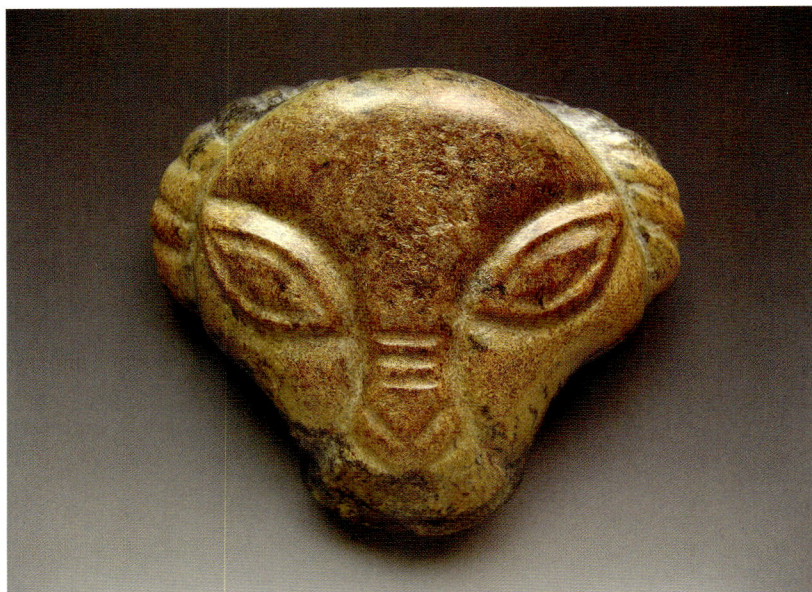

图 420 仿红山文化玉羊首
Picture 420 imitating Hongshan Culture　Jade sheep head

图 421 玉羊首器背
Picture 421 The back of Jade sheep head

这是一件以原生沁河漠玉制作的玉器。当一件玉器整体被土壤覆盖以后，土壤中所含有的能够对玉器造成侵害的元素应该是均等的，因此沁象应该是基本相同的，这就是必须要强调的玉器受沁的统一性与完整性。而此件玉羊首则不然，器表与器背沁象相差很多。这是因为原生受沁河漠玉，玉羊首正面接近地表，因此受沁较重。而器背正是玉石剥离层处，因此玉器正、背两面沁象完全不同。

This is one jade ware made of Hemo jade of raw infiltration. When a ware was wholely covered with soil coverage, the elements in the soil have the equal harm effect to the jade, essentially, it will create the same infiltration phenomenon. It must emphasize the unity and integrity of jade infiltration. But this jade sheep head is not, as surface with a difference image with the back. Because the Hemo jade receiving raw infiltration, the front side of jade sheep head is near surface of the land, the infiltration is heavier. But the back of Jade is a stripping layer, so the infiltration phenomenon is different between the two sides.

图 422 仿红山文化玦形玉兽
Picture 422 imitating Hongshan Culture   Jade Coiled
Animal

图 423 玦形玉兽另面
Picture 423 Another side of Jade Coiled Animal

以原生沁河漠玉仿制红山文化玉器极具欺骗性。因
此我们必须进行细致分析。

上图这件玉器正反两面皆有比较真实的沁象，但却
缺少完整性。玉兽背部与前脸沁象明显不同，说明兽背
处玉石生长于地下，前脸处接近或裸露地面。

下图黑色沁斑与表面沁色看起来真实性都很强，很
容易被误认为沁色为后天所形成。进行认真分析你会发
现，这两件玉器都在中间大孔处出现"断沁"现象。器
面石化斑与沁色突然中断，显然违反自然科学规律。因
此鉴定为伪器。

It has extreme deceiving with Hemo jade of raw infiltration imitating Hongshan-culture jade ware. Therefore we must
carry out careful analysis.

The front and back of this ware in above picture all has
more actual infiltration phenomenon, but it lacks integrity. The
infiltration of Jade beast back and former face is obviously
differenct, explanting that the back of beast jade grow in underground , former face is near or bare on ground.

The black spots and surface infiltration color of this ware
in picture 424 looks great authenticity, so it will
easily be mistaken for acquired infiltration formed.
Through careful analysis you will find the two
wares both appeared "not continuous infiltration"

279

图 424 仿红山文化玦形玉兽
Picture 424 imitating Hongshan Culture   Jade Coiled
Animal

phenomenon. in the middle big holes. The petrifaction spots and sudden disruption of
infiltration color, which obviously violated nature science law. Therefore we appraise it is fake
ware.

图 425 仿红山文化神人

Picture 425 imitating Hongshan Culture jade god person

图 426 仿红山文化玉神面

Picture 426 imitating Hongshan Culture Jade God Face

　　左图人物造型仿照三星堆文化，头顶冠状器依红山文化羽翅形佩所仿制。无论器形与工艺皆不符红山文化古玉特征。

　　此器制作完成后，放置高压釜内烧烤制成鸡骨白色，冒充钙化器。

　　右图人物双目与嘴部雕琢皆与红山文化"压地隐起法"工艺不符。

　　此器在烧制过程中由于火温过高而形成炸裂"火劫纹"。

In picture 425, this ware figure modeling imitate sanxingdui culture, the crest-shaped ware of the head depend on Hongshan-culture wing-shaped wear imitating. Regardless of ware shape and technology, is inconsistent with Hongshan-culture ancient jade feature.

After completing this ware, they put it in the cauldron of high voltage to roast into chicken bone white, pretending calcification ware.

In picture 426, This ware figure's two eyes and mouth carving is both different with the technology "digging hollows" of Hongshan Culture.

It is split that this ware formed "fire splitting veins" in burning course for high temperature.

图 427 仿红山文化玉鸟
Picture 427 imitating Hongshan Culture Jade Bird

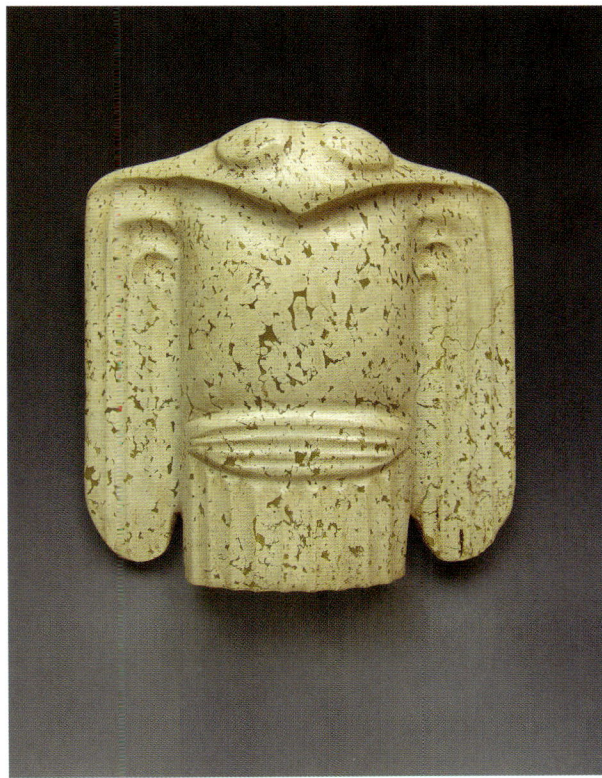

图 428 仿红山文化玉鸟
Picture 428 imitating Hongshan Culture Jade Bird

　　左图玉器制作完成后低温烧烤成鸡骨白色。在烧烤前先行在鸟腹、尾、翅处做残，以冒充自然破损。

　　经烧烤之玉器多干涩，无包浆。

　　右图玉器在制作完成后以纸蘸腊涂画玉器表面，然后在生石灰水中浸泡，直至器面呈鸡骨白色。

　　试想，当古玉器深藏地下时，玉器不可能均匀受沁，并且所露玉地皆呈锐角几何图形。

　　此器受沁变化缺乏科学性，因而失去真实感。

　　The ware of left picture roasted into chicken bone white with low temperature after complete. Before roasting they made incomplete in bird belly, tail and wings, in order to pretenc to be natural breakage.

　　The roasted ware was almost dry and not smooth, and had no baojiang.

　　In right picture, they painted the surface of jade ware with paper dipped in wax after finished, and then soaked in raw lime water untill the ware surface submitted chicken bone white r.

　　Thinking that when the ancient jade ware was deep in underground, the jade ware is impossible to receive infiltration evenly, and exposed jade texture all submitted the geometric figure of acute angle.

　　The infiltration change of this ware lacks scientificness, thus it loses actual sense.

图 429 仿红山文化虎形佩

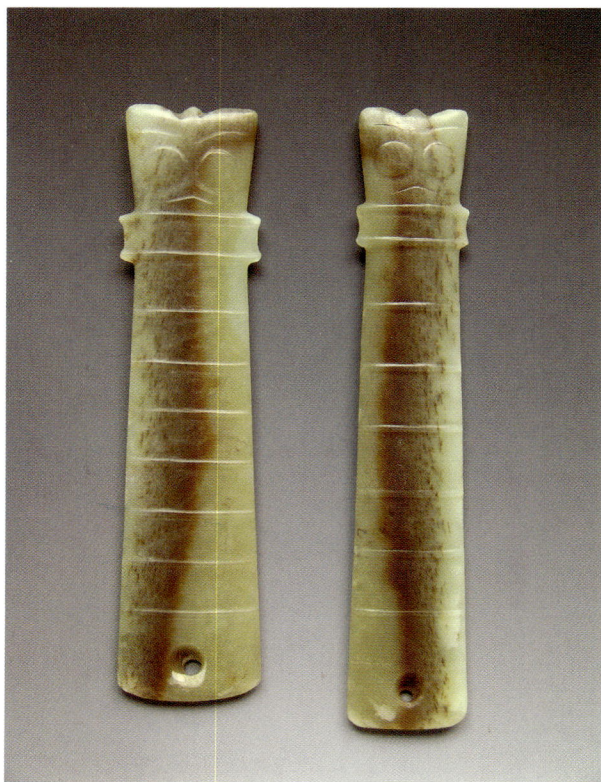

Picture 429 imitating Hongshan Culture Tiger-shaped ware

图 430 仿红山文化玦形玉兽

Picture 430 imitating Hongshan Culture Jade Coiled Animal

左图二器均为老玉新作。又称为"老玉新工"。我们所见器表赭石色沁痕为玉石原生沁，先天已有，而非后天沁成。二器取之同一块玉石，极有可能由较薄残破玉斧改制。

二器均无明显包浆，直观感觉：生、涩、新。缺少年代感。

右图玉器由岫岩玉新制玉器。全器除所见绺裂外并无其它沁后变化。绺裂只在器表一面，为原生先天形成，应取自小块岫玉所制作。

总体感觉新而生涩。

In left picture this two wares are old make new jade, and also called "old jade new technology". We see the ochre infiltration trace of the ware surface is raw infiltration for jade which had have congenitally, and not got acqueirdy. The two wares are taken from the same jade, have big possibility with more thin broken jade axe to alter.

The two wares are without obvious baojiang, straight sense: is stiff, dry, not smooth and new lacking age sense.

In right picture this ware is made of new xiu rock jade. The whole ware, besides tuft crack pattern seen, does not have the other change after infiltration. The tuft crack pattern is in one side of the ware surface, which is formed in raw, which should be made of little piece xiu rock jade.

The whole sense is new and not smooth.

图 431 仿红山文化马蹄形器
Picture 431 imitating Hongshan Culture　Jade Clevis Hoop

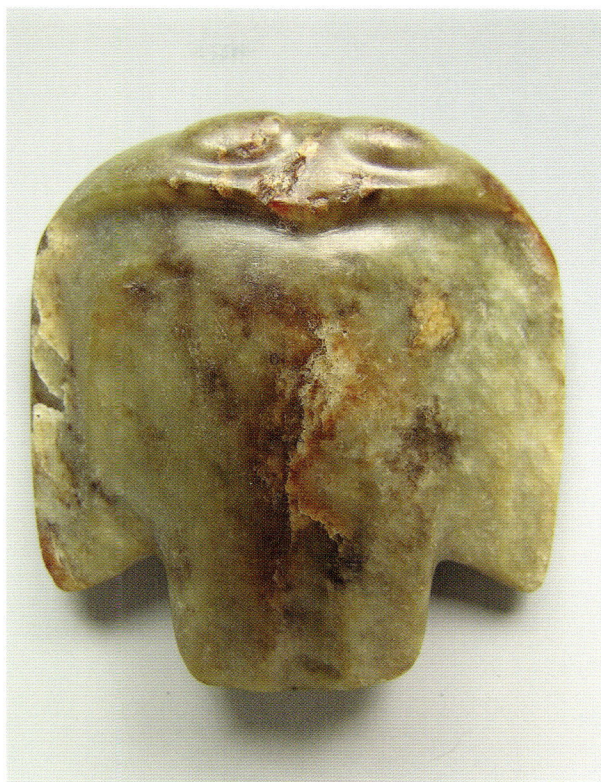

图 432 仿红山文化玉鸟
Picture 432 imitating Hongshan Culture　Jade Bird

选择绺、璺、棉、瑕疵较重玉石做色已成为制假者最常用手段。

色由孔入。无残破或玉石原生中空现象，色不能进入。此器局部经过做残，然后人为浸入颜色。

此三件仿红山文化玉器，皆采用高温下以高锰酸钾染色而成。所做沁色夸张、呆板、无过渡性。

In picture 431, selecting tuft crack、crack、cotton、the jade of heavier flaw to make colour have become the most common means.

In picture 432, the color is entered through holes. Without broken or jade raw hollow phenomenon, the color can not enter. This ware partly made incomplete, then soaked into color by artificial.

In picture 433, the three imitating Hongshan-Culture wares all adopted high temperature with Potassium Permanganate dyeing. The Color is exaggeration, rigid, and no transition.

图 433 仿红山文化玉兽
Picture 433 imitating Hongshan Culture　Jade Animal

434 仿红山文化玉怪兽
Picture 434 imitating Hongshan Culture Jade monster

图 435 仿红山文化玉怪兽
Picture 435 imitating Hongshan Culture Jade monster

图 436 仿红山文化蜜蜂
Picture 436 imitating Hongshan Culture Honeybee

图 437 仿红山文化玉人
Picture 437 imitating Hongshan Culture Jade person

　　这些以淋酸法仿制的红山文化玉器，不但造型奇特，而且皆无明显包浆。

These Hongshan–culture jade wares imitated with the method of soaked acid, which not only have peculiar modelling, but also does not have obvious baojiang.

图 438 仿红山文化龙形玉
Picture 438 imitating Hongshan Culture Dragon-shaped jade

图 439 龙形玉的另面
Picture 439 another side of Dragon-shaped jade

一件玉器在特定环境下它的沁象应该是相一致的，这就是沁象的统一性与完整性。

此器一面有黑色蚁斑，而另一面却没有。尽管局部出现绺裂仍不能认定其真实性。仔细观察，龙尾钻孔处蚁斑消失，因此断定此器由原生沁河漠玉所制作，并在器表做了仿真处理，这种明显"断沁"玉器为仿古赝品。

The infiltration of one jade ware under specific environment should be consistent, which is integrity and the unity of infiltration phenomenon.

This ware has black ant form spot, but another side doesn't have. Though part arises tuft crack pattern, we still can not believe its actuality. We observing carefully, the black ant form spots disappear on drilling hole place of dragon tail, therefore we conclude that this ware is made by raw infiltration of Hemo jade, and make emulation in ware surface. This kind of obvious jade ware of "broken infiltration" is imitating ancient fake.

图 440 龙形玉的局部放大
Picture 440 Dragon-shaped jade partly enlarged

图 441 仿红山文化玦形玉兽
Picture 451 imitating Hongshan Culture   Jade Coiled Animal

图 442 仿红山文化玉蛙
Picture 442 imitating Hongshan Culture   Jade Frog

图 443 仿红山文化玦形玉龟
Picture 443 imitating Hongshan Culture   Jade Coiled Tortoise

图 444 仿红山文化玦形玉兽
Picture 444 imitating Hongshan Culture   Jade Coiled Animal

　　这是用不同方法和手段仿制的红山文化玉器。总体感觉：工艺粗糙、干涩呆滞、沁色夸张、缺乏生机。

This is the Hongshan-culture jade ware that copied with different method and means. The whole sense: technology is rough, dry, not smooth, dull, color exaggeration, and lifeless.

图 445 仿红山文化斧形器
Picture 445 imitating Hongshan Culture   Axe-shaped ware

图 446 仿红山文化玉神祖

Picture 446 imitating Hongshan-Culture　Jade Numen

图 447 仿红山文化玉神祖

Picture 447 imitating Hongshan-Culture　Jade Numen

图 448 仿红山文化玉龙

Picture 448 imitating Hongshan-Culture　Jade Dragon

　　上图两件玉器皆以辽宁产岫岩玉制作。并经过高温酸蚀做灰沁皮壳，然后再进行局部染色处理。无论工艺、沁色、绺裂痕、包浆皆与真古玉器沁象相差甚远。

　　下图玉龙采用岫玉中含沙斑较重玉石制作，并进行过浸腊处理。从中可以看出：沁象单一、沁色无明显过渡、包浆虚假、无年代感。

The above two jade wares are made of xiu rock jade from Liaoning. And through high temperature sour etch makes grey infiltration shell, then, carry out local dyeing handling Regardless of technology, infiltration color, the mark of tuft crack pattern and baojiang, it is very far to differ with infiltration of real ancient jade ware.

The jade dragon adopted Xiu jade contained more heavy sand spots to make, and soaked by acid. From it we can find out: the infiltration phenomenon is unitary, the color do not have obvious transition, baojiang is false, do not have time sense.

图 449 仿红山文化玉兽
Picture 449 imitating Hongshan Culture　Jade Animal

图 450 仿红山文化玉鸟
Picture 450 imitating Hongshan Culture　Jade Bird

　　包浆，是鉴定高古玉器真伪的重要条件。凡出土高古玉器皆有不同程度的包浆。

　　图中这三件玉器皆为仿红山文化玉器，并做过浸酸处理。看起来无光泽、僵死、更无包浆。

Baojiang is the important condition for appraising high ancient jade wares real or false. All unearthed high ancient jade wares have baojiang of different degree.

The three jade wares in the picture are all imitating Hongshan-culture jade wares, and have made by soaking acid. Looks no reluster, dead, and even no baojiang.

图 451 仿红山文化玉神面
Picture 451 imitating Hongshan Culture　Jade God Face

图 452 仿红山文化玉人
PPicture 452 imitating Hongshan Culture　Jade Person

图 453 仿红山文化鹰兽
Picture 453 imitating Hongshan Culture　Jade Eagle beast

这是以岫岩产苍玉，又被称作玉石根子仿制的红山文化玉器。

上图二器造型光怪陆离，属凭空想象杜撰之器，这类玉器因为造型奇特往往吸引很多人上当受骗。

以苍玉所仿红山文化玉器，不但与红山文化真古玉器加工工艺相差甚远，而且皆无包浆与明显受沁变化。

This is the imitating Hongshan Culture jade ware with grey jade produced by xiu rock also called jade root.

The modelings of above two wares are grotesque in shape and gaudy in color, which belongs to the out of imaginative fabricate ware, so this kind of jade ware often attracts many persons to be deceived because its modeling is peculiar.

With grey jade imitating Hongshan-culture jade ware not only far from the Hongshan-culture real ancient processing technology, but also have no baojiang and obvious infiltration change.

图 454 仿红山文化玉蚕
Picture 454 imitating Hongshan Culture　Jade Silkworm

图 455 仿红山文化天地神佩
Picture 455 imitating Hongshan
Culture Compound Jade Baldric
for Heaven and Earth

图 456 天地神佩另面
Picture 456 another side of Compound Jade Baldric for Heaven
and Earth

　　这是一件仿红山文化天地神佩，以带有原生沁的新玉制作。此器上部巧妙的利用了原生沁色，看上去很自然。器下部为剥离层结合部无沁色，为看上去更真实，人工作了黄色沁。老玉新作之器除缺少沁色的完整性外，皆无明显包浆，给人以生涩感。

This is an imitating Hongshan-culture Compound Jade Baldric for Heaven and Earth, made by the new jade of raw infiltration. This ware is ingenious to have used raw infiltration, looks very natural. The downside of the ware is peeling off layer and does not have infiltration color, in order to look more real, they made yellow infiltration by artificial. The ware of old make new besides lacks the integrity of infiltration color, and all have no obvious baojiang, so give person the sense of not smooth..

图 457 仿红山文化玉鸟
Picrure457 imitating Hongshan Culture Jade bird

图 458 玉鸟器背
Picrure458 The back of jade bird

　　这是以原生沁青玉仿制的红山文化玉器。原料取自于河道或距地表较浅处。从玉石表层剥离已先天受沁玉皮所仿制古玉器，具有很大的欺骗性。

　　此器沁色华丽，但缺少统一性与完整性。并且无明显包浆，沁象僵滞，缺少灵动感。

This is the imitating Hongshan-culture jade ware with blue-green jade of raw infiltration. The material took from in river course or near the surface of the earth. From jade surface peeling off the imitating ancient jade ware made by jade skin that has already been infiltration, have greatly deceiving.

　　The infiltration colour of this ware is gorgeous, but lacks unity and integrity. And do not have obvious baojiang, the infiltration phenomenon is stiff, lacks lively sense.

图 459 仿红山文化玉人
Picture 459 imitating Hongshan Culture Jade person

图 460 仿红山文化玉人
Picture 460 imitating Hongshan Culture Jade person

图 459：这是青金石仿造的红山文化玉器。器面白色并非白化斑，而是原生石线。

图 460：这是以页拉石仿鸡肝玛瑙所制作成的玉器。

图 461：这是以淡青色较软玉质玉石所制作的玉器，并经过化工原料"快速金黄"染色仿黄玉玉器。

Picture 459 This is the imitating Hongshan-culture jade ware made by green golden stone. The ware surface is white and not white spot, but is raw stone line.

Picture 460 This is imitating jade ware made of chicken liver agate with yela stone.

Picture 461 This is the imitating topaz ware made by more soft light cyan jade and through industrial chemicals "fast golden" dyeing.

图 461 仿红山文化复合形玉人
Picture 461 imitating Hongshan Culture compound jade person

图 462 仿红山文化玉怪兽
Picture 462 imitating Hongshan Culture Jade monster

图 463 仿红山文化勾云形玉佩
Picture 463 imitating Hongshan Culture Cloud-shaped jade pendant

这些都是经过氢氟酸浸泡然后再染色的玉器。凡经过酸处理的玉器，皆泛白灰。白灰盘之则退，然后复出，永不能完全去除。

These are jade wares that soaking with hydrogen fluorine acid and then dyeing.

Through soaking with acid, the jade ware all arise white grey. Making the white ash would disappear, appear again then, can not exclude completely.

图 464 仿红山文化兽面人
Picture 464 imitating Hongshan Culture jade person of beast face

图 465 仿红山文化兽面人
Picture 465 imitating Hongshan Culture jade person of beast face

图 466 仿红山文化玉人
Picture 466 imitating Hongshan Culture Jade person

图 467 仿红山文化玉鸟
icture 467 imitating Hongshan Culture Jade bird

　　图 466、467：这是经过高温强酸处理过的玉器，由于全身皆白不露玉地，被称作"水泥块子"。在二十余年红山文化考古发掘中，到目前尚未发现类似沁象玉器。

　　图 468、469：这两件玉器皆经过氢氟酸浸泡再染色。

　　图 470：在仿制的红山文化玉器上雕琢奇特纹饰及象形文字，已成为造假者蒙骗人们的一种特殊手段。

Picture 466、467：This is the jade ware processed through the strong acid of high temperature, because of the whole body is white do not show jade texture, had been called "cement piece". During more than 20 years of Hongshan culture archaeological studies and excavation, until now, have not discovered the similar jade ware of this infiltration phenomenon.

Picture 468、469：This two jade wares soaked through hydrogen fluorine acid then dyeing.

Picture 470：On the imitating Hongshan culture jade ware, they carved the writing of peculiar veins and pictograph, which have become a kind of means to deceive people by fake productors.

图 468 仿红山文化鸟形器
Picture 468 imitating Hongshan Culture Bird-shaped ware

图 469 仿红山文化玉羊首
Picture 469 imitating Hongshan Culture Jade sheep head

图 470 仿红山文化圭形器
Picture 470 imitating Hongshan Culture Gui-shaped ware

图 471 仿红山文化鸟形器
Picture 471 imitating Hongshan Culture Bird-shaped ware

图 472 鸟形器另面
Picture 472 another side of Bird-shaped ware another side

这是经过微酸高温处理过的玉器。

玉石已改变原本颜色，器面可见酸处理后的炸裂璺。

凡经过微酸高温蒸煮玉石：玉石颜色改变，炸裂璺深入，璺裂处色脏。

This is the jade ware proccessed through tiny sour with high temperature.

Jade have changed former color and ware surface can be seen sour handling fry crack.

All through tiny sour with high temperature and steaming the jade: Jade color changes, cracks go deep into, and color of crack place has not clean .

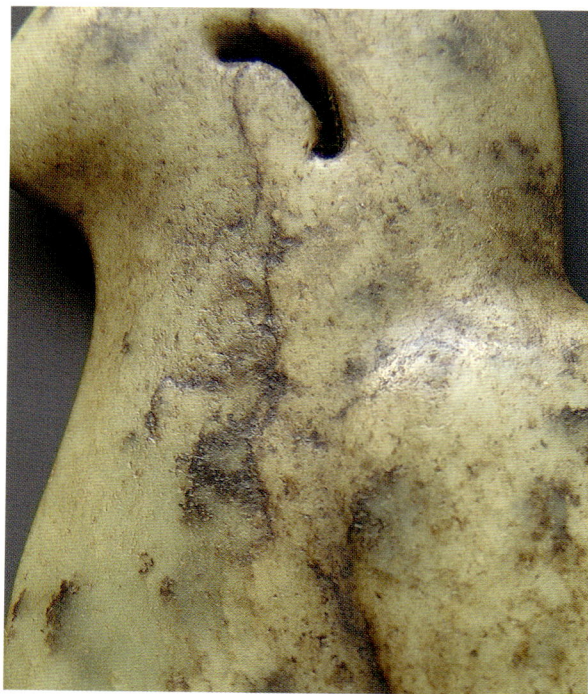

图 473 鸟形器局部放大
PPicture 473 Bird-shaped ware partly enlarged

图 474 仿红山文化玦形玉兽
Picture 474 imitating Hongshan Culture Jade coiled animal

图 475 仿红山文化玉人
Picture 475 imitating Hongshan Culture Jade person

图 476 仿红山文化玦形玉兽
Picture 476 imitating Hongshan Culture Jade coiled animal

左图,这是"老玉新作"仿红山文化玉器。
右图,这是以淋酸法仿制的红山文化玉器。
此二器皆以新玉高温染色作成的仿红山文化
玉器。

In left picture, this is "old make new" jade imitating Hongshan—culture jade ware

In right picture, this is imitating Hongshan—culture jade ware with pouring sour method.

The two wares are the new jade dyeing with high temperature to imitate Hongshan—culture jade ware.

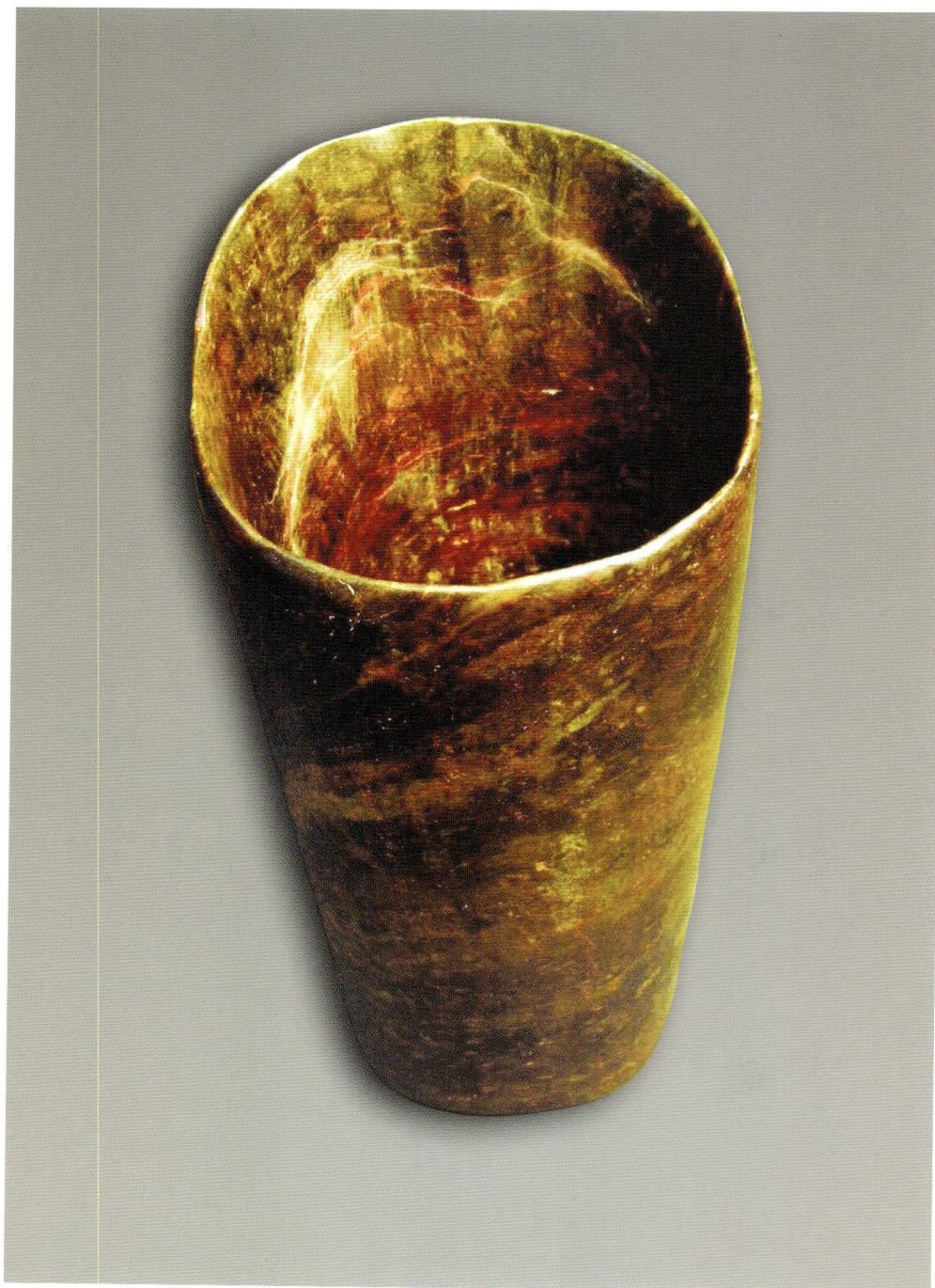

图 477 仿红山文化马蹄形器

Picture 477 imitating Hongshan-Culture Jade Clevis Hoop

图 479 仿红山文化玉神祖

Picture 479 imitating Hongshan-Culture Jade Numen

图 480 仿红山文化玉神祖

Picture 480 imitating Hongshan-Culture Jade Nume

图 481 这是以岫岩玉制作并染色的仿红山文化玉器。颜色夸张，严重失真。这是早些年仿制的玉器，已逐渐被人们所认识。

Picture 481 This is imitating Hongshan-culture jade ware made by xiu rock jade and dyeing. Color exaggeration, it lost sense seriously. This is the imitating jade ware made in early years, and had gradually been know by people.

图 482 人工做沁玉器，看起来极不自然。
Picture 482 Man-made infiltration jade ware seems not natural.

图 483 这是经过高温微酸蒸煮过的玉器，利用其麻斑和裂纹再敷以装饰土。
Picture 483 This is the jade ware through the tiny acid with high temperature to steam, and use spots and tuft crack pattern covered with soil again to make decorate.

图 484 这是以老玉改制的仿红山文化玉鸟。仔细观察你会发现：器正、背两面沁色不统一，无明显包浆。
Picture 484 This is imitating Hongshan-culture jade bird with old jade altering. You can find through carefully observing: The front and back of ware infiltration colour do not unify and do not have obvious baojiang.

图 485 玉鸟器背
Picture 485 The back of jade bird

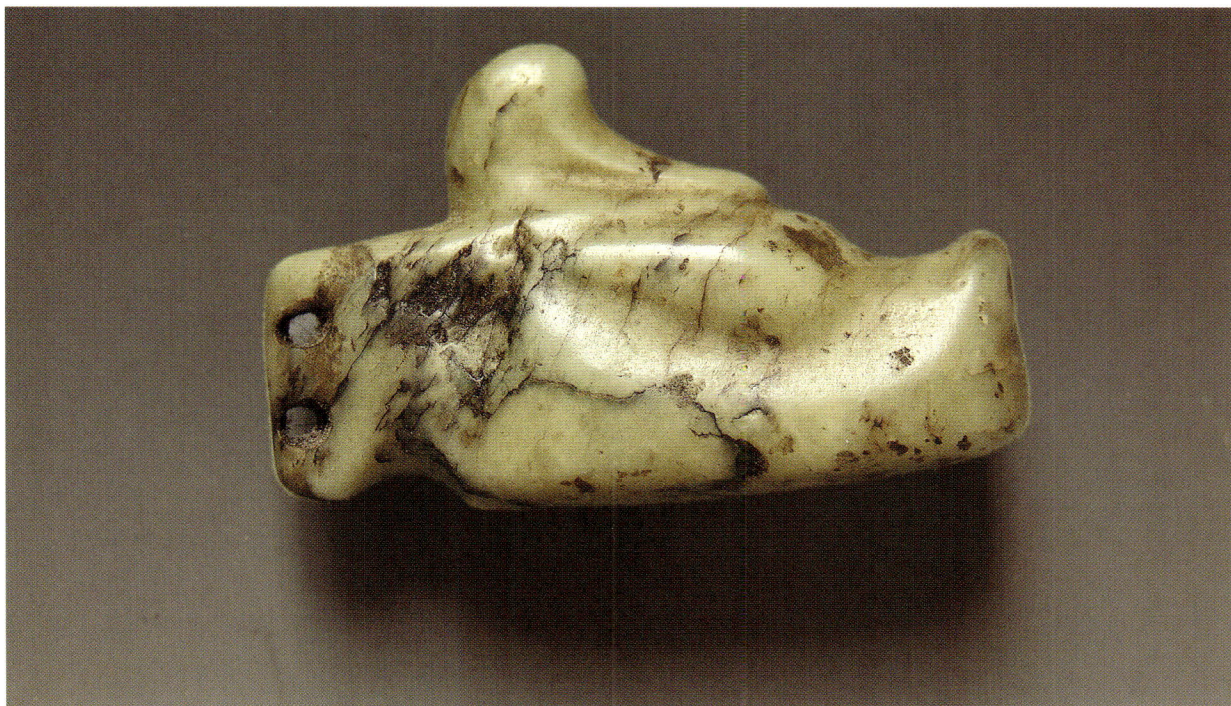

图 486 仿红山文化玉兽首
Picture 486 imitating Hongshan Culture Jade beast head

图 487 玉兽首局部放大可见炸裂纹
Picture 487 Jade beast head partly enlarged can see explosion viens

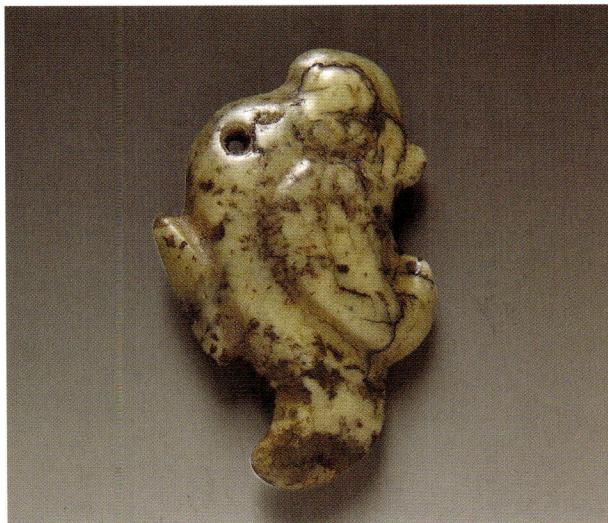

图 488 仿红山文化鸟形佩
Picture 488imitating Hongshan Culture Bird-shaped jade pendant

　　这些都是经过高温酸浸过的仿红山文化玉器。除玉石颜色改变外，器身遍布炸裂纹，然后利用炸裂纹向内充色，以炸裂纹冒充绺裂，两者进行对比具有明显差别。

　　These are imitating Hongshan-culture jade ware soaked in the acid with high temperature. Besides jade color changed, the whole of jade ware have explosion veins, and then usethe viens to put color inside in order to pretend to be tuft crack pattern, the two contrast to have obvious difference.

图 A
Picture A

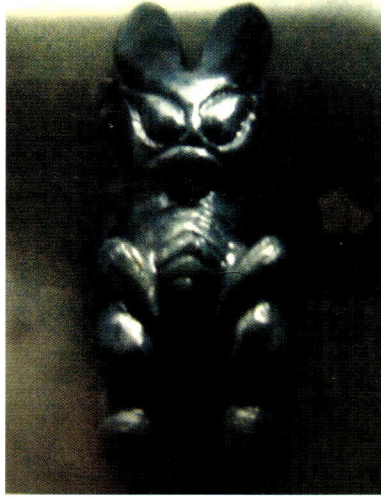

图 B
Picture B

图 C
Picture C

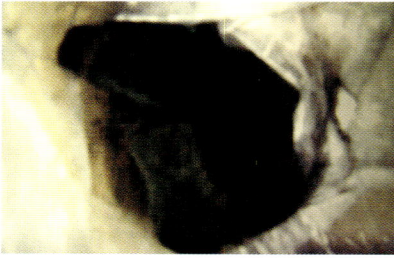

图 D
Picture D

图 E
Picture E

"黑皮玉"制作方法

图 A：选择质地松软玉材加工玉器。

图 B：放入氢氟酸溶液内进行浸泡。

图 C：经过浸泡后的玉器表面泛出白灰并出现麻斑。

图 D：将化工染料"快速金黑"用酒精兑开，涂刷在玉器表面二次以上。

图 E：被涂刷过"快速金黑"的玉器已经变黑，然后在玉器表面浸腊，以制作假包浆。

被称为含有 35 种元素的"黑皮玉"就这样完成了。

The produce method " dark leather jade"

Picture A Select soft jade material processing jade ware.

Picture B Put into hydrogen fluorine sour solution to soak

Picture C Via the surface of jade ware soaking, appear white ash and spots.

Picture D dissolve chemical dyestuff " fast gold dark " with alcohol to paint on the surface of jade ware more than twice.

Picture E The ware have been painting with " fast gold dark " have changed black, then soak wax on the surface of jade ware in order to make false baojiang.

Being called "dark leather jade" containing thirty-five kinds of elements, have just so been completed.

图 489 仿红山文化鸟形器

Picture 489 imitating Hongshan Culture bird-shaped jade ware

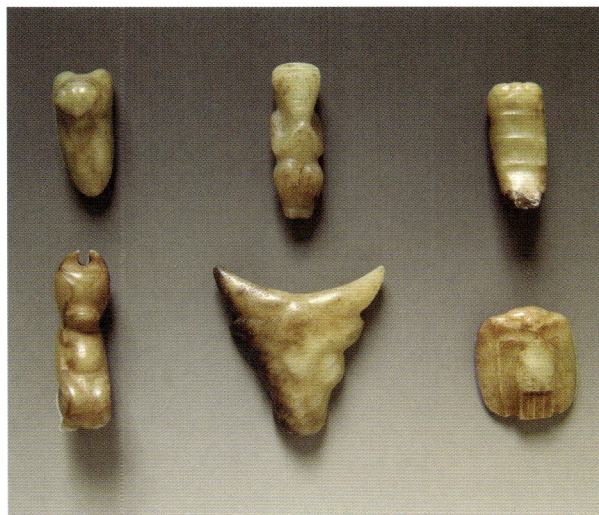

图 491 仿红山文化玉器

Picture 491 imitating Hongshan Culture jade ware

这些玉器皆经过酸腐蚀，看上去器表脏乱，无光泽。

选择与红山文化真古玉器相类似玉材，仿照真品器型与工艺，高仿品基本可以达标。但真古玉器的包浆与沁色，制假者却永远望尘莫及。

These jade wares are corroded by acid, looks ware surface dirty, disorder, and have no luster.

They choose the similar jade material with Hongshan-culture real ancient jade ware imitating ware type and technology of real ware, so high imitating ware can pass basically. But real jade ware's baojiang and infiltration colour, make fake producer forever do not arrive.

图 492 仿红山文化玉器

Picture 492 imitating Hongshan Culture jade ware

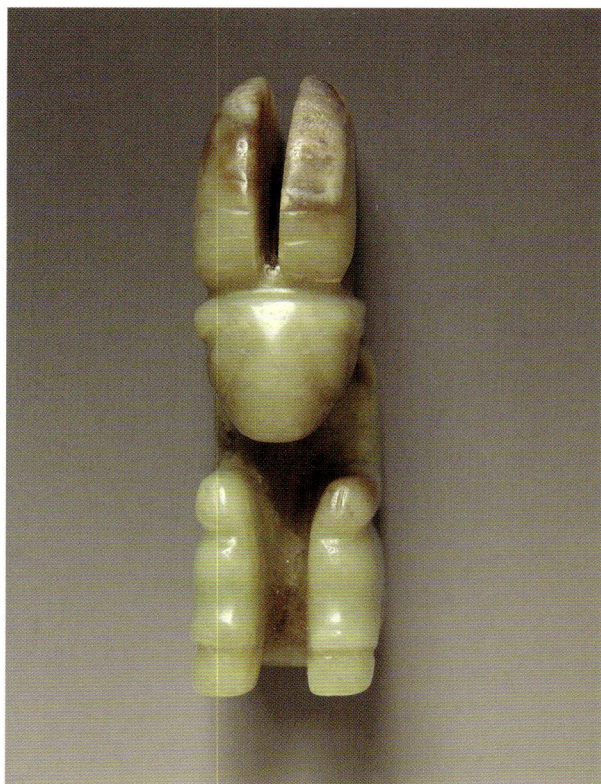

图 493 仿红山文化玉神祖
Picture 493 imitating Hongshan-Culture Jade Numen

图 494 仿红山文化玉神祖器背
Picture 494 imitating back of Hongshan-Culture Jade Numen

图 495 仿红山文化玉熊
Picture 495 imitating Hongshan-Culture Jade Bear

目前市场上出现的岫岩玉仿制红山文化玉器，多在玉器局部烧烤注色，以冒充自然形成糖色。此类器物沁色不具过渡性，并且器表出现炸裂痕。

Now, appearing on market xiu rock jade imitating Hongshan–Culture jade ware, and in the local of jade ware roasting to circulate colour to pretend to be nature form sugar color. A lot of infiltration colours of this kind of wares, have no transition, ware surface appears explosion trace.

结　语

在《红山文化古玉精华》出版时，曾许下诺言，说将要出版《红山文化古玉鉴定》一书。在几年酝酿的时间里，国内外的红山文化古玉收藏家、爱好者电话不断，紧追不舍，在热切企盼中所带着的真诚与厚爱深让我感动。在此谨表谢意。

《红山文化古玉鉴定》与其他类书籍有所不同，很有可能将被作为工具书长期阅读和应用。所以在编撰过程中几易其稿，生怕有丝毫的疏忽而给红山文化爱好者造成误导。因此竭尽全力以求最大可能的避免错误发生，以达到理想的宣传效果，希望能给红山文化玉器收藏与研究者提供可靠的帮助或有所启迪。

在编写本书过程中，由于考古发掘出土玉器资料甚少，远不能详尽阐述古玉鉴定多方例证，因而在诸多鉴定要点中选用了"听雨堂"珍藏的红山文化玉器作为进行剖析与鉴别样品。在此郑重向读者承诺：凡《听雨堂》提供玉器，作者将以法律责任绝对保证每件藏品的真实性。如发生错误，愿意承担经济赔偿责任。

本书中所有考古发掘图片均选自"辽宁省文物考古研究所"编《牛河梁红山文化遗址与玉器精粹》与《牛河梁遗址》两书，对所给予的帮助，深表谢意。

《红山文化古玉鉴定》是作者历经 20 多年收藏与研究红山文化玉器的经验总结，是汗水与泪水交织而成的劳动成果，任何人不得随意侵占其著作权。如有盗版侵权发生，必将诉诸法律严厉追究其经济赔偿责任。

计划于明年出版《红山文化古玉研究与收藏》，以满足广大红山文化古玉爱好者与了结作者多年之愿望。

本书在编撰过程中尽管做了最大努力，但由于作者才疏学浅，仍然避免不了存在这样或那样的不足甚至错误，恳请国内、外广大红山文化玉器收藏爱好者和专门从事红山文化研究的专家学者提出宝贵意见。并愿意以国家利益为重，以学术研究为根本，为探究中国古代文明历史与弘扬中国的传统文化共同做出努力。

《中国文化管理学会红山文化古玉收藏研究俱乐部》《北京听雨堂文化发展中心》，聘请《北京小耘律师事务所》国际知名律师王自豪先生为法律顾问，如遇假冒、侵权、恶意攻击诽谤等行为，将诉请法律保护。

徐强于　《中国文化管理学会红山文化古玉收藏研究俱乐部》

咨询热线：13911269627

网址：www.hongshanclub.org.cn

2007.3.5

Final Language

In the publication of "Hongshan antiquated jade", I made a promise that will publish a book "Hongshan cultural ancient jade is appraised". During those years, I received many calls from domestic and international collectors and fans of Hongshan cultural ancient jade, they are eager, sincere and be love, which moved me deeply.

The book "Hongshan cultural ancient jade appraisal" is different with other books, which will be used as a reference book for a long period. So when I write volume draft, for fear that there is slightest necligence cause to misleading with Hongshan cultural fans. Therefore I devoted the biggest attention to avoid mistake wish to reach ideal propagative effect and collected Hongshan cultural jade article, which can offer reliable help with researcher or enlightenment.

When the book was in compiling, because there was a few data of archaeology can be excavated, so can not elaborate the ancient jade appraisal thoroughly in many illustration, thus the book "Hear rain hall" be chosen to use to collect Hongshan cultural jade article as analyse and distinguish sample. To make promise to readers: All jade articles offered by "hear rain hall", author will guarantee the actuality of each most-prized holding absolutely with legal responsibility. If there are any mistakes, the author willing to undertake economic responsibility of compensation.

All the pictures of excavation were choosed from " Niuheliang site" and "Jade article is shrewd and pure" two books, which edited by The Liaoning province archaeology research institute.

"Hongshan cultural jade apprise" is the summary of author's 20 years experience of collecting and studying Hongshan cultural jade article, it is wovened by sweat and tear intersectly, any person can not occupy its copyright at will. If any pirate occurs, the person must take the responsibility of economic compensation sternly.

In order to satisfy with the fans of Hongshan cultural ancient jade, the book will be published in next year.

Author spared his biggest effort to avoid mistakes, but since little knowledgable, still can not avoid existence or any mistakes, so any suggestions welcomed from domestic and international of Hongshan cultural jade article experts and scholar who is engage in Hongshan cultural research and willing to continue to make effort together with you for probing Chinese ancient civilized history and promoting the traditional culture of China.

《Research and Collection Club of HongShan-Culture Jade Articles of China Culture Administration Association》《Beijing "listening to rain" hall culture develop center》, appointed international famous lawyer Wangzihao from 《Beijing Richard Wang & Co》 for law adviser, if meet counterfeit、tort、malice attack libel etc behavior, will take the law protection.

Xuqiang

Research and Collection Club of HongShan-Culture Jade Articles of China Culture Administration Association .

Consult telephone : 13911269627

www.hongshanclub.org.cn

2007.3.5